CONNECTING PEOPLE THROUGH ENGLISH

with Workbook

Joan Saslow
Allen Ascher

Connectivity: Connecting People through English   Level 5B with Workbook

Copyright © 2023 by Pearson Education, Inc.

All rights reserved. No part of this publication may be reproduced, stored in a retrieval system, or transmitted in any form or by any means, electronic, mechanical, photocopying, recording, or otherwise, without the prior permission of the publisher.

Pearson Education, 221 River Street, Hoboken, NJ 07030 USA

Text composition: EMC Design Ltd

Library of Congress Cataloging-in-Publication Data: A catalog record for the print edition is available from the Library of Congress.

Printed in the United States of America
ISBN-13: 978-0-13-746408-1

1 2022

pearsonenglish.com/connectivity

CONTENTS

About the Authors iii
Learning Objectives for 5A and 5B iv
Components viii
Key to Icons in the Student's Book x
To the Teacher xi

UNIT 6   On the Move 56
UNIT 7   Belief and Reality 68
UNIT 8   Achievement and Intelligence 78
UNIT 9   Looking Ahead 90
UNIT 10   Global Ties 100

Reference Charts 112
Grammar Expander 127
Pronunciation Lessons 139
Writing Handbook 149
Soft Skills Booster 159

WORKBOOK

UNIT 6 .... W47
UNIT 7 .... W57
UNIT 8 .... W66
UNIT 9 .... W75
UNIT 10 .... W84

Photo Credits

Cover

10'000 Hours/Digital Vision/Getty Images; Thomas Barwick/Digital Vision/Getty Images; PeopleImages/E+/Getty Images.

Frontmatter Page viii (accountant): Andrey_Popov/Shutterstock; viii (teller): YinYang/E+/Getty Images; viii (salesperson): Iakov Filimonov/Shutterstock; viii (nurse): Shutterstock; viii (lawyer): RichLegg/E+/Getty Images; viii (mechanic): Wavebreakmedia/Shutterstock; viii (secretary): Elena Elisseeva/Shutterstock; viii (tour guide): SolStock/E+/Getty Images; ix (mobile top): Brovko Serhii/Shutterstock; ix (p. 86 top): Fizkes/Shutterstock; ix (p. 86 bottom): Marvent/123RF; ix (p. 87): Insta_photos/Shutterstock; ix (mobile left): Brovko Serhii/Shutterstock; ix (image on mobile left): Mentatdgt/Shutterstock; ix (image on mobile right): Iakov Filimonov/Shutterstock; ix (desktop bottom) Evgeny Karandaev/Shutterstock; xix (image on mobile left): Mentatdgt/Shutterstock; xix (image on mobile right): Iakov Filimonov/Shutterstock.

Unit 6 Page 56: Westend61/Getty Images; 58 (woman in car): Antonio Diaz/123RF; 58 (man walking): Prod-akszyn/Shutterstock; 58 (woman texting): Comzeal/123RF; 61 (background): James R. Martin/Shutterstock; 61 (two women): Mangostar/123RF; 62 (luggage carousel background): Anek.soowannaphoom/Shutterstock; 62 (Tom): Antonio Diaz/123RF; 62 (luggage carousel): Anek.soowannaphoom/Shutterstock; 62 (Tom): Antonio Diaz/123RF; 62 (Tom): Antonio Diaz/123RF; 63: CRAFT24/Shutterstock; 64 (man): Olga Yastremska/123RF; 64 (security concept): Jijomathaidesigners/Shutterstock; 65: Shutterstock.

Soft Skills Work Shop 3 Page 66 (dentist): Sergey Mironov/Shutterstock; 66 (airplane): Kickers/ E+/Getty Images; 66 (students): J.D. Dallet/Agefotostock/Alamy Stock Photo; 66 (laptop): Cobalt88/Shutterstock; 66 (laptop, man on couch): Selimaksan/ E+/Getty Images; 66 (hotel): Pixelparticle/Shutterstock; 67: Mentatdgt/Shutterstock.

Unit 7 Page 68: MStudioImages/E+/Getty Images; 69 (A): Santiago Marquez/Shutterstock; 69 (B): Elnour/Shutterstock; 69 (C): Mypokcik/Shutterstock; 69 (D): Megan Betteridge/Shutterstock; 69 (E): Mark Grenier/Shutterstock; 69 (G): Til Vogt/Shutterstock; 71: Chuanpis/Shutterstock; 72 (Elliot): Vladimir Gjorgiev/Shutterstock; 72 (Brooke) Jon Barlow: Jon Barlow/Pearson Education Ltd; 73 (spider): Alex Stemmer/Shutterstock; 73 (viewing platform): Sashamol/Shutterstock; 74 (top): Vanatchanan/123RF; 74 (bottom): Sherry Yates Young/123RF; 06 (woman): Katarzyna Białasiewicz/123RF; 76 (bracelet): Hugh Threlfall/Alamy Stock Photo.

Unit 8 Page 78: Mihailomilovanovic/E+/Getty Images; 79 (office): Marvent/Shutterstock; 79 (hourglass): Motortion Films/Shutterstock; 79 (Do Not Disturb sign): Akemaster/Shutterstock; 79 (student studying): Ashish_wassup6730/Shutterstock; 79 (woman stretching): TORWAISTUDIO/Shutterstock; 80 (George): SB Arts Media/Shutterstock; 80 (Sue Lin): Leungchopan/Shutterstock; 80 (Vivian): Wavebreakmedia/Shutterstock; 80 (Narcisco): Leungchopan/Shutterstock; 80 (Sophie): Oscarhdez/Shutterstock; 81: Fizkes/123RF; 82 (man studying): Brandon Blinkenberg/Shutterstock; 82 (woman studying): Follow Focus/Shutterstock; 83: Gorodenkoff/Shutterstock; 84 (top): Constantine Pankin/123RF; 85 (reading): Pixelheadphoto digitalskillet/Shutterstock; 85 (guitar lesson): Primagefactory/123RF; 85 (science students): Wavebreakmedia/Shutterstock; 85 (baby at doctor): Tomsickova Tatyana/Shutterstock; 85 (butterfly study): Acik/123RF; 86 (top): Fizkes/Shutterstock; 86 (bottom): Marvent/123RF; 87: Insta_photos/Shutterstock.

Soft Skills Workshop 4 Page 88 (fear of flying): Milkovasa/Shutterstock; 88 (cooking together): Art_Photo/Shutterstock; 88 (volunteers): Wavebreakmedia/Shutterstock; 89 (students in library): Vitchanan Photography/Shutterstock; 89 (presentation): Mediaphotos/ iStock/Getty Images.

Unit 9 Page 90: Iammotos/Shutterstock; 91 (robot): Miriam Doerr Martin Frommherz/Shutterstock; 91 (flags): Andykazie/123RF; 91 (woman walking): Westend61/Getty Images; 91 (vaccination): Prostock-studio/Shutterstock; 92 (man): Fizkes/Shutterstock; 92 (woman): WAYHOME studio/Shutterstock; 93: Fabrice Lerouge/ONOKY-Photononstop/Alamy Stock Photo; 94 (man top): Fizkes/Shutterstock; 94 (woman top): Fizkes/Shutterstock; 94 (Ken Olsen): Carol Francavilla/AP/Shutterstock; 94 (Mary Barra): M Astar/Sipa/Shutterstock; 95 (Clifford Stoll): Rob Crandall /Alamy Stock Photo; 95 (Jane Goodall): ALESSANDRO DELLA VALLE/EPA-EFE/Shutterstock; 95 (hand scan): Aleksandra Chalova/123RF; 95 (space tourist): Mike_shots/Shutterstock; 95 (monorail): Volodimir Zozulinskyi/Shutterstock; 95 (stressed driver): DimaBerlin/Shutterstock; 96: Jillian Cain Photography/Shutterstock; 97: Boyloso/Shutterstock; 98 (baby nursery): Ben Edwards/ Stockbyte/Getty Images; 98 (college lecture): ESB Professional/Shutterstock.

Unit 10 Page 100 (man left): Prostock-studio/Shutterstock; 100 (man right): Aslysun/Shutterstock; 101 (stop sign): Lester Balajadia/Shutterstock; 101 (girl student): Maroke/Shutterstock; 101 (class instructor): Piranka/E+/Getty Images; 103 (drug trafficking): Macor/123RF; 103 (conflict): Thomas Hengge/Shutterstock; 103 (migration): Ververidis Vasilis/Shutterstock; 103 (drought): Edgar G Biehle/Shutterstock; 103 (street crime): Jacob Lund/Shutterstock; 103 (hunger): StanislauV/Shutterstock; 103 (terrorism): Everett Collection/Shutterstock; 104 (woman): Dabyki.nadya/Shutterstock; 104 (man): Maridav/Shutterstock; 105 (martial arts): Westend61 GmbH/Alamy Stock Photo; 105 (clothing label): JohnKwan/Shutterstock; 105 (tapas illo): DiViArt/Shutterstock; 106 (woman): Antonio Diaz/123RF; 106 (man): AlenD/Shutterstock; 108 (Ever Given ship): Corona Borealis Studio/Shutterstock; 108 (camel train): Rolf_52/Shutterstock; 109: Tirachard Kumtanom/123RF.

Soft Skills Workshop 5 Page 110 (salad): Olena Danileiko/123RF; 110 (teenage boy): Suzanne Tucker/Shutterstock; 110 (street crime): Jacob Lund/Shutterstock; 110 (map): Qvasimodo art/Shutterstock; 111: Rawpixel/123RF.

ABOUT THE AUTHORS

Joan Saslow

Joan Saslow is a foreign language teaching specialist and author. She is co-author with Allen Ascher of a number of award-winning* best-selling English-language textbook series for adults and teenagers, most recently Pearson's *Top Notch* and *Summit*.

In addition, Ms. Saslow is author of the *Workplace Plus*, *Ready to Go*, and *Literacy Plus* series, as well as of *English in Context: Reading Comprehension for Science and Technology*. Earlier, she was series director of *True Colors* and *True Voices*.

Ms. Saslow is a frequent speaker at international teachers' conferences and participates in the English Language Specialist Program of the US Department of State's Bureau of Educational and Cultural Affairs. She has lived and taught in Chile and is fluent in Spanish.

Ms. Saslow has a BA and MA in French from the University of Wisconsin, Madison.

Allen Ascher

Allen Ascher has been an ELT teacher, teacher-trainer, academic director, consultant, and publisher. He is co-author with Joan Saslow of the award-winning* six-level *Top Notch* and *Summit* series for adults and young adults. He also authored the "Teaching Speaking" module of *Teacher Development Interactive*, Pearson's online multimedia teacher-training program. In addition to living and teaching in Beijing, China, he served as academic director of the intensive English language program at Hunter College and taught in the teaching certificate program at the New School in New York City.

Mr. Ascher has an MA in Applied Linguistics from Ohio University and has been a frequent presenter at professional conferences and teacher training events around the world.

**Top Notch* and *Summit* are each recipients of the Association of Educational Publishers' Distinguished Achievement Award, as well as the TAA (Textbook and Academic Authors Association) Textbook Excellence Award.

AUTHORS' ACKNOWLEDGMENTS

The authors wish to thank Katherine Klagsbrun for her contribution to the *Connectivity* series, notably the Soft Skills Boosters; the Vocabulary Booster in Foundations level; the Grammar Expanders and Writing Handbooks in levels 1-3, and the Extend-It Phrase Books and Extra Challenge Reading Activities in levels 4 and 5.

The authors are indebted to these reviewers, who provided extensive and detailed feedback and suggestions during the development of *Connectivity*, as well as the hundreds of teachers who completed surveys and participated in focus groups.

Jorge Aguilar, Centro de Estudio de Idiomas, Universidad Autónoma de Sinaloa, Mexico • **Manuel Wilson Alvarado Miles**, Quito, Ecuador • **Cris Asperti**, CEL LEP, São Paulo, Brazil • **Edwin Bello**, PROULEX, Guadalajara, Mexico • **Mery Blum**, CBA, Cochabamba, Bolivia • **Sandra Vargas Boecher Prates**, Programa Cursos de Línguas-UFES, Brazil • **Pamela Cristina Borja Baltán**, Quito, Ecuador • **Jorge Braga**, IBEU, Brazil • **Esther María Carbo Morales**, Quito, Ecuador • **Jorge Washington Cárdenas Castillo**, Quito, Ecuador • **Luis Angel Carrillo**, UNID, Mexico • **Angela de Alencar Carvalho Araújo**, Colégio Militar de Fortaleza, Fortaleza, CE, Brazil • **Angélica Chávez Escobar**, Universidad de León, Mexico • **Gemma Crouch**, ICPNA Chiclayo, Peru • **Mrs. Elizabeth Cruz Flores**, Tecnológico de Monterrey, Cuernavaca, Mexico • **Martin Del Castillo Palomino**, CIVIME Language School, Lima, Peru • **Ingrid Valverde Diaz del Olmo**, ICPNA Cusco, Peru • **Edith Espino Inadeh**, ITSE, Panama • **María Amparo García**, ICPNA Cusco, Peru • **Octavio Garduño Ruiz**, IPN Escuela de Turismo, Mexico • **Martha Angelina González Párraga**, Guayaquil, Ecuador • **Michael Hood**, Nihon University College of Commerce, Tokyo, Japan • **Zoe Hsu**, National Tainan University, Taiwan • **Segundo Huanambal Díaz**, ICPNA Chiclayo, Peru • **Jesse Huang**, National Central University, Taiwan • **Sara Iza Pazmiño**, Universidad Técnica de Ambato, Ecuador • **David Jiménez Huarhua**, CIVIME Language School, Lima, Peru • **Eleanor S. Leu**, Soochow University, Taiwan • **Yihui Li (Stella Li)**, Fooyin University, Taiwan • **Chi-Fan Lin**, Shih Hsin University, Taiwan • **Linda Lin**, Tatung Institute of Technology, Taiwan • **Patricio David López Logacho**, Quito, Ecuador • **Patricia Martins**, IBEU, Rio de Janeiro, Brazil • **Patricia McKay**, CEL LEP, São Paulo, Brazil • **María Teresa Meléndez Mantilla**, ICPNA Chiclayo, Peru • **Maria Helena Meyer**, ACEU, Salvador, Brazil • **Johana Melo**, Centro Colombo Americano, Bogotá, Colombia • **José Manuel Mendivil**, CBA, La Paz, Bolivia • **José de Jesús Mendoza Rivas**, Universidad Tecnológica de León, Mexico • **José Minaya Minaya**, CIVIME Language School, Lima, Peru • **Hiroko Miyake**, Tokyo Kasei University, Japan • **Luis Fernando Morales Severiche**, CBA, Santa Cruz Bolivia • **Andy Morera Calzada**, B-able-2 Academy, Quito, Ecuador • **Jason Moser, PhD**, Kanto Gakuin University, Japan • **Adrián Esteban Narváez Pacheco**, Cuenca, Ecuador • **Mónica Nomberto**, ICPNA Chiclayo, Peru • **Jaime Núñez**, Universidad Católica de Honduras, Honduras • **Tania Elizabeth Ortega Santacruz**, Cuenca, Ecuador • **Juan Camilo Ortegón**, Colombo, Cali, Colombia • **Lcdo. Javier Ortiz**, Project Santo Domingo de los Tsachilas (PUCESD), Ecuador • **Joselineth Padrón López**, Charlotte English School, Quito, Ecuador • **Martha Patricia del Carmen Páez**, Universidad Politécnica Salesiana, Quito, Ecuador • **Giuseppe Paldino Mayorga**, Jellyfish Learning Center, San Cristóbal, Ecuador • **Luis Antonio Paredes**, Universidad Central de Ecuador, Ecuador • **Tarik Preston**, Saudi Arabia • **Neusa Pretzel**, Skylimit Idiomas, Santa Cruz do Sul, Brazil • **Leni Puppin**, Programa Cursos de Línguas-UFES, Brazil • **Allen Quesada-Pacheco, Ph.D**, University of Costa Rica, San José, Costa Rica • **MA Rocío Isabel Rivera Cid**, Pontificia Universidad Católica de Valparaíso, Viña del Mar, Chile • **Luis Rodriguez Amau**, ICPNA Chiclayo, Peru • **Llilyan Rodríguez Conesa**, Charlotte English School, Quito, Ecuador • **Amalia Elvira Rodríguez Espinoza De Los Monteros**, Guayaquil, Ecuador • **Rolando Rodríguez Serra**, CIVIME Language School, Lima, Peru • **Melany Rodríguez-Cáceres**, Bogotá, Colombia • **Majid Safadaran Mosazadeh**, ICPNA Chiclayo, Peru • **Abutarab Saleem**, Hampson English, China • **Héctor Sánchez**, PROULEX, Guadalajara, Mexico • **Mónica Alexandra Sánchez Escalante**, Quito, Ecuador • **Jorge Mauricio Sánchez Montalvan**, Quito, Ecuador • **Cinthia S. Schmiedl Cornejo**, CBA, La Paz, Bolivia • **Judith Silva**, Universidad Técnica de Ambato, Ecuador • **Anamarija Skoda**, Pontificia Universidad Católica de Chile, Santiago de Chile, Chile • **Silvia Solares**, CBA, Sucre, Bolivia • **María Julia Suárez**, CBA, Cochabamba, Bolivia • **Mercedes Tapia Avalos**, CIVIME Language School, Lima, Peru • **Prof. Matthew Taylor**, Kinjo Gakuin University, Nagoya, Japan • **Eric Anthony Tejeda Evans**, PROULEX, Guadalajara, Mexico • **Blanca Luz Terrazas Zamora**, ICPNA Cusco, Peru • **Christian Juan Torres Medina**, Guayaquil, Ecuador • **Raquel Torrico**, CBA, Sucre, Bolivia • **Ana María de la Torre Ugarte**, ICPNA Chiclayo, Peru • **Magdalena Ullauri**, Universidad Nacional del Chimborazo, Riobamba, Ecuador • **Universidad Galileo**, Guatemala City, Guatemala • **Juan Omar Valdez**, DR-TESOL, Santo Domingo, Dominican Republic • **Susana Valdivia Marcovich**, URP, CIDUP and Euroidiomas, Lima, Peru • **Erika Valdivia de Souza**, CIVIME Language School, Lima, Peru • **Jay Veenstra**, Toyo University, Japan • **Solange Lopes Vinagre Costa**, SENAC, São Paulo, Brazil • **Magno Alejandro Vivar Hurtado**, Universidad Politécnica Salesiana, Cuenca, Ecuador • **Dr. Wen-hsien Yang**, National Kaohsiung Hospitality College, Kaohsiung, Taiwan • **Holger Zamora**, ICPNA Cuzco, Peru

LEARNING OBJECTIVES

Unit	COMMUNICATION GOALS	VOCABULARY	GRAMMAR
1 **Planning for a Career** page 2	• Describe someone's background • Discuss career and study plans • Discuss the qualities of a good résumé • Interview for a job	• Collocations for career and study plans **Word Study:** • Collocations with have and get for qualifications	• Simultaneous and sequential past actions: Review and expansion • Completed and uncompleted past actions closely related to the present **GRAMMAR EXPANDER** • Describing past actions and events: review • Stative verbs: non-action and action meanings
2 **Building Character** page 12	• Discuss when telling a lie might be acceptable • Accept responsibility and express regret • Identify the origins of moral principles • Describe the values you live by	• Accepting or avoiding responsibility • Some values	• Adjective clauses: review and expansion • "Comment" clauses introduced with which **GRAMMAR EXPANDER** • Adjective clauses: overview • Grammar for Writing: adjective clauses with quantifiers • Grammar for Writing: reduced adjective clauses
3 **Confronting Difficulty** page 24	• Describe how fear affects you physically • Express frustration, empathy, and encouragement • Explore the nature of heroism • Discuss overcoming disabilities	• Physical effects of fear • Expressing frustration, empathy, and encouragement **Word Study:** • Expanding vocabulary by using parts of speech	• Using so . . . (that) or such . . . (that) to explain a result • Clauses with no matter **GRAMMAR EXPANDER** • Count and non-count nouns: review and expansion • Embedded questions: review and common errors
4 **Building Relationships** page 34	• Introduce and respond to criticism • Give someone positive feedback • Explain how you handle anger • Explore your relationships with friends	• Shortcomings • Expressing and handling anger	• Cleft sentences: review and expansion • Adverb clauses of condition **GRAMMAR EXPANDER** • Cleft sentences: more on meaning and use • Grammar for Writing: more conjunctions and transitions
5 **What's Funny?** page 46	• Respond to humor • Explore the potential benefits of laughter • Analyze what makes people laugh • Discuss when joking "crosses the line"	• Types of humor • How to respond when someone tells a joke • Common types of jokes	• Questions in indirect speech • Indirect speech: statements: backshifts in tense and time expressions **GRAMMAR EXPANDER** • Indirect speech: review and expansion • Say, tell, and ask • Grammar for Writing: other reporting verbs

CONVERSATION STRATEGIES	LISTENING / PRONUNCIATION	READING	WRITING / SOFT SKILLS BOOSTER
• Ask, "What brings you here today?" to formally invite someone to request help or express a need. • Use "Correct me if I'm wrong, but . . ." to confirm something you believe to be true. • Say, "I've given it some thought, and . . ." to introduce a thoughtful opinion or change of mind. • Informally ask for advice with "I was hoping you could steer me in the right direction." • Formally express willingness to do something with "I'd be more than happy to . . ."	**Listening Skills:** • Listen to activate vocabulary • Listen for main idea • Listen to confirm content • Listen for supporting details **Pronunciation:** • Sentence stress and intonation: review	**Texts:** • A questionnaire about dreams, goals, and plans • An article about someone's career decision • An article on résumé writing • A résumé **Skills / strategies:** • Understand from context • Infer information • Apply ideas	**WRITING HANDBOOK** **Task:** • Write a cover letter for a job application **Skill:** • A formal cover letter **SOFT SKILLS BOOSTER** • Positive attitude: Encourage and offer suggestions to support others.
• Introduce an admission that you made a mistake with "I'm really sorry, but . . ." • Accept responsibility for a mistake with "It was totally my fault." • Express remorse for one's actions with expressions like "I'm so embarrassed," "I feel awful about it, etc." • Relieve someone's self-blame with "Look, these things happen." • Offer to make good on financial harm one has caused with "I insist on paying for it."	**Listening Skills:** • Listen to draw conclusions • Make personal comparisons • Listen to summarize • Understand from context • Listen for main idea and supporting details • Critical thinking **Pronunciation:** • Emphatic stress and pitch to express emotion	**Texts:** • A survey about taking or avoiding responsibility • An article about being truthful • An article about core values **Skills / strategies:** • Classify vocabulary • Understand vocabulary from context • Relate to personal experience	**WRITING HANDBOOK** **Task:** • Write a college application essay **Skill:** • Restrictive and non-restrictive adjective clauses **SOFT SKILLS BOOSTER** • Integrity: Indicate when your values are similar or different.
• Express concern for someone's state of mind with "Is everything OK?" • Begin an explanation with "Well, basically" to characterize a problem in just a few words. • Express empathy with "That must be tough." • Say "Hang in there" to offer encouragement to someone facing a difficulty. • Say "Anytime" to acknowledge someone's expression of gratitude.	**Listening Skills:** • Listen to activate vocabulary • Word study practice • Listen for supporting details • Listen to summarize a story **Pronunciation:** • Vowel reduction to /ə/	**Texts:** • A self-test about how chicken you are • A description of how fear affects someone physically • An article about Stevie Wonder and Evelyn Glennie **Skills / strategies:** • Relate to personal experience • Understand from context • Infer information	**WRITING HANDBOOK** **Task:** • Write a report about an event **Skill:** • Reducing adverbial clauses **SOFT SKILLS BOOSTER** • Effective communication: Use self-correction to repair errors or slips of the tongue.
• Politely introduce criticism or an uncomfortable topic with "There's something I need to bring up." • Say "I didn't realize . . ." to acknowledge your acceptance of someone's criticism. • Say "I didn't mean to . . ." to acknowledge how your behavior might have been interpreted. • Say "On the contrary" to assure someone you don't feel the way they think you might. • Express gratitude for someone's negative yet helpful feedback with "You've done me a favor."	**Listening Skills:** • Listen to activate grammar • Listen for main idea • Listen to infer **Pronunciation:** • Shifting emphatic stress	**Texts:** • Descriptions of people's shortcomings • Perspectives on feedback for employees • An interview about friendship **Skills / strategies:** • Identify main idea • Summarize	**WRITING HANDBOOK** **Task:** • Write an essay troubleshooting a common shortcoming **Skill:** • Transitional topic sentences **SOFT SKILLS BOOSTER** • Adaptability: Use hesitation expressions to prepare for unanticipated questions.
• Say "Come see this" to invite someone to look at something you think he or she will find interesting. • Say "Wait, what?" to informally express incredulity at what someone has just said. • Say "That cracks me up, actually" to admit that you find something pretty funny.	**Listening Skills:** • Listen to activate vocabulary • Listen for details • Listen to paraphrase • Listen to summarize **Pronunciation:** • Intonation of sarcasm	**Texts:** • An article about the health benefits of laughter • An article about what makes people laugh **Skills / strategies:** • Critical thinking • Understand main idea • Understand from context • Identify supporting details	**WRITING HANDBOOK** **Task:** • Write a story with dialogue **Skill:** • Writing dialogue **SOFT SKILLS BOOSTER** • Decisiveness: Offer a strong or weak hypothesis.

Unit	COMMUNICATION GOALS	VOCABULARY	GRAMMAR
6 **On the Move** page 56	• Describe how you deal with commuting • Help others avoid hassles while traveling • Talk about property lost, damaged, or stolen on a trip • Discuss protecting Internet security	• Travel hassles • Ways to politely ask for a favor **Word Study:** • Participial adjectives as noun modifiers	• The unreal conditional: continuous forms for actions in progress • The unreal conditional: statements with If it weren't for . . . / if it hadn't been for . . . **GRAMMAR EXPANDER** • Real and unreal conditionals: summary and expansion
7 **Belief and Reality** page 68	• Describe a scam • Describe fears and phobias • Talk about the power of suggestion • Discuss superstitions	• Phobias • Superstitions **Word Study:** • Noun and adjective forms	• Nouns: Indefinite, definite, unique, and generic meaning (review and expansion) • Reporting beliefs: It + a passive reporting verb **GRAMMAR EXPANDER** • Article usage: summary • Definite article: additional uses • Non-count nouns with both a countable and an uncountable sense • Grammar for Writing: passive reporting verbs with an infinitive phrase
8 **Achievement and Intelligence** page 78	• Identify your unique strengths • Talk about how you study • Discuss the effect of the environment on intelligence • Evaluate your emotional intelligence	• Ways to describe strengths and talents • Interpersonal and intrapersonal intelligence	• Using auxiliary do for emphatic stress • The subjunctive **GRAMMAR EXPANDER** • Grammar for Writing: emphatic stress • Infinitives and gerunds in place of the subjunctive
9 **Looking Ahead** page 90	• Discuss the pros and cons of innovative technologies • Make predictions about science and technology • Talk about preparing for future pandemics • Explain social and demographic trends	• Expressing and dismissing concern • Demographic and social trends	• The passive voice in unreal conditional sentences • The passive voice: the future, the future perfect, and the future as seen from the past **GRAMMAR EXPANDER** • Grammar for Writing: when to use the passive voice
10 **Global Ties** page 100	• React to international news events • Talk about the influence of foreign imports • Discuss the ways your culture might cause culture shock • Understand the impact of globalization	• Phrasal verbs for discussing events and issues • Discussing culture shock	• Separability of transitive phrasal verbs **GRAMMAR EXPANDER** • Phrasal verbs: expansion

Reference Charts .... page 112
Grammar Expander .... page 127
Pronunciation Lessons .... page 139

CONVERSATION STRATEGIES	LISTENING / PRONUNCIATION	READING	WRITING / SOFT SKILLS BOOSTER
• Ask a stranger for help with "I wonder if you could do me a favor." • Agree to offer assistance with "How can I help?" • Confirm willingness to perform a favor with "I'd be happy to." • Announce your return with "I'm back."	**Listening Skills:** • Listen to activate vocabulary • Listen to activate grammar • Listen for main idea • Listen to confirm content • Listen for supporting details **Pronunciation:** • Regular past participle endings • Reduction in perfect modals	**Texts:** • A travel hassles self-test • Interview responses about commuting hassles • An article about laptop disasters while traveling **Skills / strategies:** • Identify supporting details • Summarize • Discussion	**WRITING HANDBOOK** **Task:** • Write an essay comparing and contrasting two means of transportation **Skill:** • A comparison and contrast essay **SOFT SKILLS BOOSTER** • Problem solving: Give constructive feedback non-judgmentally.
• Indicate you've guessed someone's news with "Don't tell me . . ." • Say "Why am I not surprised?" to suggest an outcome should have been predictable. • Respond to a question with "Don't ask" to imply that the answer will be disappointing. • Begin a statement with "Let's just say . . ." to indicate you're going to make a long story short.	**Listening Skills:** • Listen for main idea • Listen for details • Listen to confirm content **Pronunciation:** • Linking sounds	**Texts:** • A fact sheet about scams • Two accounts of phobias • An article about placebos and nocebos **Skills / strategies:** • Understand from context • Infer information • Critical thinking	**WRITING HANDBOOK** **Task:** • Write an essay about superstitions **Skill:** • Subject-verb agreement: expansion **SOFT SKILLS BOOSTER** • Leadership: Encourage others to support their ideas.
• Indicate that you have prior knowledge about a situation with "So I understand (that) . . ." • Use "Would you say you . . . ?" to encourage someone to express a point of view. • Say "So here's what I'd suggest" to announce you're going to propose a plan. • Say "You can't go wrong" to support someone's tentative decision.	**Listening Skills:** • Listen to confirm content • Listen to clarify • Listen to draw conclusions **Pronunciation:** • Emphatic stress with auxiliary verbs	**Texts:** • A questionnaire on ability to focus and stick to a task • Descriptions of strengths and talents • Study tips • An article on measuring intelligence **Skills / strategies:** • Understand main idea • Understand details • Find supporting details	**WRITING HANDBOOK** **Task:** • Write an essay about staying focused on a task **Skill:** • Explaining cause and result **SOFT SKILLS BOOSTER** • Respectfulness: Interrupt and delay an interruption.
• Respond with "Seriously?" to express disbelief. • Use "I'd think twice before . . ." to advise cautiousness about a decision. • Agree with someone's statement of personal belief with "That makes two of us!"	**Listening Skills:** • Listen for point of view • Listen to summarize • Listen to activate vocabulary • Listen for facts and figures • Listen to draw conclusions **Pronunciation:** • Reading aloud	**Texts:** • A survey on beliefs about the future • An article on preparing for future pandemics **Skills / strategies:** • Understand writer's purpose • Understand from context • Activate language	**WRITING HANDBOOK** **Task:** • Write a formal essay about future trends **Skill:** • The thesis statement in a formal essay **SOFT SKILLS BOOSTER** • Conflict resolution: Respectfully acknowledge disagreement.
• Say "You name it" to indicate the list could be a lot longer. • To add to an already long list, say "To say nothing about . . ." • Begin a statement with "At least . . ." to express mild approval or relief.	**Listening Skills:** • Listen to infer meaning • Listen to summarize • Listen for details **Pronunciation:** • Intonation of tag questions	**Texts:** • A quiz on English today • An article on efforts to reduce hunger • People's opinions about foreign imports • An interview about the effects of globalization **Skills / strategies:** • Activate prior knowledge • Identify supporting details	**WRITING HANDBOOK** **Task:** • Write an essay about globalization **Skill:** • Rebutting an opposing point of view **SOFT SKILLS BOOSTER** • Negotiation: Attempt to come to agreement by supporting your view with respect.

Writing Handbook .... page 149
Soft Skills Booster .... page 159

COMPONENTS

For the Teacher

Connectivity makes lesson preparation easier with a wide array of time-saving tools for presentation and planning all in one place.

Presentation Tool

A digital tool for presenting the content of the Student's Book (and optional Workbook) in class, accessible through the Pearson English Portal.

Allows you to:
- navigate easily between units, lessons, and activities.
- pop up all activities from the page, for display and to show answers.
- play all the audio files from the page.
- present all the *Connectivity* videos, including Keep Talking Videos and *Connect TV* sitcom (lower levels) and authentic video (upper levels).
- plan dynamic lessons using the embedded teacher's notes.
- assign homework and tests.
… and much more!

The Presentation Tool is also available to download, enabling you to teach offline.

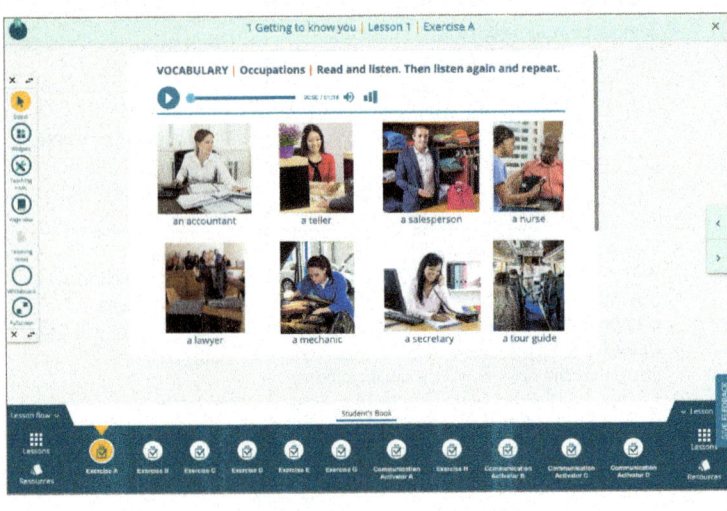

Teacher's Book and Lesson Planner

Detailed interleaved lesson plans, language and culture notes, optional activities, and more. Available in print and as a pdf in the Teacher's Resources on the Portal.

- Ideas for extension activities, differentiated instruction, teaching tips, alternative ways to do activities, advice on dealing with tricky language items, and notes on how to remediate and motivate students.
- Annotated answers on the facing Student's Book pages.

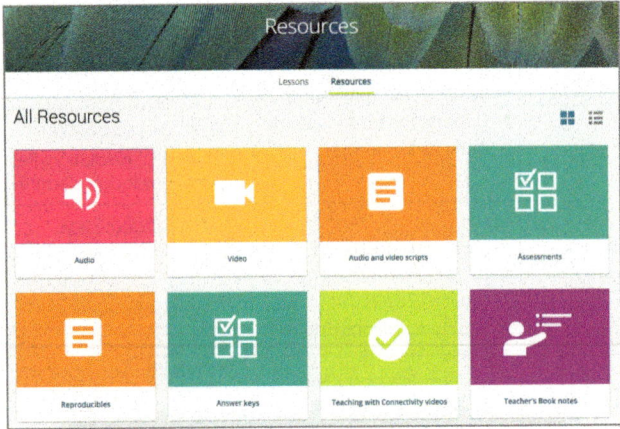

Teacher's Resources

Comprehensive, easy-to-access resources for planning, teaching, and professional development.

Includes:
- a wide variety of downloadable worksheets to enhance and extend each lesson.
- a dedicated *Connectivity* Methods Handbook which highlights *Connectivity's* course pedagogy and offers best practices for teaching a communicative course.
- *Teaching with Connectivity* videos, for overview, planning, and teacher support.
- answer keys and audio/video scripts.
- Global Scale of English mapping booklets, for efficient planning.
- Soft Skills Mapping Document to build awareness of the essential soft skills students are acquiring as they engage in course activities.
- ready-made Unit, Midterm, and Final achievement tests, with a test generator.

For the Student

A code gives students access to the digital components: the Student's eBook, a Student's app, and Online Practice. A separate print Workbook is also available.

Student's eBook

The Student's Book in digital format.

The eBook enables students to access their Student's Book materials on their computer and mobile devices, wherever and whenever they want. The digital format enhances student engagement with interactive activities, and audio and video at the point of use.

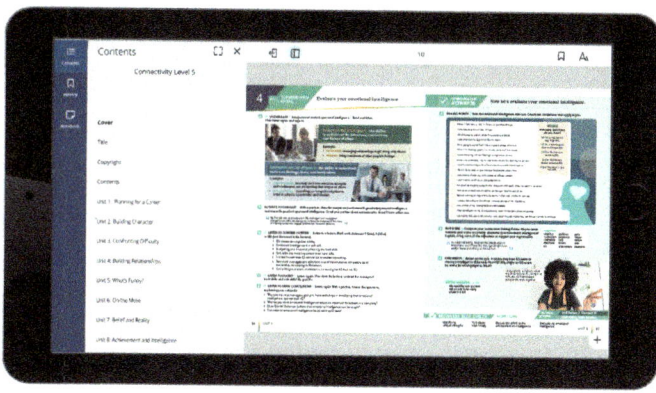

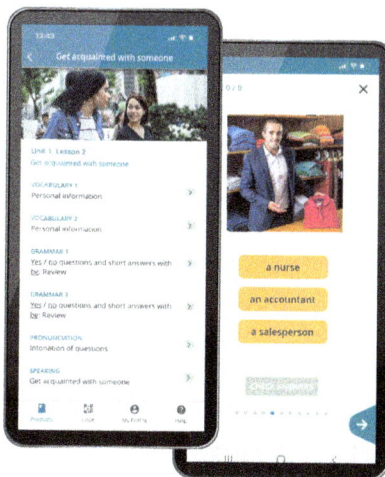

Student's app

Digital practice that empowers students to take charge of their learning outside of class, online and offline.

It gives students access anytime, anywhere to the complete *Connectivity* audio and video program as well as hundreds of activities for grammar, vocabulary, pronunciation, listening comprehension, and speaking practice. The app content is available on the Pearson Practice English App.

Online Practice

Lesson-by-lesson exercises to accompany the Student's Book with an abundance of interactive practice activities in all skills.

Offers:
- immediate feedback on wrong answers.
- a listen-and-record feature that allows students to compare their pronunciation to a model.
- extra reading and writing practice.
- a perfomance area that helps students keep track of their progress and plan future practice.

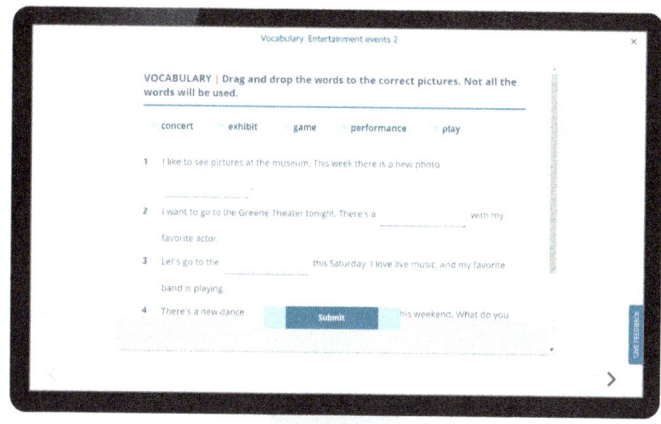

Workbook

Lesson-by-lesson written practice activities to accompany the Student's Book, providing extra practice for vocabulary, grammar, conversation, social language, reading, and writing.

Offers:
- open-ended, personalized activities to increase student engagement.
- full-color design with numerous illustrations and photos.
- additional exercises for the Grammar Expander and Writing Handbook.

KEY TO ICONS IN THE STUDENT'S BOOK

Digital resources are available on the **Pearson English Portal** (the access code is provided on the inside front cover). Audio and video are also available in the **Student's eBook** and **Pearson Practice English App**.

CORE MATERIAL

Student's Book icon	What is it?
(audio icon)	Student's Book audio
KEEP TALKING! — Watch the video for ideas!	*Keep Talking* videos that provide dramatized models of extended conversation, discussion, and role play to accelerate students' communicative competence

SUPPLEMENTAL MATERIAL

Student's Book icon	What is it?
FOR MORE PRACTICE, GO TO YOUR DIGITAL RESOURCES	An abundance of digital resources comes with every *Connectivity* Student's Book: • Pearson Practice English App: A mobile app that provides additional language practice activities, and gives students quick access to course audio and video • Online Practice: Additional practice activities tied to a gradebook (these activities are different from the ones included on the app)
For more practice...	End-of-unit review and extension material offered in several formats: • Unit Review: Printable exercises for extra listening comprehension and language practice • *Connect TV*: Engaging authentic video for language consolidation and fun • Test-Taking Skills Booster: Practice for skills typically included in standardized proficiency tests
GRAMMAR EXPANDER PRONUNCIATION LESSONS SOFT SKILLS BOOSTER WRITING HANDBOOK	Optional lessons that align with the content in each unit, covering grammar, pronunciation, writing, and soft skills. These lessons appear at the back of the Student's Book.

TO THE TEACHER

Connectivity is a six-level course for adults and young adults who need to use English fluently and confidently in their life and work, and to interact with people from a variety of language backgrounds and cultures.

Ideal for students who lack opportunities to observe or practice English outside of class, *Connectivity* creates a highly enriched blended language learning experience by ensuring:

- rich exposure to natural authentic spoken and written language models.
- thorough coverage of form, meaning, and use.
- continual integration, recycling, and activation of new language.
- ongoing confirmation of progress and self-assessment.

With two alternative entry points—*Connectivity Foundations* for true beginners and *Connectivity 1* for false beginners—the course is benchmarked to the Global Scale of English and tightly correlated to the Can-do Statements of the Common European Framework of Reference. All six levels are available in full and split formats.

Each full level of *Connectivity* provides 60–90 hours of instruction and is designed for use in traditional, hybrid, flipped, and blended settings. An unequaled array of printable, digital, and online resources makes it easy to vary and tailor the course to your teaching style, your learners' needs, your available time, or even to extend the hours of instruction to up to 120 hours.

SIGNATURE FEATURES

A Systematic Speaking Pedagogy

Connectivity rigorously develops learners' linguistic, socio-linguistic, and pragmatic competence and fluency. Socially authentic model conversations systematically encourage improvisation and extension, and discussion preparation activities recycle language and build confidence. Soft skills practice—woven throughout—prepares learners for employability and workplace success in English. Mediation activities ensure students can use English to interact with people from diverse language and culture groups and are able to react to, summarize, and paraphrase spoken and written texts in English. An optional Soft Skills Booster (Levels 1–5) provides spoken practice of a selected soft skill for each unit. Level 4 also offers an Extend-It lesson after every two units that consolidates and applies previously learned language through collaboration on a variety of motivating tasks, such as projects and role plays. In Level 5, a Soft Skills Workshop after every two units provides opportunities to put collaboration, teamwork, and presentation into practice.

Explicit Grammar and Vocabulary

Connectivity takes the guesswork out of form, meaning, and use. Clear charts illustrate grammar and usage in context and *Notice the Grammar* activities increase learners' grammar awareness. *Pronounce the Grammar* activities promote spoken mastery. Clear captioned picture-dictionary-style vocabulary illustrations with accompanying audio ensure understanding and accurate pronunciation of new words. Interactive digital vocabulary flash cards provide continual practice and recycling for memorability.

Individualized Teaching and Learning

Respecting teachers' individual styles and preferences, as well as their limited time to prepare material, *Connectivity* offers over a thousand extra ready-to-use printable extension activities so that teachers never have to search for or create supplements. A wide choice of extra speaking activities, unit reviews, supplementary pronunciation activities, inductive grammar charts, unit study guides, writing process worksheets, video worksheets, flash cards, extra grammar exercises, test-taking skill builders, and more are available for every unit.

A Multi-faceted Audio and Video Program

Connectivity includes a wealth of audio and video features for the modeling of authentic speech, conversation pair work activation, listening comprehension practice, pronunciation practice, and fun. So that students will be prepared to understand English as an international language, the audio includes a variety of native and non-native accents. *Connectivity's* listening comprehension syllabus builds key skills and strategies to improve listening proficiency. Practi-chants (*Foundations*) develop fluency and confidence with the support of a fun and engaging beat. For further guidance, Pronunciation and Grammar Coach videos accompany levels Foundations to 3. The *Keep Talking* video increases oral production and fluency. *Connect TV* (Foundations–Level 3) is a hilarious situation comedy that keeps students laughing and learning. *Connect TV* (Levels 4–5) offers authentic video that has been curated for the student's level.

We hope that *Connectivity* maximizes your enjoyment and success!
We wrote it for you.

Joan Saslow and Allen Ascher

UNIT 6

On the Move

PREVIEW

A 🔊 **LOST PROPERTY** | Listen to a podcast about a common hassle in airline travel. What is the problem the speaker is discussing? What does the speaker suggest doing?

B 🔊 **ZOOM-IN** | Read and listen to two colleagues discussing Internet security. Notice the <u>featured</u> words and phrases.

> **UNDERSTAND A VARIETY OF ACCENTS**
> **Jason** = American English (standard)
> **David** = American English (regional)

Jason: Oh no. Not again. <u>Can't they just leave me be</u>?
David: What's the matter?
Jason: This pop-up asking me to enable two-factor authentication. It's like <u>the umpteenth time</u>.
David: You mean you don't have it? <u>You're playing with fire</u> if you don't.
Jason: David, I'm pretty careful about my passwords. I even have a password manager. What could go wrong?
David: Plenty.
Jason: Like what?
David: You could get hacked.
Jason: Even with a password manager? How likely is that?
David: What if you forget your master password? And I've heard password managers aren't 100% secure. They say they can be hacked if your device is infected with malware.
Jason: Come on. I'm a pretty careful guy. I don't ever click on links or download files from a source I don't trust. <u>What are the odds</u> of getting infected if I'm that careful?
David: I'm not sure, but they say that adding two-factor authentication really increases security. <u>You just can't be too careful these days</u>.
Jason: No offense, but I think that's <u>a little over the top</u>. That two-factor authentication is a real pain in the neck. You can't get into anything without waiting for a 4-digit code. Some of those things even ask you to answer a bunch of security questions!
David: Jason, <u>take my word for it</u>. A little hassle's nothing compared to dealing with identity theft. Get the two-factor. <u>You just can't beat</u> the security it provides.

C **UNDERSTAND FROM CONTEXT** | With a partner, discuss and complete the definition for each <u>featured</u> word or phrase from Zoom-In. Then use them in your own sentences.

1. If something happens for "the umpteenth time," it has happened ....
2. If you ask, "What are the odds," it means you don't think something is very ....
3. If you call something "a little over the top," you mean that it's ....
4. If you tell someone to "take your word for it," you mean you want the person to ....
5. If you say, "You just can't beat" something, you mean that it's ....

D **THINK AND EXPLAIN** | Answer the questions.

1. Why does Jason say, "Can't they just leave me be?"
2. Why does David tell Jason he's "playing with fire"?
3. Why does David say, "You just can't be too careful these days"?

E **LOOK IT UP AND SHARE** | Find a word or phrase in Zoom-In that was new to you. Look it up and use it in a sentence. Share your sentence with a partner.

....

F **DISCUSSION** | Do you think having both a password manager and using two-factor authentication is over the top? Is David too much of a worrywart? Explain.

UNIT 6
COMMUNICATION GOALS

Lesson 1 Describe how you deal with commuting
Lesson 2 Help others avoid hassles while traveling
Lesson 3 Talk about property lost, damaged, or stolen on a trip
Lesson 4 Discuss protecting Internet security

G TALKING POINTS | Take the self-test.

ARE YOU AN EXPERIENCED TRAVELER?

Check the travel hassles you've faced on trips you've taken by car, plane, bus, or train.

- [ ] inedible or disgusting airline food
- [ ] no meals on a long flight
- [ ] insufficient room in overhead bins
- [ ] an overbooked flight
- [ ] lost luggage
- [ ] a long line
- [ ] a long delay
- [ ] a flat tire
- [ ] a mechanical breakdown
- [ ] poor air-conditioning or heating
- [ ] no cell phone service or Wi-Fi
- [ ] uncomfortable seating
- [ ] an aggressive driver
- [ ] a huge traffic jam
- [ ] finding a bathroom
- [ ] finding something to eat
- [ ] getting towed
- [ ] getting lost
- [ ] missing a connection
- [ ] other _____

HOW MANY HASSLES DID YOU CHECK?

1–5	**Novice traveler:** You have a lot to learn.
6–10	**Intermediate traveler:** You're getting better at dealing with hassles.
11–15	**Experienced traveler:** You know how to avoid trouble.
16–20	**Seasoned traveler:** You've seen it all! Nothing freaks you out.

H PAIR WORK | Compare scores on Talking Points. Which of you has experienced more hassles? Tell your partner about your worst experience while traveling. Ask and answer questions about your partner's experiences.

START TALKING

DISCUSSION Discuss the questions.

- How can travelers plan for and avoid some of the hassles in Talking Points?

> " It's a good idea to schedule enough time between connecting flights. You just can't be too careful about that. "

- Are you more like Jason in Zoom-In, and hassled by security reminders and pop-ups on your phone? Or are you more like David, and appreciative of reminders? Explain.

> " I'm more like Jason. If you ask me, David's attitude is a little over the top. "

1 COMMUNICATION GOAL | Describe how you deal with commuting

A 🔊 **GRAMMAR CLOSE-UP** | Read about each person's commute. Notice the <u>featured</u> grammar.

Tell us about your commute to work or school.

There are other options, but I choose to drive to work every day in the comfort and safety of my own car. If I <u>weren't driving</u>, <u>I'd have to take</u> three buses to get there. And unfortunately, in this town the buses aren't always safe. I've been pickpocketed on the bus twice. There's sometimes traffic on my route during the evening rush hour, but parking is probably the biggest hassle I have to deal with. Just last week I got a parking ticket because I had forgotten to renew my parking pass. If I <u>hadn't been working</u> such long hours, I probably <u>wouldn't have forgotten</u> to renew that pass.

There are never enough hours in the day to both work and exercise, so I have to multi-task to stay fit. How? I walk to work. I figure if I <u>weren't walking</u> to work and back five days a week, <u>I'd be huffing and puffing</u> on a treadmill—<u>and paying</u> for an expensive gym membership. The downsides? It takes me about forty minutes door-to-door, and the bus only takes ten. But my worst hassle is that drivers are inconsiderate and don't always respect the pedestrian right of way, which can be dangerous. But if I <u>hadn't made</u> a resolution to get my exercise this way, <u>I'd be spending</u> all my exercise hours in a car in traffic <u>or waiting</u> around for a bus or train. I prefer it my way.

I use a rideshare app to get to my job at the university. I only work three days a week, so it doesn't cost me an arm and a leg, and I don't have to own a car. I <u>would take</u> the subway if the city <u>weren't</u> constantly <u>making</u> track repairs <u>and rerouting</u> trains. And if it <u>weren't</u> for my rideshare, <u>I'd be</u> constantly <u>worrying</u> about how long it would be till the next train arrived.

B **PAIR WORK** | Is your commute a hassle? Tell your partner about its upsides and downsides.

C **GRAMMAR** | The unreal conditional: continuous forms for actions in progress

Unreal conditional sentences can describe actions in progress. You can use the continuous in one or both clauses, depending on your meaning.

Present unreal conditional sentences
 Use <u>were</u> / <u>weren't</u> + a present participle in the <u>if</u> clause.
 Use <u>would</u> / <u>wouldn't</u> + a present participle in the result clause.
  If they **were driving** home right now, they **wouldn't be wasting** time at that bus stop! [continuous in both clauses]
  If buses were more frequent, we**'d be riding** on one now. [continuous only in the result clause]

Past unreal conditional sentences
 Use <u>had</u> / <u>hadn't been</u> + a present participle in the <u>if</u> clause. Use <u>would</u> / <u>wouldn't have been</u> + a present participle in the result clause.
  If I **hadn't been talking** on the phone, I **would have been watching** the news of the bridge collapse on TV. [continuous in both clauses]
  We **would have been parking** there every day if they hadn't closed the garage. [continuous in the result clause only]

Sentences with mixed time frames
 All unreal conditional sentences can mix present and past time frames within the same sentence to reflect meaning. The continuous form can be in one or both clauses, depending on meaning.
  If the travel agent **had been** honest about how much time is needed between flights, I **wouldn't be spending** the night in the airport waiting for the next flight. [past condition / present result]
  I **would have had to join** a gym if I **weren't walking** to work every day. [past result / present condition]

> **Remember:** Conditional sentences contain an <u>if</u> clause and a result clause.
>
> **Real conditional sentences** describe the present or future results of real conditions.
> If I **go** to sleep early, I **wake up** early. (present)
> If you **take** the bus, you**'ll arrive** late. (future)
>
> **Unreal conditional sentences** describe the present or past results of unreal conditions.
> If I **were** you, I **would take** the train. (present)
> If he **had driven**, he **would have gotten** lost. (past)

> **Be careful!** Don't use <u>would</u> in the <u>if</u> clause in any unreal conditional sentence.
> If **I were taking** the late train, . . .
> NOT If I ~~would be taking~~ the late train . . .

GRAMMAR EXPANDER p. 127
Real and unreal conditionals: summary and expansion

UNIT 6

D UNDERSTAND THE GRAMMAR | Choose the sentence that best explains the meaning of each quotation. Then, with a partner, make a statement with <u>should have</u> to indicate what could have prevented the problem.

1 "If I'd taken the subway, I wouldn't be waiting around for a driver to confirm my rideshare."
   a I took the subway, so I don't have to wait for the rideshare driver's confirmation.
   b I didn't take the subway, so I'm waiting for the rideshare driver's confirmation.
   c I took the subway, and I'm waiting for the rideshare driver's confirmation.

2 "If I'd been walking to work instead of driving, I wouldn't have gotten a parking ticket."
   a I was walking to work, and I got a parking ticket.
   b I wasn't walking to work, but I didn't get a parking ticket.
   c I wasn't walking to work, and I got a parking ticket.

3 "I wouldn't be paying extra for my luggage if the airline didn't have a weight limit."
   a I'm paying extra for my luggage because the airline has a weight limit.
   b I'm not paying extra for my luggage because the airline doesn't have a weight limit.
   c I would pay extra for my luggage if the airline had a weight limit.

> If I'd bought gas yesterday on my way home, I wouldn't be walking to the gas station now!
>
> You should have at least checked the gas gauge before you left this morning.

E GRAMMAR PRACTICE | Circle the correct verb or verb phrase to complete each statement.

1 If you (would be / were) driving home now, you (would be / would have been) sitting in traffic.

2 If my phone battery (weren't / isn't) dead, I'd (be calling / have called) the rideshare now.

3 She (wouldn't be paying / would have paid) a parking fine if she (wouldn't be parking / hadn't parked) in a no-parking zone.

4 If he (hadn't been / wouldn't have been) riding the subway during rush hour, he wouldn't (get / have gotten) pickpocketed.

5 If Jill (hadn't been / had been) paying attention to the time, she wouldn't (be waiting / wait) for a train that had already left.

F PAIR WORK | Take turns completing the unreal conditional statements, using continuous verb forms.

1 If it were the weekend, I ....
2 I wouldn't have been late to class if ....
3 We would be watching a game right now if ....
4 If I were on vacation, I ....
5 I'd have seen the accident if ....

1 If it were the weekend, I'd be taking a walk right now.

COMMUNICATION ACTIVATOR

Now let's describe how we deal with commuting.

A TALKING POINTS | Write about two commuting hassles you have (or someone you know has) experienced. Include statements about how each problem could have been avoided or prevented.

What was the hassle?	How I could have avoided or prevented it
On my way to an interview, I had a flat tire, and I was late.	I should have checked my tire pressure.
What was the hassle?	How I could have avoided or prevented it

Common hassles
- getting stuck in traffic
- a mechanical breakdown
- no parking spaces available
- crowded public transportation
- a flat tire
- rush hour traffic
- inconsiderate drivers
- getting pickpocketed
- other: ___

KEEP TALKING! ●●●
- Ask about how your partner handled each hassle.
- Suggest ways the problem could have been avoided.
- Say as much as you can.
- ▶ Watch the video for ideas!

B DISCUSSION | Tell your partner about your two experiences from Talking Points in more detail. Include one statement beginning with <u>If I had been</u> + a present participle and / or one with <u>If I hadn't been</u> + a present participle.

> "If I'd been checking the tire pressure regularly, I wouldn't have had a flat tire."

2 COMMUNICATION GOAL Help others avoid hassles while traveling

A 🔊 **VOCABULARY** | Ways to politely ask for a favor | Read and listen. Then listen again and repeat.

Would you mind giving me a hand with this?

Do you think you could point me in the right direction?

Could I ask you to keep an eye on my things?

Could you possibly grab that for me?

Would you be nice enough to save my place in line?

Would you please let me through?

B 🔊 **LISTEN TO ACTIVATE VOCABULARY** | Listen to each conversation and write the letter of the favor that you predict the speaker will request.

..... 1 a Could you possibly save my place in line?
..... 2 b Would you mind giving me a hand with it?
..... 3 c Do you think you could point me in the right direction?
..... 4 d Would you please let me through?
..... 5 e Would you be nice enough to grab it for me?
..... 6 f Would you be nice enough to keep an eye on them?

C **GRAMMAR** | The unreal conditional: statements with <u>If it weren't for</u> . . . / <u>If it hadn't been for</u> . . .

Use <u>If it weren't for</u> . . . or <u>If it hadn't been for</u> . . . + an object in a present or past unreal conditional statement to express relief or regret that the circumstances didn't lead to a different outcome.

Relief
  If it weren't for your help, we'd still be at the airport waiting for our bags. (But, in fact, you *did* help us. So everything turned out fine.)
  I think I would have gotten lost **if it hadn't been for** my GPS. (But, in fact, I *didn't* get lost, thanks to my GPS.)

Regret
  If it weren't for the rain, we would eat lunch outside. (But it's raining, so we won't.)
  If it hadn't been for the terrible traffic, they wouldn't have been so late. (But they *were* late because the traffic was terrible.)

> **Remember:** You can also express strong regret with <u>If only</u> + <u>were</u> or a past perfect form.
> **If only** you **were** here.
> **If only** it **hadn't been** raining!
> **If only** the traffic **hadn't been** so terrible.

D **NOTICE THE GRAMMAR** | Find and underline examples of the unreal conditional expressing either relief or regret in Grammar Close-Up on page 58. Which does each express?

E **UNDERSTAND THE GRAMMAR** | Listen to the conversations and infer whether the speakers are expressing relief or regret.

1 relief / regret
2 relief / regret
3 relief / regret
4 relief / regret
5 relief / regret
6 relief / regret

F **LISTEN TO ACTIVATE GRAMMAR** | Listen again. Complete the paraphrase of what happened in each conversation. Use <u>if it weren't for</u> or <u>if it hadn't been for</u>.

1 .... the fact that they saw the other car, they might have had an accident.
2 Millie would love to go on the tour .... her cold.
3 They might still be in line .... the fact that she speaks Spanish.
4 They wouldn't be late for the play .... the flat tire.
5 .... her thoughtlessness, she thinks they wouldn't have divorced.
6 He might still be waiting for the bus .... Ben.

G **GRAMMAR PRACTICE** | On a separate sheet of paper, restate each sentence as an unreal conditional statement with <u>if it weren't for</u> or <u>if it hadn't been for</u>.

Example: Because of the weather, they have to reschedule the game. | *If it weren't for the weather, they wouldn't have to reschedule the game.*

1 Because I have this terrible backache, I can't take you to the airport this evening.
2 Because I got a wake-up call, I didn't miss our appointment.
3 Because they made the announcement, we didn't go to the wrong departure gate.
4 Because of the flight attendant's help, I was able to put my bag in the overhead bin.
5 Because of the airline's automatic text message, we didn't arrive late.

H **GRAMMAR PRACTICE** | Complete the statements with true information, using <u>if it weren't for</u> or <u>if it hadn't been for</u>. Then, with a partner, take turns reading your statements aloud.

1 ...., I wouldn't be able to speak English as well as I can today.
2 I wouldn't have chosen to study English ....
3 ...., I would have chosen a different career path.
4 I would have slept late today ....

Now let's help others avoid hassles while traveling.

A **CONVERSATION MODEL** | Read and listen.
A: Excuse me. I wonder if you could do me a favor.
B: Sure. How can I help?
A: I think I left my boarding pass at the counter. Would you mind keeping an eye on my things?
B: Not at all. I'd be happy to. The lines are so long today.
...
A: I'm back. Thanks so much.
B: No problem.
A: I'm not sure what I would have done if it hadn't been for your help.

Social language
Respond willingly to a request for a favor with "How can I help?"

B **PRONUNCIATION PRACTICE** | Listen again and repeat. Then practice the Conversation Model with a partner.

C **IN YOUR OWN WORDS** | Create a similar conversation, using the Vocabulary. Start like this: *Excuse me. I wonder if you could do me a favor?* Be sure to change roles and then partners. (Option: Use the Unit 6 Energizer Worksheet.)

KEEP TALKING! •••
- Say more about why you need help.
- Explain the possible consequences if you don't get help.
- Continue the conversation with small talk.
- Say as much as you can.

▶ Watch the video for ideas!

3 COMMUNICATION GOAL: Talk about property lost, damaged, or stolen on a trip

A 🔊 **READING** | Read about two losses. Which do you think was worse?

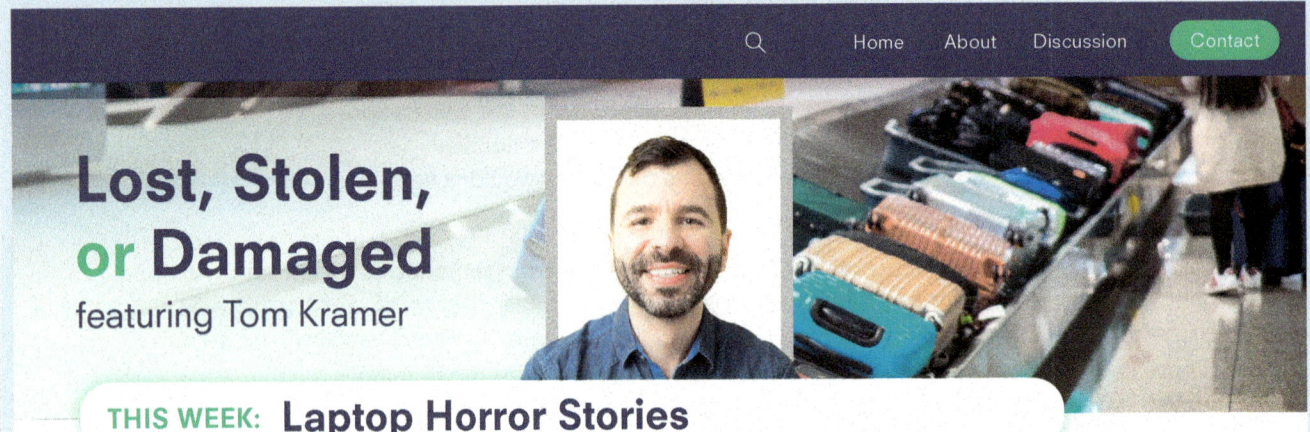

Lost, Stolen, or Damaged
featuring Tom Kramer

THIS WEEK: Laptop Horror Stories

Here are two tales about laptop disasters on the road.

Dear Tom,

I recently visited Peru on business and had an early morning flight from Lima to Trujillo, so I stayed in the airport hotel. I unfortunately overslept and ended up rushing through security to catch my plane. Of course, I had to remove my laptop from my carry-on for inspection. It wasn't until I unpacked my bag in Trujillo that I realized the laptop wasn't in it. And then it dawned on me: Duh! I must have forgotten to put it back in my bag at Lima security. Since I don't speak Spanish, I had a local colleague contact the airline, but no one had turned in the lost device. On my way back to Lima, I checked again. I was able to inquire in English, but there was no record of anyone having found it. I could just kick myself. If it hadn't been for oversleeping and rushing through security, this never would have happened. Do you have any suggestions to help me keep my wits about me next time?

Kim Ho-suk, Seoul, South Korea

 Sorry to hear about your misfortune. If it makes you feel any better, the US Transportation Security Administration (TSA) reports that between $800,000 and $1,000,000 in loose change is left behind by passengers going through security in U.S. airports in a typical year. Other items typically left behind are belts, keys, glasses, and . . . yes, laptops. Seasoned travelers make a short mental checklist they automatically review before leaving security for their gate. (Laptop? Wallet? Phone? Keys? . . .) Even better, when you get around to replacing the device, consider getting laptop tracking software that will locate it for you if you ever get separated from it again. The extra cost is well worth it.

Dear Tom,

Two months ago, I was attending a conference in Los Angeles and I had a freak accident with my laptop. I needed to do some work in my hotel room, so I set up my laptop on the coffee table in front of the sofa. Fortunately, I got up to make myself a cup of coffee. I say fortunately because as soon as I got up a big chunk of the ceiling crashed down right onto my laptop! If it hadn't been for that cup of coffee, the ceiling would have fallen onto my head. I called the front desk, and they sent up a repair crew—for the ceiling. But my laptop? Since it's still working, they offered to pay for a repair instead of a replacement. Tom, don't you think that's wrong? The screen is badly cracked and it's an absolute mess.

Helena Elyakim, Minneapolis, US

 Well, you can thank your lucky stars for that coffee break, but shame on the hotel for not offering to cover the cost of a replacement! Even though you apparently didn't insist, it's not too late. I suggest you get a lawyer to contact them. I'm sure the hotel has insurance to pay for damages they cause to property. In the meantime, let this be a warning to all our readers to always look around your hotel room for any potential problems—such as cracks in the ceiling! Good luck, and let me know if this gets resolved.

B **IDENTIFY SUPPORTING DETAILS** | Mark each statement T (true) or F (false). With a partner, correct the false statements, using information from the article.

.... 1 Mr. Kim had to rush through security because he left his laptop behind.
.... 2 Mr. Kim realized that his laptop was missing after he arrived at the hotel in Lima.
.... 3 Mr. Kim realized that he had forgotten to put the laptop back into his carry-on.
.... 4 Mr. Kramer suggests a mental checklist to avoid leaving things behind.
.... 5 Mr. Kramer points out that it's common for people to leave property behind at airport security.
.... 6 Ms. Elyakim's hotel agreed to pay for a replacement laptop.
.... 7 Mr. Kramer suggests Ms. Elyakim's situation is hopeless and she should just learn from the experience and buy a new laptop.

C **SUMMARIZE** | With a partner, take turns summarizing the two stories. Say as much as you can.

D **DISCUSSION** | Discuss the questions.

1 What would you do if you discovered that your laptop was missing when you arrived at your hotel?
2 What do you think is a good method to avoid leaving things behind when you are distracted or in a hurry?
3 What do you think the hotel should have done in response to Ms. Elyakim's situation with the damaged laptop?

Now let's talk about property lost, damaged, or stolen on a trip.

A **TALKING POINTS** | Write notes about a time your property (or the property of someone you know) was lost, stolen, or damaged on a trip or a commute.

> What happened? *I left my watch behind.*
> When? *last year*   Where? *at a hotel in Chicago*
> Write a brief summary and what the outcome was: *I was in a hurry for my flight home and accidentally left it on the dresser. I contacted the hotel and they sent it to me the next day.*

What happened?
When?   Where?
Write a brief summary and what the outcome was:

B **DISCUSSION** | Describe the events you wrote about in Talking Points. Ask about your partner's experience and discuss how to avoid having it happen again. (Option: Use the Unit 6 Soft Skills Booster, p. 159.)

> When did you discover that your watch was missing?

> When I was in line at the airport, I looked at my wrist to check the time, and it wasn't there.

→ RECYCLE THIS LANGUAGE
I [lost it] for the umpteenth time!
What are the odds of that?
You can't beat [making a list].
Take my word for it. . . .

4 COMMUNICATION GOAL Discuss protecting Internet security

A **WORD STUDY** | Participial adjectives as noun modifiers | The past participles of transitive verbs can function as noun modifiers. Read and listen. Then listen and repeat.

a **hacked** email account → The email account was **hacked**.
a **damaged** reputation → His reputation is **damaged**.
an **encrypted** website → The website is **encrypted**.
a **required** username → The username is **required**.
a **lost** password → The password was **lost**.
stolen credentials → The credentials were **stolen**.
a **canceled** credit card → The credit card was **canceled**.
a **trusted** source → The source is **trusted**.

The airline called to tell me they'd found my **lost** cell phone. Duh! I didn't even realize it was **lost**!

PRONUNCIATION LESSON p. 139
• Regular past participle endings
• Reduction in perfect modals

B **WORD STUDY PRACTICE** | Rewrite each sentence that contains an underlined pronoun, using a participial adjective as a noun modifier.

I asked the hotel to replace my damaged laptop.

1 (My laptop was damaged.) I asked the hotel to replace it.
   ....
2 (Her identity was stolen.) She repaired it by going through a lot of complicated steps.
   ....
3 (The plane was delayed.) It caused us to miss our connecting flight.
   ....
4 (The hotel Wi-Fi was broken.) I couldn't log on to it for two hours.
   ....
5 (My phone was lost.) I told the airline about it as soon as I arrived.
   ....

C **LISTEN FOR MAIN IDEA** | Listen to Part 1 of a podcast interview. What's Steve Lingen's main idea?
☐ 1 When credit card fraud is detected, your card is canceled and replaced.
☐ 2 Sending personal information over the Internet can be dangerous.
☐ 3 Some people use the same username and password across many sites.

D **UNDERSTAND FROM CONTEXT** | Read the words and phrases. Then listen to Part 1 again and, with a partner, explain the meaning of each one.

1 connectivity   2 a fraud alert   3 log-on credentials   4 identity theft

E **LISTEN TO CONFIRM CONTENT** | Now listen to Part 2 of the podcast. Mark each of the following statements T (true), F (false), or NI (no information).

.... 1 Encrypted information is unintelligible.
.... 2 Unintelligible information is inaccessible to hackers.
.... 3 The three main ways we access the Internet while traveling are never secure.
.... 4 Airport public Wi-Fi hotspots are safer than the ones in cafés.
.... 5 Hotel Wi-Fi networks can be safe, but it's impossible to know.
.... 6 A VPN is worthwhile for people who travel a lot.
.... 7 Malware can protect your device from hackers.

UNIT 6

F 🔊 **LISTEN FOR SUPPORTING DETAILS** | Discuss these questions with a partner. Listen to Part 2 again to confirm your conclusions.

1 Why should you not log on to financial institutions and online retailers while you're on a public Wi-Fi?
2 Why should we not assume a hotel's Wi-Fi network is secure?
3 What are three possible consequences of providing information on an unencrypted site?
4 What are two common ways you might enable hackers to install malware on your device?

Now let's discuss protecting Internet security.

A **TALKING POINTS** | Complete the chart by indicating your Internet habits at home or on the move.

	Always	Sometimes	Never or rarely
I use public Wi-Fi hotspots.			
I check to see if the websites I visit are encrypted.			
I use a different password for each site that requires one.			
I use two-factor authentication.			
I use a password manager.			
I set my portable devices to automatically connect to Wi-Fi in the area.			
I set my device to automatically remember and fill in my passwords.			
I take actions to protect myself from identity theft.			
Add any other steps you take (or think you should take):			

B **GROUP WORK** | Compare your responses in Talking Points. Discuss which practices you think best keep users secure. What practices are new to you? Explain the importance of protecting one's security on the Internet and the consequences of ignoring good practices.

> " I think changing my passwords is really important. Using one password all the time is playing with fire. You just can't beat having secure passwords. "

WRITING HANDBOOK p. 149
- **Skill:** A comparison and contrast essay
- **Task:** Write an essay comparing and contrasting two means of transportation.

PROGRESS SELF-CHECK **NOW I CAN**   For more practice... **Unit Review** / *Connect TV* **Test-Taking Skills Booster**

☐ Describe how I deal with commuting.
☐ Help others avoid hassles while traveling.
☐ Talk about property lost, damaged, or stolen on a trip.
☐ Discuss protecting Internet security.

UNIT 6 | 65

Soft Skills Workshop 3
A Sales Presentation

Outcome
You will make a sales presentation to convince people to buy a product or service.

1 TEAMWORK Choose a type of product or service and describe its features.*

Choose one of the products or services in the photos below for your team's sales presentation.

Create a name for the product or service, e.g., the name of your hotel.

Brainstorm the profile of your target clients and list the features you think would be appealing to them. Concentrate on ones you think are unique or better than competing products or services, e.g. *The Splendid Hotel has its own private air taxi.*

Tips for TEAMWORK
Respectfully confirm understanding of your colleagues' ideas.
If I understand correctly, you think ___. Right?
Correct me if I'm wrong, but do you mean ___?
Let me get this straight. Are you saying that ___?

a dental clinic
an airline
a virtual psychotherapist
a private language school
a resort hotel

*a feature: what a product or service has, is, or does

Tips for COLLABORATION
Provide constructive feedback.
I love [your benefit statement], but you might want to ___.
This is very good. However, I wonder if it would be [clearer] if ___.
I think [that]'s great, but I wonder if it would be better to ___.
That's so well said. I couldn't have done better myself.

2 COLLABORATION Create benefit* statements for each feature.

Discuss and agree on the three to five most appealing features you identified in Activity 1. Support your reasoning with examples.

In pairs, draft at least one benefit statement for each feature and write it on the board, a screen, or a shared piece of paper. For example, *The Splendid Hotel has a private air shuttle to the international airport* [feature], *so you'll never miss your flight back home.* [benefit]

Take turns reading each pair's benefit statements aloud to the team. Decide which benefits would be the most convincing to your clients. Revise any statements that could be improved.

*a benefit: how the feature will make a client's life better or prevent something bad from happening

🖨 Print out the **Evaluation Chart**.

3 PRESENTATION Rehearse the sales presentation and present it to the class.

Rehearse: Elect an "announcer" who will tell the class what product or service your group is presenting. Brainstorm a short script for the announcer.

Decide which team member will present each feature and benefit. Decide on the order in which the features will be presented. Resequence them during the rehearsal if necessary.

Practice the presentation several times so you will sound convincing and enthusiastic and won't need to read your notes.

Present: Present your product or service to the class. Make sure the audience is convinced you believe in what you are saying. At the end, have the "announcer" make a brief summary of the features and benefits that were presented.

Tips for PRESENTATION

- Act as if the audience were potential clients of your team's product or service. Describe the features and benefits with enthusiasm.
- Speak slowly and clearly so the audience can understand the connection between each feature and benefit.
- Make eye contact from person to person in the audience.
- Ask for confirmation from time to time.
  Does that make sense?
  How does that sound?
  Is that important to you?

EVALUATE Improve your presentation skills.

Use the Key to answer the questions and evaluate each sales presentation. Discuss strengths and weakness and make suggestions about how each presentation might be improved.

☐ Did the presenters make a strong argument for why their product or service was better than what their competition offered?

☐ Did the presenters speak slowly enough to make the connection between each feature and benefit clear?

☐ Did the presenters speak with enough enthusiasm to convince the audience that they believed what they said about the product?

☐ Did the presenters ask the audience to confirm they were addressing their needs?

☐ Did the final presenter remind the audience of the product or service's most important features and benefits in the summary?

KEY
Y = yes
U = usually
S = sometimes
N = no

UNIT 7

Belief and Reality

PREVIEW

A 🔊 **FEARS AND PHOBIAS** | Listen to a description of fears and phobias. What's the difference between a fear and a phobia?

B 🔊 **ZOOM-IN** | Read and listen to a conversation about a situation that might be too good to be true. Notice the <u>featured</u> words and phrases.

UNDERSTAND A VARIETY OF ACCENTS
Dan = American English (standard)
Eliana = Portuguese

Dan: Hey, Eliana, got a minute? <u>I'd like to run something by you</u> . . . get your opinion.
Eliana: Sure, Dan. What's up?
Dan: So, Kate and I went to Florida for the weekend last Friday, and at the airport we were offered a free day pass to a resort on Saturday: lunch, access to their private beach, etc. <u>There was only one catch</u>: We had to take a tour of one of their model apartments and listen to a sales pitch.
Eliana: Uh-oh. <u>This raises a red flag for me</u>. Whenever I hear about a "free lunch," I think of that old saying, "There's no free lunch."
Dan: Understood. Anyway, the resort people sent a limo to pick us up, took us to the resort's restaurant for a gorgeous lunch, showed us to the beach . . . just as they had promised.
Eliana: So far so good. Then what?
Dan: And, as agreed, at the end of the day, they showed us an awesome model apartment and photos of some others. The prices were surprisingly low, but they explained it was a special offer since construction is still underway.
Eliana: Let me guess. You had to decide right away.
Dan: That's right. By this Friday, and then the price goes up.

Eliana: Pressure tactics. Never a good sign.
Dan: That's true, but it sounds like a great deal. You don't actually buy the apartment in the traditional sense. It's a "time share." You buy the rights to use it for two months out of the year. Other people buy the other months. And if you decide you don't want to use it for your two months, you can rent it out to someone else to cover the cost of your mortgage—maybe even make a little money.
Eliana: But how can you be sure you'll be able to rent it?
Dan: Well, the company owns a lot of properties, and they claim they've never had an apartment that didn't get rented. <u>It really sounds like a safe bet</u>.
Eliana: Dan, <u>I'd take that claim with a grain of salt</u>.
Dan: What could go wrong? The place is awesome and the rental is guaranteed.
Eliana: I hate to say it, but <u>that might be wishful thinking on your part</u>. Sometimes when an offer looks too good to be true, it is.

C **UNDERSTAND FROM CONTEXT** | Find a <u>featured</u> sentence in Zoom-In with a similar meaning.

1 I would be suspicious of that. ....
2 This makes me worry about something. ....
3 There was a downside. ....
4 You might be hoping it's true without really knowing if it's realistic. ....
5 I don't think there's any way I could lose. ....
6 I'd like your opinion about something. ....

D **LOOK IT UP AND SHARE** | Find a word or phrase in Zoom-In that was new to you. Look it up and use it in a sentence. Share your sentence with a partner.

....

E **THINK AND EXPLAIN** | With a partner, discuss the questions.

1 What's the difference between buying and owning an apartment and buying a time share in an apartment?
2 How do you think Dan should proceed in deciding whether the offer is truly a good deal?

UNIT 7 COMMUNICATION GOALS

Lesson 1 Describe a scam
Lesson 2 Describe fears and phobias
Lesson 3 Talk about the power of suggestion
Lesson 4 Discuss superstitions

F TALKING POINTS | Take the illusions self-test.

Stare at each image for one minute. Describe what the illusion is. Then check your answer.

Answers

A. Two people of impossibly different sizes appear to be interacting with each other.   B. The horizontal lines appear to be sloping, creating uneven rows. But the lines are actually parallel.   C. If we count the boards on their left side, there appear to be seven, but when we count them on the right side there appear to be five.   D. We see half a woman's face. Depending on how we look at it, she appears either to be looking out at us or in profile, looking to the right.   E. The image appears to be moving, but it isn't.   F. Part of the image that should be in the back appears to be in the front.   G. There are two zebras, but we only see one head. Depending on how we look at the image, the head appears to belong to the zebra on the left or the one on the right.

G PAIR WORK | Together write a definition of the word "illusion."
(Option: Try to explain how each illusion in Talking Points was created.)

START TALKING

PAIR WORK

1 It's said that "seeing is believing," but can we trust our first perceptions? Why or why not?

2 Which of the following would you take with a grain of salt? Explain why.
   - a photo on your favorite news site that shows a politician accepting a cash bribe
   - a TV documentary about governmental corruption
   - a surprise email announcing you've won a large prize
   - a text, email, or call from a relative in trouble, asking for cash
   - a profile photo of a person on a dating website

1 COMMUNICATION GOAL: Describe a scam

A **GRAMMAR** | Nouns: indefinite, definite, unique, and generic meaning (Review and expansion)

A noun (or noun phrase) is "indefinite" when it doesn't refer to a specific person, place, thing, or idea. Use the indefinite articles (<u>a</u> / <u>an</u>) with indefinite singular count nouns. Don't use articles with indefinite non-count nouns.

You can get <u>a vacation house</u> for very little money. [indefinite: not a specific vacation house]

A noun (or noun phrase) is "definite" when it refers to a specific person, place, thing, or idea. An indefinite noun becomes definite when mentioned a second time. Use the definite article (<u>the</u>) with definite singular and plural count nouns and with definite non-count nouns.

We're going to <u>the vacation house</u> we told you about. [definite: a specific vacation house]
We bought a new car, but <u>the car</u> was a piece of junk. [definite: second mention]

A count or non-count noun can represent a person, place, thing, or idea that is unique; in other words, there's only one. Use <u>the</u>.

<u>The theory of relativity</u> was developed by Albert Einstein. [It was his theory, no one else's.]
Some people mistakenly think climate change isn't affecting <u>the environment</u>. [It's the Earth's environment, not another one.]

Count nouns can be used in a generic sense to represent all members of a class or group of people, places, or things. There are three ways a noun can be used generically, with no difference in meaning.

<u>Elephants</u> are
<u>An elephant</u> is } believed to bring good luck.
<u>The elephant</u> is

> **Remember:**
> Non-count nouns name things you cannot count. They are neither singular nor plural, but they always use a singular verb.
> Common categories of non-count nouns are abstract ideas, sports and activities, illnesses, academic subjects, and foods.

> **GRAMMAR EXPANDER** p. 128
> - Article usage: summary
> - Definite article: additional uses
> - Non-count nouns with both a countable and an uncountable sense

B **UNDERSTAND THE GRAMMAR** | Read each statement and choose the phrase that describes the underlined word or phrase.

1. <u>The offer</u> in the email seemed too good to be true.
   a refers to offers people receive in general
   b refers to a specific offer received in an email

2. My family thinks <u>pizza</u> should be made from all organic ingredients.
   a refers to all pizzas
   b refers to some pizzas

3. <u>The president</u> will sign the law that was just passed.
   a refers to a specific president
   b refers to presidents generically

4. <u>A president</u> can sign laws that have been passed.
   a refers to a specific president
   b refers to presidents generically

5. <u>Fire</u> is one of the greatest dangers to old wooden houses.
   a refers to fire in general
   b refers to a specific fire

6. It used to be thought that <u>the cat</u> was domesticated by humans, but this turns out not to be true.
   a refers to a specific cat
   b refers to cats in general

C **GRAMMAR PRACTICE** | Complete the statements about doubtful advertising claims. Insert <u>a</u>, <u>an</u>, or <u>the</u> before a noun or noun phrase where necessary. Write <u>X</u> if the noun shouldn't have an article.

1. .... British company claims to have invented .... machine that allows .... people to talk with their pets. .... company says .... machine, called the PetCam, will be available later in .... year.

2. It's well known that .... carrots are a good source of .... vitamins. In fact, ... research has determined that drinking .... glass of carrot juice every day can add .... years to your life.

3. .... WeightAway diet plan promises to help you lose .... weight fast. .... company guarantees that people following .... plan can lose up to 10 kilograms per week.

4. Last week, the news reported that thousands of people had sent .... money to .... organization advertising a shampoo that .... organization claimed would grow .... hair overnight.

D **GRAMMAR PRACTICE** | With a partner, create sentences for two of the following nouns used in a generic sense: <u>car</u>, <u>shoe</u>, <u>scam</u>, <u>horse</u>.

COMMUNICATION ACTIVATOR

Now let's describe a scam.

A **TALKING POINTS** | Read about four international scams. Add one of your own if you can. With a partner, discuss why you think people fall for each scam.

⚠️ **Romance scam**

Someone you haven't met in person offers friendship, romance, and / or marriage. Shortly after, the person asks for money for hospital bills, legal expenses, or some other sudden problems.

⚠️ **Grandparent scam**

A person contacts grandparents and claims to be their grandchild or other family member who needs money right away for an emergency. The scammer asks the grandparent to keep it a secret.

⚠️ **Drug trafficking scam**

Someone offers you a job overseas, the opportunity to do charity work, or requests that you transport documents or other items for him or her. The scammer offers to pay travel expenses and offers free luggage. What you don't know is that the luggage contains drugs.

⚠️ **Foreign lottery scam**

Someone informs you that you've won prize money in a foreign lottery, but that you must pay taxes and other fees before you can collect your money.

⚠️ **Another scam you've heard of**

_____
_____
_____

B 🔊 **CONVERSATION MODEL** | Read and listen.

A: Did you hear what happened to Pat?
B: No, what?
A: He wanted to meet someone, so he went on an international dating site.
B: Oh, no. Don't tell me he fell for the romance scam—the one where you fall in love online . . . but then the person needs money?
A: That's exactly what happened! She said she had to have a medical procedure, so he sent her a bunch of money to help out. He hasn't heard a thing from her since.
B: Why am I not surprised? How much did he lose?
A: Don't ask. Let's just say he's learned a lesson.
B: Right. I wonder why he fell for it in the first place.

Social language
Indicate you've guessed someone's news with "Don't tell me ___ ."

C 🔊 **PRONUNCIATION PRACTICE** | Listen again and repeat. Then practice the Conversation Model with a partner.

D **IN YOUR OWN WORDS** | Role-play a conversation similar to the one in Exercise B, using one of the scams from Talking Points or another scam you know. Start like this: _Did you hear what happened to . . . ?_ Be sure to change roles and then partners. (Option: Use the Unit 7 Energizer Worksheet.)

KEEP TALKING! •••
- Say more about what happened.
- Speculate about why the person fell for it.
- Talk about other scams you know about.
- Say as much as you can.

▶️ Watch the video for ideas!

↪️ **RECYCLE THIS LANGUAGE**

There was one catch.
There's no free lunch.
That should have raised a red flag.
People can be so gullible.
It was wishful thinking on [his] part.

We all need to be a bit skeptical.
We need to take things like that with a grain of salt.
That seems a little fishy.
It doesn't add up.

2 COMMUNICATION GOAL Describe fears and phobias

A 🔊 **GRAMMAR CLOSE-UP** | Read and listen to two people talk about their phobias. Notice the <u>featured</u> grammar.

Elliot Phillips, 26

" I got stuck on an elevator when I was eleven and ever since then, I've been terrified of being in one—or in any small or crowded spaces. No matter that elevators and small spaces don't pose any real danger—what I have is more than plain old fear. I have claustrophobia—an *irrational* fear. So the danger is all in my mind. <u>It used to be believed that</u> phobias would invariably be a lifelong problem, but <u>it's now understood that</u> certain types of therapy can actually cure them, and I'm in something called "exposure therapy." In my therapy, I'm forced to repeatedly confront my claustrophobia by spending short periods of time in small or crowded spaces and seeing that nothing bad happens. <u>It's estimated that</u> exposure therapy can take a few months to work. Wish me luck! "

Brooke Dawson, 34

" I used to have acrophobia. But now I'm over my fear of heights. Well, I shouldn't call it fear. It was a full-blown phobia. I used to have to make excuses any time I needed to go above the second floor of a building. And airplanes? Forget about it. Only a few years back, <u>it was thought that</u> acrophobia was incurable except through exposure therapy, but when I heard about that, I said no thanks—too scary. But then someone told me about "counter conditioning." Apparently, <u>it's been argued that</u> it can be equally effective, so I changed my mind. I was taught to substitute relaxation techniques for my anxiety, and that did the trick! Guess what? I'm flying to the Grand Canyon tomorrow and plan to ride a donkey down the trails, from the heights down into the valley below. Can you believe it? "

B **PAIR WORK** | Discuss the questions.
1. In your opinion, can a phobia ever be a rational (as opposed to an irrational) fear? Explain.
2. Do you have any fears? Do you know anyone with a full-blown phobia?

C **GRAMMAR** | Reporting beliefs: <u>It</u> + a passive reporting verb

To report what is often or generally said or believed (but which you don't know to be true or you are not personally asserting), use <u>it</u> + the passive form of a reporting verb. Follow with a noun clause beginning with <u>that</u>. As in indirect speech, the verb tense in the noun clause reflects the meaning being expressed. This structure is common in news reports and formal writing.
  It's said that phobias **are** common.
  It was widely **believed that** some phobias **were** incurable.
  Before effective therapy became available, **it had been estimated that** more than 80% of phobics **had** never **tried** to overcome their fears.
  It might be argued that some therapeutic techniques **are** just too frightening for the average phobic.
  It used to be felt that one **would** just **have to live** with a phobia, no matter how much inconvenience it caused.

Common reporting verbs
argue	estimate
assert	feel
assume	hold
believe	say
claim	think

Remember: You can also report generalized statements and beliefs with <u>people</u> and <u>they</u>:
  People [or **They**] **say** arachnophobia—an irrational fear of spiders—is pretty common.

GRAMMAR EXPANDER p. 130
Passive reporting verbs with an infinitive phrase

D **GRAMMAR PRACTICE** | On a separate sheet of paper, replace the subject and active reporting verb in each statement with <u>it</u> + a passive reporting verb.
1. They claim that a phobia is an extreme irrational fear.
2. People now believe that there is hope for many phobics.
3. They used to say that exposure therapy was more difficult to endure than counter-conditioning.
4. They say that some phobias last a lifetime.
5. Some assert that therapy for phobias isn't worth it and that it's better just to accommodate the fear by avoiding what gives you such extreme anxiety.
6. In the past, they estimated that approximately 10% of people in the U.S. suffered from phobias.

E WORD STUDY | Noun and adjective forms
Read the noun and adjective forms that name and describe a person who suffers from acrophobia. Use the same spelling pattern to complete the chart for the other phobias. Then listen and repeat.

Name of phobia	What you call a person who suffers from it	How you describe the person
acrophobia [heights]	an acrophobe	acrophobic
agoraphobia [being outside of the home]		
arachnophobia [spiders]		
aerophobia [flying]		
claustrophobia [enclosed spaces]		
ophidiophobia [snakes]		
xenophobia [foreigners]		

COMMUNICATION ACTIVATOR

Now let's describe fears and phobias.

A TALKING POINTS | On the notepad, write some of the things you are afraid of. You can use the phobias in Word Study or your own fears or phobias. Do you think your fears are run-of-the-mill fears or could they be full-blown phobias?

Fear	Are you just afraid, or phobic?	What happens?
bees	I'm totally phobic!	I get sweaty palms and palpitations.

Fear	Are you just afraid, or phobic?	What happens?

B PAIR WORK | Compare Talking Points. Describe your fears and how they affect you. Ask and answer questions and offer advice. Say as much as you can.

> Why do you think you're so afraid of snakes? Have you ever seen one?

> Actually no, I haven't. And I don't think I have a full-blown phobia. Snakes just freak me out.

> Well, if it's not a real phobia, maybe it would help to learn more about snakes. Most are harmless, and they're helpful in the garden.

C DISCUSSION | Discuss the most common fears your classmates have and how the fears affect them in their everyday and professional lives. Provide examples.

↪ **RECYCLE THIS LANGUAGE**
My hands shake.
I get sweaty palms / palpitations / sick to my stomach.
I lose my voice.
I get butterflies in my stomach.
I'm just a worrywart.

3 Talk about the power of suggestion

COMMUNICATION GOAL

A **READING** | Read the article about placebos and nocebos. What do they have in common?

THE PLACEBO AND NOCEBO EFFECTS

Two of the most fascinating examples of the power of suggestion in medicine are the placebo effect and the nocebo effect. These two opposite phenomena are two sides of the same coin. And while the placebo effect has been widely known for many years, the nocebo effect has been largely overlooked until recently and is thus less well understood.

The word *placebo* refers to a fake medication (one that contains no active ingredients) or to a medical procedure that patients believe will help them and then, as a result of that expectation, it does. For example, in one well-known study, three groups of patients who were told they needed knee surgery underwent one of three procedures. One group had the usual standard surgery. In a second group, the knee was opened surgically but the interior was only washed. In the third group, the doctor made three tiny cuts in the skin, but didn't perform any surgery inside the knee at all. All patients believed they had had the standard surgery. At the end of a year, the patients who had had no surgery reported the same good results as those who *had* had the surgery. It's not known if the placebo effect is caused by the power of wishful thinking, but it is known to be common.

It has been shown repeatedly that certain factors increase the effectiveness of placebos. If a pill, for example, looks like a genuine medicine, the person taking it is likely to believe it contains medicine. It has also been found that patients think larger pills contain larger doses of medicine, and thus must be more effective. Similarly, it has been demonstrated that taking two pills has a greater therapeutic effect than taking only one. Another important determiner of placebo effectiveness is the doctor-patient relationship. If the patient trusts the doctor administering the "medication," he or she is more likely to be helped or cured by it.

The *nocebo* effect is also based on the power of suggestion or expectation. If a patient has been told that a medication is likely to cause an adverse reaction (such as dizziness or headache), he or she is more likely to experience one. This has been demonstrated both in experiments and in actual medical practice. One dramatic non-medical experiment is often cited as an example of the nocebo effect: When given a non-alcoholic beverage that subjects were told was beer, they believed and acted as if they were drunk. They slurred their speech, acted silly, and even fell and hurt themselves. Simply believing a substance will make one drunk can result in drunkenness.

What are the implications of the placebo and nocebo effects for medical practice? Placebos can be used in research to help evaluate the effectiveness of real medications. If two groups of patients are treated with either a placebo or a real medication and both achieve the same result, it is clear that the medication lacks real effectiveness. Also, it is well known that some patients ask doctors for medications that are ineffective and potentially harmful (such as antibiotics for the common cold). Doctors can prescribe such patients a placebo, knowing that it may be effective and will cause no harm.

The nocebo effect, on the other hand, can present doctors with an ethical dilemma. Adverse reactions to particular medications are typically experienced by a very small percentage of patients. Doctors wonder if they should inform patients of these potential adverse reactions since they know they are very unlikely to occur. The power of suggestion of the nocebo effect could interfere with the more likely positive effects of a necessary medication, depriving patients of an effective treatment.

In conclusion, although we believe the body and the mind are separate, the existence of the placebo and nocebo effects suggests that the distinction between the two might be more complicated than we as yet understand. All humans are probably somewhat susceptible to the power of suggestion.

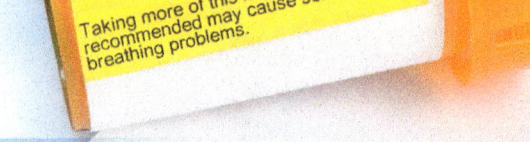

B **UNDERSTAND FROM CONTEXT** | Choose the correct word or phrase to complete each statement.

1. The placebo and nocebo effects are both thought to be caused by (the power of suggestion / two sides of the same coin).
2. Something that is (investigated / overlooked) hasn't come to our attention before.
3. A (placebo / phenomenon) appears to be a real medication.
4. (A placebo / An adverse reaction) is an unwanted side effect of a medication.
5. (Antibiotics / Nocebos) are not effective medications for the common cold.

UNIT 7

C INFER INFORMATION | Complete each statement, based on the information in the article.

1. The factor that doesn't contribute to the placebo effect is ……. .
   a. the appearance of the medication
   b. scientific research
   c. trust in the doctor
   d. the expectation that it will work

2. The knee surgery experiment demonstrates ……. .
   a. the power of suggestion that surgery was performed
   b. the value of washing the interior of the knee
   c. the harmful effects of fake procedures
   d. the need for procedures in surgery

3. The drunkenness experiment is an example of ……. .
   a. the placebo effect
   b. the nocebo effect
   c. an ethical dilemma
   d. the harmful effects of beer

4. …… is one factor that might cause a placebo to be effective.
   a. The lack of harmful adverse reactions
   b. The patient's trust in his or her doctor
   c. Their relatively low cost
   d. The high quality of the medicine

5. Under normal circumstances, adverse reactions to medications occur in ……. .
   a. most patients
   b. the sickest patients
   c. only a few patients
   d. the common cold

D CRITICAL THINKING | Discuss the questions. Explain your reasoning.

1. In what way are the placebo effect and the nocebo effect "two sides of the same coin"?
2. Is it ethical to give a patient with a cold a placebo instead of an antibiotic?
3. What are the pros and cons of telling a patient about potential adverse reactions to a medication?

COMMUNICATION ACTIVATOR

Now let's talk about the power of suggestion.

A TALKING POINTS | Complete the chart with questionable claims people are likely to believe. Then speculate about why people are susceptible to each claim.

Some possible reasons
cultural traditions
advertising
sexism
racism
peer pressure

Claim	Why people want to believe it
You can lose weight without dieting.	People don't want to stop eating what they like.

Claim	Why people want to believe it

B DISCUSSION | With a partner, discuss your Talking Points, providing specific examples you have seen or know about. (Option: Use the Unit 7 Soft Skills Booster, p. 160.)

> " I saw a medical testimonial from a patient who claims he lost half of his body weight by drinking apple cider vinegar three times a day. I think people want to believe this is possible because it seems so much easier than months of diet and exercise. "

RECYCLE THIS LANGUAGE
I'd take that claim with a grain of salt.
That raises a red flag for me.
That might be wishful thinking on [your] part.
It sounds like a safe bet.
There's only one catch.

4 COMMUNICATION GOAL | Discuss superstitions

A 🔊 **VOCABULARY** | Superstitions | Read and listen. Then listen again and repeat.

a superstition: a belief that some objects or actions are lucky or unlucky

Many cultures have **superstitions** about the power of certain numbers to protect people from harm.

bad luck: a misfortune that happens by chance

There's a superstition that breaking a mirror can bring you 7 years of **bad luck**.

a good luck charm: an object that some people believe can bring them good luck

Some people like to wear **good luck charms** on a bracelet.

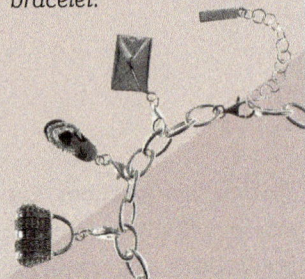

a curse: the expression of a wish that someone will face a misfortune

Some people believe that when they are sick it's the result of **a curse** someone put on them.

B **ACTIVATE VOCABULARY** | Discuss the questions about the Vocabulary with a partner.
1 Do you know the origin of the superstition about breaking a mirror? If not, look it up on the Internet and discuss what you find.
2 Do you have any good luck charms? Describe those you have or ones you are familiar with. Do you think good luck charms work?
3 Do you believe it's possible for someone to put a curse on another person? Who, if anyone, is capable of cursing other people or things?

C 🔊 **LISTEN FOR MAIN IDEA** | Listen to a podcast about superstitions. What is the main idea of the podcast?
☐ 1 Some superstitions may be rooted in scientific principles.
☐ 2 A delusion is a typical superstition.
☐ 3 Many people carry out the traditions of local superstitions even though they don't believe in them.

D 🔊 **LISTEN FOR DETAILS** | Listen again to complete the statements, according to the podcast.
1 Magical thinking is the basis of most ....
   a cultures   b superstitions   c symbols
2 The purpose of most superstitions is to cause a particular ....
   a outcome   b belief   c thinking
3 Many superstitions are based on the belief that certain symbols, ... , or events can cause or prevent something from happening.
   a delusions   b outcomes   c actions
4 Many people conform to the ...... prescribed by a superstition, even if they don't truly believe it will bring them luck or protect them from danger.
   a behavior   b charm   c misfortune
5 Some ...... are believed to be capable of preventing misfortunes.
   a good luck charms   b curses and omens   c delusions and superstitions
6 Famous physicist Neils Bohr ...... the superstition that a horseshoe can bring good luck.
   a believed   b created   c didn't truly believe
7 In Estonia, there are three common superstitious beliefs about determining the ...... of a baby.
   a gender   b health   c death
8 In the Philippines, some of the most well-known superstitions relate to ....
   a grains   b funerals   c household chores

E 🔊 **LISTEN TO CONFIRM CONTENT** | Listen again. Check the topics that were discussed in the podcast and write X next to the ones that weren't. Then, with a partner, summarize what was said about each topic that you checked.

☐ 1 what a superstition is
☐ 2 why superstitions are untrue
☐ 3 whether there's a logical or scientific basis for most superstitions
☐ 4 what the difference is between a delusion and a superstition
☐ 5 why we believe in superstitions even though we might not believe them to be true
☐ 6 why there are so many superstitions about animals
☐ 7 why Estonians are so superstitious
☐ 8 why Filipinos eat out before going home after a funeral

PRONUNCIATION LESSON p. 140
Linking sounds

COMMUNICATION ACTIVATOR

Now let's discuss superstitions.

A **TALKING POINTS** | Ask three classmates about superstitions they are familiar with. Write the information on the notepad.

name: Diana
superstition: If you spill salt, there will be an argument.

name:
superstition:

name:
superstition:

name:
superstition:

Topics superstitions are often about:
- foods / drinks
- good luck / bad luck
- brides and grooms
- particular months, days, or dates
- dreams
- birth / death
- your own idea: ___

B **DISCUSSION** | With a partner, discuss whether or not you believe in any of the superstitions you wrote about in Talking Points—or if someone you know does. Discuss why people might or might not be superstitious.

KEEP TALKING! •••
- Tell your partner more about one of the superstitions.
- Talk about someone you know who believes in it.
- Express your opinion about that superstition or about superstitions in general.
- Say as much as you can.

▶ Watch the video for ideas!

Diana, do you believe in that superstition?

Actually, no I don't. But my grandparents do!

C **ROLE PLAY** | With a partner, role-play a discussion in which you describe a superstition to a visitor to your country. If you are the visitor, ask questions.

WRITING HANDBOOK p. 150
- Subject-verb agreement: expansion
- Task: An essay about superstitions

➡ **RECYCLE THIS LANGUAGE**

You don't really buy that, do you?	Oh, come on!
It just doesn't add up.	That might be wishful thinking.
It doesn't make sense.	Why do people fall for stuff like that?
It's a little far-fetched.	Some people are just gullible.
	I'd take that with a grain of salt.

PROGRESS SELF-CHECK — **NOW I CAN**

For more practice...
Unit Review / *Connect TV*
Test-Taking Skills Booster

☐ Describe a scam.
☐ Describe fears and phobias.
☐ Talk about the power of suggestion.
☐ Discuss superstitions.

UNIT 8

Achievement and Intelligence

PREVIEW

A 🔊 **ENVIRONMENT AND INTELLIGENCE** | Listen to a lecture. What are the arguments for and against the effect of the environment on extreme intelligence?

B 🔊 **ZOOM-IN** | Read and listen to a conversation between two students on the verge of making career and study plans. Notice the featured language.

> **UNDERSTAND A VARIETY OF ACCENTS**
> Ian = British English
> Amal = Arabic

Ian: So have you narrowed down your plans for next year?
Amal: Well, not exactly. I do know it'll be something in the sciences, but I'm having a hard time making up my mind about what direction to take.
Ian: What are your options? I mean, what are you thinking of?

Amal: So, lab research is kind of at the top of the list—particularly plant genetics. I love the idea of being on the cutting edge of new discoveries. But I'm having second thoughts about working in a lab.
Ian: What kind of second thoughts?
Amal: Well, I know myself. I'm thinking lab work can be pretty solitary, and I enjoy working with people, collaborating, you know. My gut feeling is that research might not be the best fit. It could get lonely.
Ian: What other options are you considering?
Amal: Don't laugh, but teaching also interests me. Sounds like the polar opposite, doesn't it?
Ian: Well, that certainly isn't solitary. Is there some way to combine research and teaching—having the best of both worlds?
Amal: That's what I'm asking myself. And there might be. I figure if I get my doctorate in chemistry, I could take a professorship at a research university and conduct research there as well as teach.
Ian: But a doctorate. Wow. That takes years.
Amal: I know. And I'm not totally sure I'm cut out for it. But here's the thing: it's now or never.
Ian: Right. You don't want to have to start from scratch later. I suggest you go for it. You can't go wrong.

C **UNDERSTAND FROM CONTEXT** | Paraphrase these statements and questions containing featured words and phrases from Zoom-In. Then compare paraphrases with a partner.

1. So, have you narrowed down your plans for next year? ....
2. I'm having a hard time making up my mind about what direction to take. ....
3. I love the idea of being on the cutting edge of new discoveries. ....
4. I'm having second thoughts. ....
5. My gut feeling is that research might not be the best fit. ....
6. Sounds like the polar opposite, doesn't it? ....
7. Is there some way to combine research and teaching, having the best of both worlds? ....
8. You don't want to have to start from scratch later. ....
9. You can't go wrong. ....

D **LOOK IT UP AND SHARE** | Find a word or phrase in Zoom-In that was new to you. Look it up and use it in a sentence. Share your sentence with a partner.

....

E **THINK AND EXPLAIN** | With a partner, discuss the questions.

1. How self-aware is Amal? Explain.
2. How would you describe her personality?
3. Do you think her decision-making process demonstrates intelligence? Explain.

UNIT 8 COMMUNICATION GOALS

Lesson 1 Identify your unique strengths
Lesson 2 Talk about how you study
Lesson 3 Discuss the effect of the environment on intelligence
Lesson 4 Evaluate your emotional intelligence

F TALKING POINTS | Take the self-test.

How well do you stick to a task?

Check the adverb that describes how well you do. Then make notes of how you can do better.

I STAY ORGANIZED.
◯ Always ◯ Usually ◯ Never

Benefit A messy desk presents too many distractions. A neat one helps you stay focused on one thing at a time.

How I can do better:
_____
_____

I STICK TO A SCHEDULE.
◯ Always ◯ Usually ◯ Never

Benefit If you break up one large task into several smaller tasks and plan how much to do each day, you won't end up scrambling at the end.

How I can do better:
_____
_____

I MAKE LISTS.
◯ Always ◯ Usually ◯ Never

Benefit Making a list ensures you won't forget a key task, and as you check off the ones you've completed, you'll feel motivated by your achievement.

How I can do better:
_____
_____

I SET TIME LIMITS.
◯ Always ◯ Usually ◯ Never

Benefit Knowing how much time you have for a task ensures you won't stretch it into the time you planned for something else.

How I can do better:
_____
_____

I FIND A PLACE TO WORK WHERE I WON'T BE DISTURBED.
◯ Always ◯ Usually ◯ Never

Benefit Finding a place where others won't disturb your work enables you, and not others, to control your agenda.

How I can do better:
_____
_____

I GO OFFLINE.
◯ Always ◯ Usually ◯ Never

Benefit Confining your online time to certain periods in the day results in longer periods of uninterrupted work time.

How I can do better:
_____
_____

I TAKE BREATHERS.
◯ Always ◯ Usually ◯ Never

Benefit Short breaks can clear your mind and help you resume with better focus.

How I can do better:
_____
_____

START TALKING

PAIR WORK Tell your partner about one "never" response you made on the self-test in Talking Points. Explain what you plan to do to make it a "usually" or an "always." Ask your partner questions about how he or she plans to do better.

1 COMMUNICATION GOAL: Identify your unique strengths

A VOCABULARY | Ways to describe strengths and talents | Read and listen. Then listen again and repeat.

be good with one's hands	have the ability to use one's hands to make or do things
be mechanically inclined	be able to understand how machines work
have a head for figures	be good at mathematical calculations
have an ear for music*	be good at recognizing, remembering, and imitating musical sounds
have an eye for detail	be good at seeing or paying attention to things that others don't usually notice
have a good intuitive sense	be able to draw conclusions based on feelings rather than facts
have a way with words	be able to express one's ideas and opinions well
have a way with people	have the ability to interact well with others
have a knack for [learning languages]	have a natural skill or ability to do something well

* also: *an ear for languages*

B ACTIVATE VOCABULARY | With a partner, use the Vocabulary to describe each person below. (There may be more than one way.) Explain your reasons. Then, for each person, write three occupations or careers that would be suitable for that person.

1. George Guzmán was able to solve college-level math problems when he was 10. His high-school math team won a national competition when he was 14. George is now a math teacher in a private school but would like to change careers. He says, "I love math, but I just wasn't cut out for teaching."

2. Su Lin's parents were in the Diplomatic Corps, so she spent most of her childhood moving from post to post. Though this wasn't easy, Lin learned to speak four languages besides her native Mandarin. Wherever she lived, she was a popular student and made friends easily. She has kept in touch with most of them on social media. Lin has varied interests: organic gardening, fixing motorbikes, and finance. She has just finished her degree in economics and is looking for an unusual career that would combine some of those interests and enable her to travel and make friends.

3. Vivian Bond married young and stayed home to raise her two children. She loved cooking and in the evenings she took classes at the Culinary Institute. Over the years, Vivian perfected the art of extremely complicated cake design. Now that her children have married, Vivian would like to start a career. "Hey," she says, "Better late than never!"

4. Narciso Vidal's dad is a concert pianist, so Narciso watched him practice right from the time he was a baby. By the time he was three, Narciso surprised everyone by teaching himself to play, just by watching and imitating his father. All through school, Narciso has spent his free time on his two passions: playing piano and writing for the school newspaper. Now he's wondering what direction he should take as an adult.

5. Sophie Lane is 16. She has always loved animals, and they love her, too. As a kid, she liked to train her friends' pet dogs to do tricks. And this year, she started an after-school pet-sitting service for people's pets in her apartment building. She saves the money she earns and has contributed some to the Save the Animals Federation.

C PERSONALIZE | Use the Vocabulary to describe two people you know.

> My brother Andrei is a psychologist in a small town. He's got a good intuitive sense about what the underlying causes of people's problems are, and this enables him to help them get better quickly.

UNIT 8

D GRAMMAR | Using auxiliary do for emphatic stress

To add emphatic stress to an affirmative statement in the simple present or simple past tense, use do or did before the base form of the verb.

Even if I don't have a great eye for detail, I **do** have a knack for decorating a room.

She **did** complete the course, but she decided to take her career in another direction.

> **Be careful!**
> Use a base form after a form of the auxiliary **do**.
> She **has** an ear for languages. → She **does have** an ear for languages. NOT She does ~~has~~ ...
> He **liked** that car. → He **did like** that car. NOT He did ~~liked~~ ...

GRAMMAR EXPANDER p. 130
Emphatic stress

E PRONOUNCE THE GRAMMAR | Listen and repeat the grammar examples.

F GRAMMAR PRACTICE | On a separate sheet of paper, rewrite each item, using do or did for emphatic stress.

1. She's not the best dancer. However, she <u>likes</u> to dance.
2. Your intuition was right. You <u>learned</u> English faster than anyone expected.
3. He may not have much time during the week, but he <u>loves</u> to cook on the weekend.
4. Jane is usually pretty skeptical, but she <u>fell</u> for that romance scam.
5. Phil doesn't have a lot of run-of-the-mill fears. On the other hand, he <u>has</u> one full-blown phobia.
6. He really hated math, but in the end he <u>passed</u> the course.

PRONUNCIATION LESSON p. 141
Emphatic stress with auxiliary verbs

G PAIR WORK | Take turns making statements comparing your strengths and your weaknesses. Use the auxiliary <u>do</u> for emphatic stress.

> " I don't have much of a knack for writing, but people say I **do** have a way with words in discussions. "

COMMUNICATION ACTIVATOR

Now let's identify your unique strengths.

A CONVERSATION MODEL | Read and listen.

A: So, I understand you've been considering changing to the film program.
B: Yes, that's right. I wondering if you could help me decide.
A: I'd be happy to try. . . . So, tell me, do you have a specific career goal?
B: Actually, I'm having a hard time making up my mind between directing and editing.
A: Maybe I can help you narrow those down. Would you say you have an eye for detail?
B: I definitely do have an eye for detail, which makes me think I'd be a good editor. But I'm really kind of a people person.
A: A people person.
B: Right. I'm not sure I'm cut out for so much time in front of a computer.
A: Well, then maybe directing would be a better fit.
B: That's what I'm thinking, but I'm not sure I want to give up on editing.
A: OK. So here's what I'd suggest. Take the intro courses in both directing and editing. You'll see which you prefer. You can't go wrong.
B: That makes sense.

Social language
Indicate that you have prior knowledge about a situation with "So, I understand [that] . . ."

B PRONUNCIATION PRACTICE | Listen again and repeat. Then practice the Conversation Model with a partner.

C IN YOUR OWN WORDS | Create a similar conversation, using the Vocabulary. Change the field of study. Start like this: *So, I understand you've been considering . . .* Be sure to change roles and then partners. (Option: Use the Unit 8 Energizer Worksheet.)

KEEP TALKING!
- Ask more questions to help narrow down the options.
- Say more about your talents, strengths, and passions.
- Say as much as you can.

▶ Watch the video for ideas!

→ RECYCLE THIS LANGUAGE
I was hoping you could steer me in the right direction.
I'm [good at / not so good at] ___ .
I wish I [were / weren't] ___ .
I wish I [had / hadn't] ___ .
My gut feeling is ___ .
I'm having second thoughts.
It would be the best of both worlds.
They're polar opposites.
I say go for it.
You can't go wrong.
It's now or never.
You wouldn't have to start from scratch.

FOR MORE PRACTICE, GO TO YOUR DIGITAL RESOURCES   UNIT 8   81

2 COMMUNICATION GOAL | Talk about how you study

A 🔊 **GRAMMAR CLOSE-UP** | Read about three research-based study tips for preparing for an exam. Notice the featured grammar.

Study Smarter
Debunking the Myths

Myth #1: It's better to study harder.

Wrong! Recently, it's being recommended that studying be spaced out over several short periods instead of in one or two long ones. Moreover, it's preferable that each short study session be intense. The total study time might be the same, but you'll understand what you've learned better and will retain it longer.

Myth #2: You should study in silence.

Not true! We now know that it's not essential the study environment be quiet. Though many libraries insist that music not be played, some students say a little background noise cuts down on distractions and helps them concentrate. And one language student reports that her teachers always suggest she say new words aloud and write them in a notebook to help make them memorable. So it's important that sound not be totally banned.

Myth #3: The Internet makes studying more efficient.

Nope! Some tout the value of multi-tasking, but research suggests that be taken with a grain of salt. In a recent study, a group of college students sent an average of 97 text messages per day, with 71 of those messages being sent while doing homework. When this group's study results were analyzed, it was found that it increased the time they needed to learn material and decreased the quality of their learning. Some people suggest that if a computer isn't needed for homework, it not be used.

B **DISCUSSION** | Which of the study tips did you know about? Do you agree or disagree with them? Explain.

C **GRAMMAR** | The subjunctive

Use the subjunctive form of a verb in a noun clause that follows a verb or adjective of urgency, obligation, or advisability. The subjunctive form is the same as the base form and doesn't change, no matter what the subject of the clause is. Use **not** before the verb for the negative.

    She suggested that her daughter **study** in a quiet room.
    It's crucial that we **be** early on the day of the exam.
    They're demanding that students **leave** their phones in their lockers during class.
    My friend recommended I **not accept** the lab job unless they offer me a higher salary.

The passive form of the subjunctive is **be** + a past participle
    He asked that music **be turned off** in the study hall.
    I'm proposing the rules for cell phone use in class **not be changed**.

The continuous form of the subjunctive is **be** + a present participle.
    It's important that they **be waiting** in the room before the teacher arrives.

Note: The subjunctive in the noun clause doesn't change, no matter what the time frame of the entire sentence is.
    It **was** essential the research **include** (NOT ~~included~~) students from different cultures.
    The school psychologist **recommended** that all students **be tested** (NOT ~~were tested~~) for learning disabilities.
    She **will request** that students **not be told** (NOT ~~will not be told~~) their scores on the last test.
    The professor **had demanded** that no one **be looking at** (NOT ~~was looking at~~) a device during her lecture.

Verbs and adjectives of urgency, obligation, and advisablity

Verbs	Adjectives
ask	critical
demand	crucial
insist	desirable
propose	essential
recommend	important
request	necessary
suggest	

Be careful!
If a noun clause doesn't follow a verb or adjective of urgency, obligation, or advisability, don't use the subjunctive.
    Students agree that calendar apps **are** useful.
    It's interesting that multi-tasking **reduces** study success.

GRAMMAR EXPANDER p. 131
Infinitives and gerunds in place of the subjunctive

D **GRAMMAR PRACTICE** | With a partner, decide whether to use the subjunctive and circle the correct form. Explain each answer.

1. Matt and Emilie were convinced their son (have / had) a good intuitive sense.
2. It's suggested that every new student (takes / take) a language aptitude test.
3. It was requested that new teachers (arrive / arrived) at the school office an hour early the first day of class.
4. Ms. Sills demanded that no laptops (be / were) open during class.
5. It's crucial that one (study / studies) in short intense sessions rather than cramming in one marathon session the night before the test.
6. My parents proposed that my brother (not study / didn't study) with music playing in his room.
7. Ella's supervisor will insist that no one (is / be) late to tomorrow's lunch.
8. They suggested that we (be given / were given) an opportunity to apply for a spot in next year's class.
9. She agrees that it (be / is) hard to ignore incoming text messages when doing homework.
10. They ask that guests (be wearing / are wearing) somewhat formal clothes when they enter the reception.

> *Convinced* isn't a verb of urgency, obligation, or advisability.

E **PAIR WORK** | Take turns completing these statements in your own way, using the subjunctive.

1. On the first day of class, it's important that a teacher . . .
2. I suggest that a visitor to our city . . .
3. I would recommend that the school administration . . .
4. I think it's crucial that every parent . . .
5. If I were a parent, I would insist that my children . . .

COMMUNICATION ACTIVATOR

Now let's talk about how we study.

A **TALKING POINTS** | Make a list of your strategies for successful studying. Use Grammar Close-Up or strategies from the list.

Strategy	How it contributes to my success

Some strategies
- avoid junk food
- get plenty of sleep
- study my class notes
- listen to music
- make quizzes for myself
- say new words aloud
- make to-do lists
- work with a partner
- your own idea

B **DISCUSSION** | In a small group, share your strategies from Talking Points. Provide examples of how you've used them and say as much as you can. (Option: Use the Unit 8 Soft Skills Booster, p. 161.)

3 COMMUNICATION GOAL: Discuss the effect of the environment on intelligence

A ► **READING** | Read about intelligence and the factors that might influence it. What are some of the reasons it has been difficult to accurately measure intelligence?

Measuring and understanding intelligence

What is intelligence and what factors influence it? Many define it with a numerical score referred to as the "intelligence quotient" (or IQ). Some history: the IQ was originally arrived at by dividing a child's mental age (as defined by a test) by his or her chronological age and multiplying it by 100. Using this formula, a child of 10 who does as well on the intelligence test as the average 10 year old has an IQ of 100 (or 10 ÷ 10 x 100 = IQ 100). As a comparison, a child of 7 who does as well as the average 10 year old has an IQ of 143 (10 ÷ 7 x 100).

Today, even though most modern intelligence tests don't calculate IQ in the same way, the idea of an intelligence "quotient" continues to be used popularly as synonymous with "intelligence." However, most experts suggest that intelligence be seen as more complex than something that can be measured on a test of general knowledge, mathematical and verbal ability, logic, and memory—which is where classic intelligence tests stop. It's widely agreed that current intelligence assessments fall far short of the goal of measuring or even understanding the nature of intelligence. What are some deficiencies of the tests?

While it is accepted that IQ often does predict one's academic achievement, it can't indicate one's level of creativity or practical ability—the ability to cope with everyday life or work. Nor can IQ indicate one's potential for growth.

IQ doesn't measure creativity or practical ability.

Another weakness of IQ is the fact that the tests have long been known to be culture-bound, with one's score easily affected by the culture in which one was brought up. As a result, statistics that purport to compare the intelligence of the average person in different countries should be considered flawed or, at least, to have very limited value.

Regarding one's potential for growth, while many psychometricians (experts in the measurement of intelligence) insist that IQ test scores not be seen as changeable, others have a more nuanced—or a less black-and-white—view of how fixed one's IQ remains throughout life. One way to test the hypothesis that the IQ is fixed throughout life is to look at the relative contributions that genetics and the environment (the "nature versus nurture" question) may have had on an individual's IQ score. If it can be shown that the environment has played a role, then we can conclude that one's IQ can change during the course of one's life.

Although it's well known that genetically similar individuals generally have similar IQs, a number of studies of adopted twins have sought to clarify the effect of the environment in genetically identical individuals. If intelligence comes 100% from the genes, then identical twins would have identical IQs, no matter where they were raised. It has been found, though, that identical twins who were adopted into different families do not usually have identical IQ scores, so environment must play a role.

What's not known, though, is which environmental factors are most important. One, however, consistently seems to make a difference: health. When average IQs are compared across the world, the one factor that has the greatest impact on IQ is the level of infectious, especially parasitic, disease in the population. The effect of parasitic infections in early childhood is a slowing of intellectual development, affecting children's performance on standard intelligence tests.

Finally, the health factor might explain one of the most intriguing observations about intelligence: the Flynn Effect. Since the early 1900s, scores on IQ tests have largely increased in most parts of the world, a discovery of scientist James Flynn. Based on the recent discovery of the association between intelligence and childhood health, it has been theorized that these rising scores might be due to an increase in vaccinations and improved nutrition, which tends to support the belief that the most important environmental influence on IQ is health.

B **UNDERSTAND MAIN IDEA** | Which of the following statements expresses the main idea of the article?

☐ 1 The Flynn Effect may be due to improved health around the world since the early 1900s.
☐ 2 Although scientists are learning more about what determines intelligence, there is still much to be learned.
☐ 3 Genetics appears to play a more important role in intelligence than the environment.

84 UNIT 8

C UNDERSTAND DETAILS | Choose the best word or phrase to complete the statements.
1. The fact that intelligence can change over time proves that (nurture / nature) has an effect.
2. It's not definitively known which (environmental / genetic) factor has the greatest impact on intelligence.
3. The role of childhood health in regional differences in intelligence has been (investigated / disproved).
4. Since the early 1900s, the Flynn Effect has been observed in (most / a few) countries around the world.
5. The Flynn Effect describes a rise in (IQs / vaccinations).

D FIND SUPPORTING DETAILS | Check the statements that are or might be true. Find details in the article to support your opinion.
☐ 1 Adult intelligence is determined in the same way as that of children.
☐ 2 An IQ score doesn't describe all types of intelligence.
☐ 3 Psychometricians disagree about whether intelligence can be changed.
☐ 4 General knowledge, mathematical and verbal ability, logic, and memory are used to measure intelligence around the world.
☐ 5 Comparing the intelligence of identical twins adopted into two different families is one way to observe the influence of the environment on intelligence.

COMMUNICATION ACTIVATOR

Now let's discuss the effect of the environment on intelligence.

A TALKING POINTS | Imagine that you are a new parent and that you believe environment has a role in maximizing the intellectual potential of a child. Make a list of activities you think would enhance your child's intelligence at each age of his or her early life.

| 0-12 months |
| 12-24 months |
| 3-5 years of age |
| early primary school |
| later years |

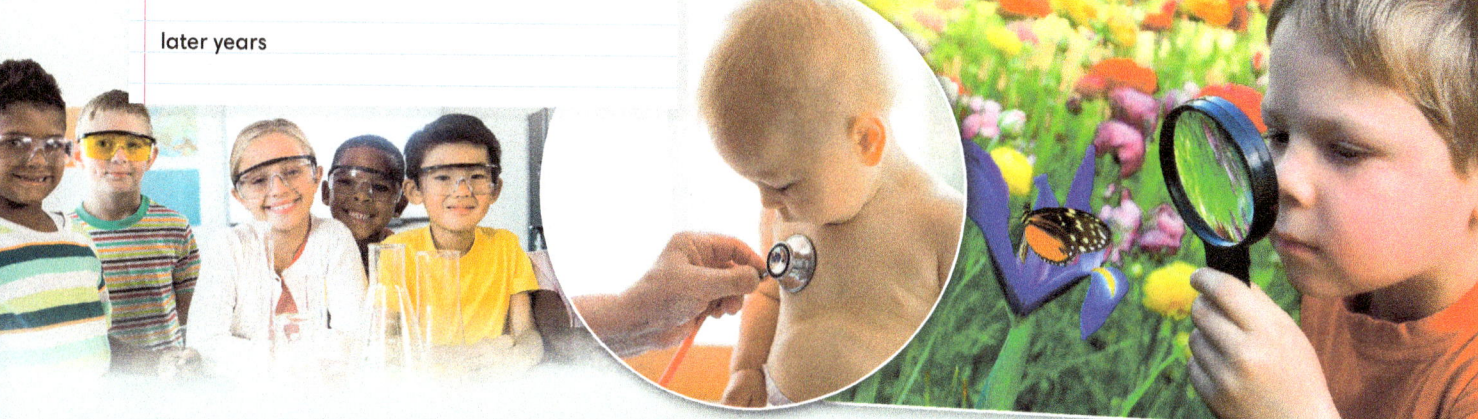

B DISCUSSION | In a small group, share your ideas from Talking Points. Explain how you think the activities would boost your child's intelligence.

❝ Personally, I believe the best way to develop children's intelligence is to read to them every night at bedtime. It builds their vocabulary and their love of learning. I would start reading to my kids even before they can talk. ❞

KEEP TALKING! ●●●
- Ask questions.
- Provide reasons for your ideas.
- Support your ideas with examples from your life, your knowledge, or the life of people you know.
- Agree and disagree.
- Say as much as you can.

▶ Watch the video for ideas!

4 COMMUNICATION GOAL | Evaluate your emotional intelligence

A **VOCABULARY** | Interpersonal and intrapersonal intelligence | Read and listen. Then listen again and repeat.

Interpersonal intelligence: the ability to understand the intentions, motivations, and desires of others

Examples
- **social skills:** managing relationships to get along with others
- **empathy:** being considerate of other people's feelings

Intrapersonal intelligence: the ability to understand one's own feelings, fears, and motivations

Examples
- **self-awareness:** knowing one's own emotions, strengths and weaknesses, and recognizing their impact on others
- **self-regulation:** controlling one's negative impulses in order to adapt to a particular environment

B **ACTIVATE VOCABULARY** | With a partner, describe one person you know with good interpersonal intelligence and one with good intrapersonal intelligence. Or tell your partner about someone who doesn't have either one.

> My first job was at a restaurant. My manager had really good interpersonal skills. He always let us know he understood the stress of making customers happy, and we felt he cared about us.

C **LISTEN TO CONFIRM CONTENT** | Listen to a lecture. Mark each statement T (true), F (false), or ND (not discussed in the lecture).

.... 1 EQ measures cognitive ability.
.... 2 Emotional intelligence is a soft skill.
.... 3 Budgeting and financial planning are hard skills.
.... 4 Soft skills are more important than hard skills.
.... 5 It is well known that IQ cannot be increased by training.
.... 6 Technical management skills form one of the emotional competencies of leadership, according to Goleman.
.... 7 Sonia Vargas is more interested in increasing her IQ than her EQ.

D **LISTEN TO CLARIFY** | Listen again. How does the lecturer contrast the concept of hard skills and soft skills? Be specific.

E **LISTEN TO DRAW CONCLUSIONS** | Listen again. With a partner, answer the questions, explaining your rationale.
1 Why are the new managers going to have workshops in developing their emotional intelligence, but not their IQ?
2 Why do you think emotional intelligence would be important for leaders in a company?
3 Does Daniel Goleman believe that emotional intelligence can be taught?
4 Can tests of emotional intelligence be as valid as IQ tests?

COMMUNICATION ACTIVATOR

Now let's evaluate your emotional intelligence.

A **TALKING POINTS** | Take the emotional intelligence self-test. Check the statements that apply to you.

- ○ When I feel down, I try to focus on positive things.
- ○ I like learning about new things.
- ○ I find it easy to admit when I've made a mistake.
- ○ I see mistakes as opportunities to learn.
- ○ Most people agree that I have a good sense of humor.
- ○ When I'm feeling upset, I'm usually aware of the cause.
- ○ Understanding others' feelings is important to me.
- ○ When I'm criticized, I try to use the criticism for self-improvement.
- ○ I don't mind talking with others about uncomfortable topics.
- ○ I find it fairly easy to get along with people I don't like.
- ○ I am aware of how my own behavior affects others.
- ○ I don't mind conflicts or disagreements.
- ○ I'm good at helping people who disagree with each other to reach a solution.
- ○ I am able to motivate myself to do things I don't want to do.
- ○ Before making an important decision, I often ask others for advice.
- ○ I always think about the ethical consequences of my decisions.
- ○ I am aware of my strengths and weaknesses.
- ○ I feel satisfied with my achievements, even if I haven't received praise.
- ○ I generally feel good about who I am, even though there may be things I'd like to change.

SCORE
How many statements did you check?

16–19 = You have a very high EQ.

12–15 = You have an above-average EQ.

8–11 = You have an average EQ.

4–7 = You have a below average EQ.

1–3 = You have a very low EQ.

B **PAIR WORK** | Compare your scores from Talking Points. Do you each feel that your score accurately measures your emotional intelligence? Explain, using some of the adjectives to support your explanation.

Adjectives
ambitious	indifferent	polite
collaborative	judgmental	relaxed
considerate	loyal	reliable
empathetic	modest	rude
fair	open-minded	trustworthy

> " It's really interesting. People have always said I'm empathetic, and it turns out that I got a high score. Maybe there's something to this EQ stuff. "

C **DISCUSSION** | Based on the quiz, in which way does EQ seem to measure intelligence differently from IQ? Why might an EQ score be useful for an employer to know?

> In my opinion, a high EQ score would contribute to a workplace with less conflict between people who work together.

WRITING HANDBOOK p. 151
- **Skill:** Explaining cause and result
- **Task:** An essay about staying focused on a task

PROGRESS SELF-CHECK — **NOW I CAN**

- ☐ Identify my unique strengths.
- ☐ Talk about how I study.
- ☐ Discuss the effect of the environment on intelligence.
- ☐ Evaluate my emotional intelligence.

For more practice... Unit Review / Connect TV
Test-Taking Skills Booster

Soft Skills Workshop 4

A "How-to" Demonstration

Outcome
You will demonstrate how to accomplish something.

How to overcome a fear or phobia

How to design and plant a garden

How to make [something to eat or drink]

MORE IDEAS
How to plan and host a party / meeting / event
How to prepare for a job interview
How to care for a cold / fever / backache
How to expand your English vocabulary
Your own idea: ___

1 TEAMWORK Choose a topic.

Form teams. Discuss and choose a topic from the photos or the More Ideas list for your how-to demonstration.

Break your team into pairs or small groups. With your partner(s), use the Planner to plan a series of steps and select the format you'd like to use in your demonstration.

PLANNER

1. Plan the steps you'd like to use in your demonstration. Write notes here, using transition words such as <u>First</u>, . . . / <u>Then</u> . . . / <u>After that</u>, . . . / <u>Finally</u>, . . .)

2. Discuss and choose the format(s) you want to use. If you want to include objects or props, discuss and decide what you would like to include.
   - ○ show slides from a deck
   - ○ make posters with drawings, photos, or magazine cut-outs
   - ○ write a list on a whiteboard
   - ○ show objects or demonstrate with props
   - ○ act out the steps or present a skit
   - ○ other: ___

Meet with the rest of the team. Share your presentation steps and format ideas from the Planner with the team. Explain the reasons for your choices.

Compare the steps from each group's planner and decide which one or ones to use in your team's how-to demonstration. Agree on the presentation format(s) as well.

Tips for TEAMWORK

Invite your colleagues to share personal experiences.
Who's ever tried to ___ ?
Has anyone had experience with ___ ?
Are any of you good at ___ ?

Offer reasons for your decisions.
We thought the class might find ___ [interesting].
I figured that this would be ___ .
We all agreed that ___ .

88

Print out the **Evaluation Chart**.

2 COLLABORATION   Write a script and assign roles.

With your teammates, write an introduction, explaining why your team chose its topic. Then write the script for what you will say as you do your demonstration.

Take turns reading the script aloud. Suggest ways to improve the script. Correct any errors.

Decide which team members will create the visuals, collect the props, or produce anything else required for the presentation format the team agreed on.

Assign roles for the demonstration. For example, one team member could introduce the demonstration topic, and the remaining team members could be assigned to present the various steps or manage the visuals.

Tips for COLLABORATION

Show willingness to accept an assignment.
I'd be happy to do that.   Got it!
Consider it done!   My pleasure.

Ask for and be open to feedback.
Can I run something by you?
How about we give [my idea] a try?
See what you think of this.

Provide colleagues with positive encouragement.
You're such [a team player / a genius]!
[Paula] is so [talented / creative / reliable], isn't she?
You really have a knack for [using digital media].

3 PRESENTATION   Rehearse the demonstration and present it to the class.

Rehearse: Provide each team member with a copy of the revised and corrected script.

Take turns rehearsing each part of the demonstration. Listen carefully to your teammates' delivery, provide feedback, and offer suggestions.

Present: Present your demonstration to the class. Introduce each new speaker. Check frequently whether your audience looks engaged with the topic or looks confused.

After your demonstration, ask the class for questions. Take turns answering, depending on which team member feels most able to respond.

Tips for PRESENTATION

Interact with the audience before you begin.
Have any of you ever tried ___ ?
What do you think of ___ ?
Are you ready to [learn something new]?

Confirm that the audience is following you.
What do you think?
Does anyone have any questions?
Is that clear?

EVALUATE   Improve your presentation skills.

Use the Key to answer the questions and evaluate each how-to demonstration. Discuss strengths and weakness and make suggestions about how each demonstration might be improved.

1. Did the introduction adequately explain why the team chose the topic?
2. Did the demonstration include a clear sequence of steps that helped achieve the desired goal?
3. Did the presentation format provide visual support that helped make the demonstration easy to follow?
4. Did the presenters interact with the audience?
5. Did the presenters make sure the audience was paying attention?

KEY
Y = yes
U = usually
S = sometimes
N = no

SOFT SKILLS WORKSHOP 4

UNIT 9

Looking Ahead

PREVIEW

A 🔊 **DEMOGRAPHIC TRENDS** | Listen to a report. What worldwide trend is the speaker describing? What reasons does she suggest might explain these changes?

B 🔊 **ZOOM-IN** | Read and listen to a husband and wife discuss the future. Notice the <u>featured</u> words and phrases.

> **UNDERSTAND A VARIETY OF ACCENTS**
> Les = American English (regional)
> Lena = American English (regional)

Les: Whoa! So listen to this: "In the next five years, more than 20% of all products will have been manufactured, packed, shipped, and delivered without ever having been touched by a human hand."

Lena: That's pretty extreme. Seriously?

Les: Well, that's what it says. . . . They call it "hyper-automation"—robots doing just about everything. So what I'm wondering is, will there be any jobs left for us humans? Seriously, Lena. <u>I'm not being facetious</u>. You're a business professor. What do you think?

Lena: I think that's <u>jumping the gun</u>. We can't know for sure where this "hyper-automation" will lead.

Les: So you don't think it'll lead to <u>massive unemployment</u>?

Lena: Maybe in jobs we know robots can <u>master</u>—things that require manual dexterity, or involve repetitive movements, and just don't need to be performed by humans anymore. It doesn't mean that other kinds of jobs are going to suddenly <u>go poof</u>.

Les: Well, I'm not convinced robots aren't capable of a lot more. Who says they can't invent things, or collaborate with each other? When will we be seeing stories about that?

Lena: Not in *our* lifetime. And there's been so much <u>hoopla</u> lately at my college about teaching students the quote unquote "soft skills"… you know: collaboration, teamwork, communication. They're going to need those in practically any job or career . . . robots or no robots.

Les: Lena, you always see the bright side. But I'm wondering if this isn't just one huge <u>slippery slope</u> to unimaginable consequences.

Lena: Well, we know robots <u>enhance</u> productivity. There's nothing wrong with that.

Les: True. Hey listen to this: "Within five years the person who purchases a product will be the first human to have touched it!"

Lena: Pretty amazing.

C **UNDERSTAND FROM CONTEXT** | Find <u>featured</u> words and phrases in Zoom-In and, with a partner, write an original sentence using each of them.

1. a word that means "excitement and discussion" ....
2. a phrase that means "a state in which huge numbers of people have no jobs" ....
3. a word that means "learn perfectly and be able to do" ....
4. a sentence that means "I'm not kidding" ....
5. a phrase that means "disappear" ....
6. a phrase that means "an event that might lead to negative changes we hadn't anticipated" ....
7. a word that means "improve or increase" ....
8. a phrase that means "coming to a conclusion before knowing all the facts" ....

D **LOOK IT UP AND SHARE** | Find a word or phrase in Zoom-In that was new to you. Look it up and use it in a sentence. Share your sentence with a partner.

E **DISCUSSION** | Where in the world do you think hyper-automation will most likely occur? Explain why.

UNIT 9
COMMUNICATION GOALS

Lesson 1 Discuss the pros and cons of innovative technologies
Lesson 2 Make predictions about science and technology
Lesson 3 Talk about preparing for future pandemics
Lesson 4 Explain social and demographic trends

F TALKING POINTS | Take the survey.

Your beliefs about the future

Read 10 optimistic predictions. Circle the response that most closely reflects your opinion. (You can circle more than one.)

1. **Robots will be a common feature in most people's homes and will enhance our lives.**
   In my city | In my country | Everywhere | Nowhere | Elsewhere (If so, where? _____)

2. **There will be opportunities for me to find a job in my chosen career.**
   In my city | In my country | Everywhere | Nowhere | Elsewhere (If so, where? _____)

3. **Women and men will be paid equally for equal work.**
   In my city | In my country | Everywhere | Nowhere | Elsewhere (If so, where? _____)

4. **Most young people will make more money than their parents and grandparents did.**
   In my city | In my country | Everywhere | Nowhere | Elsewhere (If so, where? _____)

5. **I'll be able to use English regularly in my life.**
   In my city | In my country | Everywhere | Nowhere | Elsewhere (If so, where? _____)

6. **The world will become more peaceful, and there will be fewer armed conflicts.**
   In my city | In my country | Everywhere | Nowhere | Elsewhere (If so, where? _____)

7. **Crime will decrease, and the streets will be safer at night.**
   In my city | In my country | Everywhere | Nowhere | Elsewhere (If so, where? _____)

8. **People will take action to reduce climate change, and the environment will be protected.**
   In my city | In my country | Everywhere | Nowhere | Elsewhere (If so, where? _____)

9. **Pandemics will be prevented.**
   In my city | In my country | Everywhere | Nowhere | Elsewhere (If so, where? _____)

10. **Poverty and unemployment will be reduced.**
    In my city | In my country | Everywhere | Nowhere | Elsewhere (If so, where? _____)

11. **My own prediction:** _____
    In my city | In my country | Everywhere | Nowhere | Elsewhere (If so, where? _____)

Will robots be a common feature in homes?

Will the world become a more peaceful place?

Will streets be safer at night?

Will future pandemics be prevented?

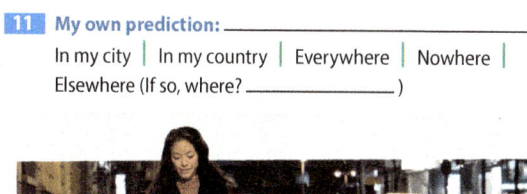

START TALKING

PAIR WORK Compare and discuss responses on the survey in Talking Points. Explain your reasoning, including details. Which one of you is more optimistic about the future?

1 COMMUNICATION GOAL
Discuss the pros and cons of innovative technologies

A **VOCABULARY** | Expressing and dismissing concern | Read and listen. Then listen again and repeat.

TO EXPRESS CONCERN
- It's a slippery slope.
- It's playing with fire.
- It's like opening a can of worms.
- It's like opening a Pandora's Box.

TO DISMISS CONCERN
- I don't see it that way at all.
- I think that's a little exaggerated.
- I guess I just see things differently.
- Don't you think you might be going overboard?

B **LISTEN FOR POINT OF VIEW** | Listen to five conversations about innovative technologies and write the correct conversation number next to each technology. Then listen again and choose the word that indicates the speaker's point of view about each technology.

.... **a** genetic engineering
  She's (concerned / not concerned) about it right now.

.... **b** remote surgery
  She's (concerned / not concerned) about it, but he (is / isn't).

.... **c** reproductive cloning
  They're (concerned / not concerned) about it.

.... **d** artificial intelligence
  They're (concerned / not concerned).

.... **e** microchip implants
  He's (concerned / not concerned) about them.

C **LISTEN TO SUMMARIZE** | With a partner, write a short summary statement in your own words about one use of each technology, based on what you learned in the conversations. Compare statements with a partner. Listen again if necessary.

Example: genetic engineering *Genetic engineering is used to enhance the disease resistance of plants.*
1. genetic engineering ....
2. remote surgery ....
3. reproductive cloning ....
4. artificial intelligence ....
5. microchip implants ....

D **GRAMMAR** | The passive voice in unreal conditional sentences

In unreal conditional sentences, the passive voice can be used in one or both clauses.

The present unreal conditional
If cancer-preventing chemicals **could be embedded** in foods through genetic modification, that technology **might be** more widely **accepted**.
If I **were offered** an unhackable microchip, I'd get it and store absolutely everything on it.

Remember: Form the passive voice with a form of **be** + a past participle.

The past unreal conditional
If remote surgery **had been approved** last year, it **would have been offered** to you when you needed your operation.
If the computer chip **hadn't been developed**, many of our most innovative technologies wouldn't be available to us now.

UNIT 9

E GRAMMAR PRACTICE | Using the prompts, write a present or past unreal conditional statement that expresses your own opinion. Use the passive voice in the <u>if</u> clause.

Example: Genetic engineering / prohibited
1. Cloning of humans / permitted
2. Everyone / trained to use soft skills
3. Surgeries / always performed by robots
4. Electricity / discovered four centuries ago
5. Astronauts / not sent to the Moon in 1969
6. Buses driven by people / replaced by driverless vehicles
7. The way to start fires / not discovered by early humans

> *If genetic engineering were prohibited, farmers wouldn't be able to take advantage of the methods that have been developed to enhance crop disease resistance.*

F PAIR WORK | Compare the statements you wrote for Exercise E. Explain your opinions and provide examples.

COMMUNICATION ACTIVATOR

Now let's discuss the pros and cons of innovative technologies.

A CONVERSATION MODEL | Read and listen.
A: What do you think about people implanting computer chips under their skin?
B: They do that? Why?
A: Well, they say you could identify yourself instantly just by passing your hand through a scanner. You wouldn't need a wallet, money, credit cards, your driver's license . . .
B: Seriously? That gives me the willies. Nothing's foolproof. Couldn't the chip be hacked?
A: You've hit the nail on the head. If the chip were hacked, your personal information could fall into the wrong hands.
B: Well, I value my privacy. I'd think twice before getting chipped, to tell you the truth.
A: That makes two of us!

Social language
Agree informally with someone's strong opinion with "That makes two of us!"

B PRONUNCIATION PRACTICE | Listen again and repeat. Then practice the Conversation Model with a partner.

C TALKING POINTS | List two innovative technologies from Exercise B on page 92. Describe a positive or possibly negative application for each.

Innovative technology	Positive (and / or negative) application
1 *genetic engineering*	*develop plants that are unappealing to insects*

Innovative technology	Positive (and / or negative) application
1	
2	

D IN YOUR OWN WORDS | Create a similar conversation to the one in Exercise A, using your notes from Talking Points. Start like this: *What do you think about ___?* Be sure to change roles and then partners. (Option: Use the Unit 9 Energizer Worksheet.)

KEEP TALKING! •••
- Provide more reasons why you are for or against a particular technology.
- Evaluate the pros and cons of other technologies.
- Express and dismiss concern.
- Say as much as you can.

▶ Watch the video for ideas!

RECYCLE THIS LANGUAGE
I'm not being facetious.
There's been so much hoopla about [it].
It's a slippery slope.
[Safety] will just go poof.

2 COMMUNICATION GOAL | Make predictions about science and technology

A GRAMMAR CLOSE-UP | Read about some predictions. Notice the featured grammar.

Maybe I jumped the gun, but I thought that gas-fueled cars would all be replaced by electric vehicles by now. When the electrics first came on the market, their price was out of range for the average consumer, and it took a while for the price to come down. However, I read that starting this year, prices have become more competitive, and the electrics are going to be sold much more widely. I didn't realize it would take so much time for charging stations to be provided. But it looks like many will have been added by the end of the year. That'll make electric vehicles more appealing to own.

It's interesting that several countries have been sending rockets to the Moon in recent years. Some experts say that by 2035 a human settlement will have already been established there. Apparently, it's not a question of having the right technology, but rather having the will to do it. One article I read noted that the cost of such a venture would probably be shared by more than one country, which would help a lot. One thing's for sure . . . By the time there's a settlement on the Moon, plans will have been created for a settlement on Mars. Now *that's* exciting.

B DISCUSSION | Discuss the questions.

1. Will electric cars ever completely replace gas-fueled cars? Explain your reasons.
2. What do you think the purpose of a settlement on Mars might be? Do you think a settlement on Mars is worth the money it will take to create? Why or why not?

C GRAMMAR | The passive voice: the future, the future perfect, and the future as seen from the past

The passive voice is often used when discussing science and technology.

The future: will be (or be going to be) + a past participle
It's likely that human settlements **will be established** on the Moon in the near future.
Climate change **isn't going to be stopped** unless we do something about it soon.

The future perfect: will have been (or be going to have been) + a past participle
By the end of this century, the world's population explosion **will have been reversed**.
Cures for many of today's major diseases **are going to have been discovered** by 2060.

The future as seen from the past: would be (or was / were going to be) + a past participle
Leonardo Da Vinci correctly **predicted** (that) ships **would be designed** to travel underwater.
No one really **believed** (that) the COVID-19 pandemic **was going to be spread** around the world so quickly.

> **Remember:** Use a **by** phrase when it's important to name the agent (the performer of the action).
> Our lives will be enhanced **by new technology**.

GRAMMAR EXPANDER p. 131
When to use the passive voice

D GRAMMAR PRACTICE | Read the predictions. On a separate sheet of paper, change them from active to passive voice.

1. Technicians will use robots to mine the Moon's natural resources.
2. India is going to surpass the U.S. as the world's second largest economy by 2050.
3. If climate change isn't addressed, the ocean will flood low-lying island nations such as Fiji.
4. Robots are going to perform the majority of microsurgeries.
5. A 3D printer will make replacement car parts for you at home.

E GRAMMAR PRACTICE | Read each prediction. Then complete the statement below it, using would be or was / were going to be + a past participle.

Computers are never going to be used in the home.

1. In the 1970s, Kenneth Olsen, CEO and founder of Digital Equipment, predicted that computers ....

General Motors will mass-produce self-driving cars by 2025.

2. General Motors CEO Mary Barra announced in 2020 that self-driving cars ....

UNIT 9

No online database will replace the newspaper.

③ In 1995, American astronomer, author, and teacher Clifford Stoll predicted the newspaper ....

Over-farming and logging will destroy the world's rainforests.

④ Primatologist Jane Goodall argued that the world's rainforests ....

F **GRAMMAR PRACTICE** | Read about four travel innovations. Write your own prediction for each one, using the future perfect in the passive voice.

Example: *By the second half of the 21st century, . . .*

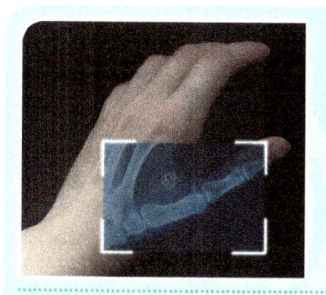

1 Getting your passport stamped may be a thing of the past. Customs agents will require a card with an electronic chip that can be swiped. Or they may rely on implanted microchips for ID.

2 How would you like to stay in a space hotel with a spectacular view? Decades of space travel innovations have made the construction and maintenance of the International Space Station a reality. It won't be long before you can buy tickets for the vacation of a lifetime. When will the first space hotel be built?

3 Tired of arriving at airports far outside the city? Transportation alternatives such as the Hyperloop may replace those long trips to and from airports. A Hyperloop pod runs through a tunnel at about the same speed as an airplane and takes you to and from the heart of the city.

4 Imagine if your car could sense your emotions and calm you down, perhaps preventing you from going ballistic when another driver cuts you off. Or imagine that this same car could keep you awake when you get drowsy. Cars of the future might be equipped with AI technology called "affective computing," which is said to be a promising safety feature that can even be programmed to adapt to the different ways people from different cultures express emotions.

COMMUNICATION ACTIVATOR

Now let's make predictions about science and technology.

A **TALKING POINTS** | Write at least three predictions in the passive voice about science and technology. Use <u>will</u>, <u>be going to</u>, or the future perfect.

In the future . . .	By 2050 . . .	By the end of the century . . .

B **DISCUSSION** | Share your predictions from Talking Points. Which of your classmates' predictions do you think are likely to come true? Do your predictions paint an optimistic or pessimistic view of the future? Explain.

KEEP TALKING! •••
- Ask your classmates questions about their predictions.
- Provide reasons for why you think a prediction will or won't come true.
- Say as much as you can.

▶ Watch the video for ideas!

RECYCLE THIS LANGUAGE

It's like opening [a can of worms / a Pandora's Box].
It's playing with fire.
It gives me the willies.
It isn't foolproof.
I'd think twice before I ____ .
That makes two of us.
I'd take that with a grain of salt.

I'm not being facetious.
You've hit the nail on the head.
You're jumping the gun.
Don't you think you might be going overboard?
I guess I just see things differently.
I think that's a little exaggerated.

FOR MORE PRACTICE, GO TO YOUR DIGITAL RESOURCES

3 COMMUNICATION GOAL: Talk about preparing for future pandemics

A READING | Read the article. What are the three main points the writer makes?

How will we stay safe when the next pandemic hits?

When Chinese scientists identified COVID-19 in 2019, and the virus began to spread across the world like wildfire, experts warned world leaders of the need for an immediate, united response to contain it and save lives. Instead, the response was slow and chaotic, and millions of people died. The pandemic's shock waves brought the global economy to its knees. It had a devastating impact on tourism and the hospitality industry, caused a catastrophic rise in unemployment, and forced countless businesses to close forever. While some countries fared better than others, most were woefully unprepared for an event of this magnitude and were compelled to take drastic measures to try to contain the spread.

The COVID-19 pandemic was a global wake-up call. Since we know that COVID-19 won't be the last pandemic, how can we do better next time?

Improve warning systems

Countries in East Asia, where 87% of the deaths from the SARS epidemic in the early 2000s occurred, had learned from that experience. As soon as their first COVID-19 cases were confirmed, they were able to respond quickly with a system of digital contact tracing—a procedure for containing and isolating the virus by identifying all the people who had had contact with infected individuals. Those people were then quarantined to ensure they didn't infect anyone else. From that experience, it is clear that all countries should follow that proactive model and make testing kits abundantly available to better inform authorities of critical decisions they must make, such as when and how to impose a lockdown in schools, nursing homes, and non-essential businesses and whether, when, and how to mandate social distancing and the use of masks.

Restore public trust

COVID-19 revealed political and social tensions in a number of countries. Inadequate government responses and the lack of adequate medical facilities led to dramatic increases in COVID-19 deaths. Some national leaders downplayed the seriousness of the disease in spite of its well-known deadliness, causing a massive loss in public trust. In some countries, the spread of misinformation caused people to keep their loved ones at home rather than take them to the emergency room. In the future, world leaders must have a plan to ensure adequate hospital space and must prevent a breakdown in public trust by identifying experts who can provide fact-based public information. False conspiracy theories posted on social media will have to be swiftly and clearly refuted, and penalties assessed against people and sites that promote lies.

Ensure the supply chain of necessities

In the early days of the pandemic, people were shocked to see how quickly basic necessities, such as toilet paper, cleansers, and frozen vegetables vanished from supermarket shelves. Manufacturers struggled to keep up with the sudden increased demand. Even more concerning was the dilemma faced by health workers, who put themselves at risk to care for others. Basic medical supplies such as personal protective equipment (PPE) became more and more difficult to locate, and a number of nurses, doctors, and other key staff came down with the disease themselves—some fatally. While development of a vaccine was successfully achieved in record time, early distribution was confusing and difficult, and there were injustices in the availability of vaccines between richer and poorer regions and countries. In the next pandemic, shortages of consumer and medical supplies can be anticipated and prevented by intelligent planning. And plans for distribution of vaccines will ensure that countries with less developed economies won't be left behind.

Basic necessities disappeared early in the pandemic.

B UNDERSTAND WRITER'S PURPOSE | Which of the following is the purpose of the article?

1 To present all the things that went wrong in the response to the COVID-19 pandemic.
2 To identify ways that the world can be better prepared for the next pandemic.
3 To help governments prevent the breakdown in public trust.

C UNDERSTAND FROM CONTEXT | Paraphrase each statement containing a word or expression from the article.

1 Contagious diseases often "spread like wildfire."

....

2 This country's economy was "brought to its knees."

....

3 The COVID-19 pandemic was "a wake-up call" to countries around the world.

....

UNIT 9

4 Initially, some government leaders "downplayed" the seriousness of COVID-19.
....

5 Conflicting information and governmental advice caused a "breakdown" in public trust.
....

6 All kinds of consumer products quickly "vanished" from store shelves.
....

7 The spread of misinformation over social media is extremely "concerning."
....

8 Some countries in the less developed world were "left behind" when richer countries quickly received vaccine supplies.
....

D ACTIVATE LANGUAGE FROM A TEXT | With a partner, discuss the meaning of each of the following words and phrases. Use each of them in your own original sentence.
1 contact tracing ....
2 a lockdown ....
3 social distancing ....
4 misinformation ....
5 a quarantine ....
6 a conspiracy theory ....

PRONUNCIATION LESSON p. 142
Reading aloud

COMMUNICATION ACTIVATOR

Now let's talk about preparing for future pandemics.

A TALKING POINTS | With a partner, identify what you think were the three most important ways in which the world was unprepared for the COVID-19 pandemic.

1
2
3

B GROUP WORK | Compare your lists from Talking Points and explain why each item on your list had a devastating impact on the situation. Ask and answer questions.

C DISCUSSION | If you were in a position of authority in your town or national government, what policies would you put into effect to prepare for the next pandemic, if one occurs?

Topics to consider
- working remotely from home
- learning remotely
- virtual visits with doctors
- social distancing
- vaccine development and distribution
- treatment development
- financial support of businesses that have to close
- early warnings
- screening and testing
- travel restrictions
- other

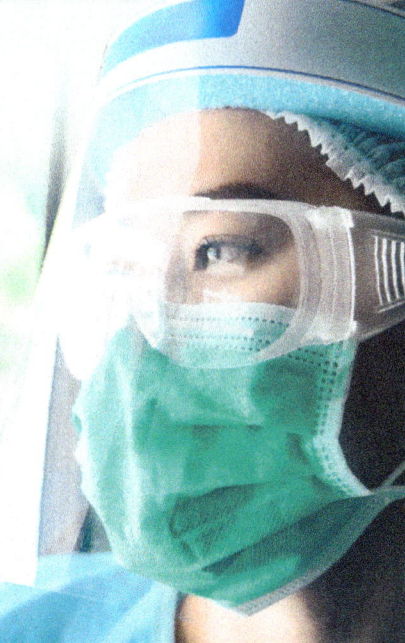

Medical worker in PPE

FOR MORE PRACTICE, GO TO YOUR DIGITAL RESOURCES

4 COMMUNICATION GOAL | Explain social and demographic trends

A 🔊 **VOCABULARY** | Demographic and social trends | Read and listen. Then listen again and repeat.

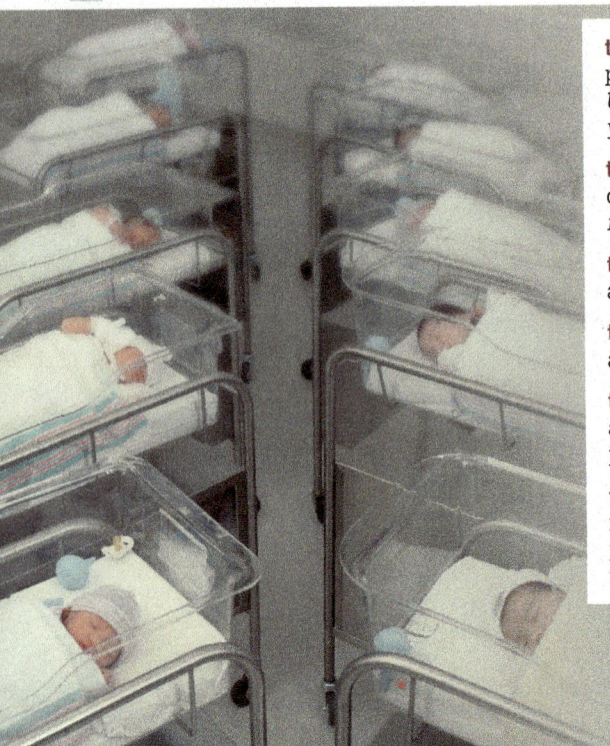

the fertility rate the average number of births per female in a particular place or population (e.g., The 2020 fertility rate in the U.K. was 1.75 births per adult woman, an increase of .06% over the year before.)

the birth rate the average number of births during a particular period of time in a particular place or population (e.g., The 2020 U.K. birth rate was 11.4 births per 1000 people, a decrease of 49% from 2019.)

the mortality rate the average number of deaths that occur during a particular period of time in a particular place or population

the divorce rate the average number of divorces that occur during a particular period of time in a particular place or population

the crime rate the average number of violent crimes or crimes against property that occur during a particular period of time in a particular place or population

the literacy rate the average number of people in a particular population who can read and write

a demographic a part of the population that is considered as a specific group within a population, such as people over the age of 65, ethnic minorities, teenagers, etc.

a trend a general tendency in the way a situation is changing or developing

a statistic a single number which represents a fact or measurement

B **UNDERSTAND THE VOCABULARY** | Write whether each example is a demographic, a statistic, a rate, or a trend. Explain your choices.

1. Even before the pandemic, more and more people began watching movies at home rather than in movie theaters. ....
2. The majority of social media site Pinterest's users are women. ....
3. The number of births per family is lower in richer, more developed nations and regions. ....
4. Fifteen percent of people over the age of 65 in the U.S. are living in poverty. ....

C 🔊 **LISTEN TO ACTIVATE VOCABULARY** | Listen to four conversations about rates and trends. Complete each statement with the name of the rate. Then listen again and circle the trend.

1. The .... rate has (risen / fallen).
2. The .... rate is (rising / falling).
3. The .... rate has (risen / fallen).
4. The .... rate has been (rising / falling).

D 🔊 **LISTEN FOR FACTS AND FIGURES** | First read the questions. Then listen to a lecture on demographic trends and answer the questions. Listen again to confirm your answers.

1. What has been happening to the world's population since 1804?
2. By 2030, what country will have the largest population?
3. What recently happened to the percentage of the world's population living in rural and urban areas?
4. What is happening to the percentage of the world's population that are seniors?

E 🎧 **LISTEN TO DRAW CONCLUSIONS** | Complete each statement by drawing a conclusion from the information in the lecture. Support your answers with reasons, based on the lecture.
1. The greatest need for resources in Africa, based on the predicted demographic, will be in the (agricultural / educational / health) sector.
2. China's economy might suffer from the rise in the (older / younger / poorer) demographic because there will be (fewer / more / the same number of) people in the workforce.
3. The largest percentage of Nigeria's population will most likely be (children / seniors / working-age citizens).

F **SUPPORT AN OPINION** | Which of the demographic trends mentioned in the lecture concern you the most? Explain your reasons to your classmates.

COMMUNICATION ACTIVATOR
Now let's explain social and demographic trends.

A **TALKING POINTS** | Make notes about social and demographic trends taking place in your country and their possible benefits or consequences. Check the ones that concern you.

☑ Marriage and divorce: *People are getting married later than before. Families will probably get smaller.*

☐ Marriage and divorce

☐ Education

☐ Family life

☐ Seniors' quality of life

☐ Children's social interactions

☐ Other:

B **GROUP WORK** | Compare notes from Talking Points. For the trends you are concerned about, discuss the consequences you have noted. Explore possible solutions. Then present the ideas you discussed to your classmates. (Option: Use the Unit 9 Soft Skills Booster, p. 162.)

❝ If families continue to decrease in size, fewer schools will be needed. ❞

RECYCLE THIS LANGUAGE
It's a slippery slope.
I'm not being facetious.
That makes two of us.
I think that's a little exaggerated.
I guess I just see things differently.
You've hit the nail on the head.
That gives me the willies.

WRITING HANDBOOK p. 152
- **Skill:** The thesis statement in a formal essay
- **Task:** Write a formal essay about future trends

PROGRESS SELF-CHECK — **NOW I CAN**

For more practice... **Unit Review / Connect TV / Test-Taking Skills Booster**

☐ Discuss the pros and cons of innovative technologies.

☐ Make predictions about science and technology.

☐ Talk about preparing for future pandemics.

☐ Explain social and demographic trends.

UNIT 10

Global Ties

PREVIEW

A **GLOBALIZATION** | Listen to one person's mixed impressions of the impact of globalization. What's one benefit she feels globalization has provided? And at the same time, what does she miss about the past?

B **ZOOM-IN** | Read and listen to two foreign university students in Marseille, France. Notice the <u>featured</u> language.

UNDERSTAND A VARIETY OF ACCENTS
Tariq = Arabic
Oki = Japanese

Tariq: Hey, Oki, long time no see! Everything OK? Everyone missed you in class today.
Oki: Hey, Tariq. Yeah, I'm fine. Just feeling a little <u>out of sorts</u>.
Tariq: What do you mean out of sorts? Are you sick?
Oki: No, nothing like that. Things have been kind of <u>getting to me</u> lately. I think I've just needed a little alone time.
Tariq: Are you homesick for Japan? France is a long way from home. I know I miss my parents in Egypt!
Oki: Well, I am definitely missing my family, but I video chat with them just about every day, so I don't think it's that. I'm just feeling kind of <u>like a fish out of water</u> these days—like I just don't belong here. I've been having trouble sleeping and all that.
Tariq: You sure you haven't picked something up? Maybe you should get a check-up at the student clinic. They're really nice there.
Oki: Thanks, Tariq, but I'm OK. <u>I'll get over it</u>. I'm just not used to the culture here. It's been getting on my nerves.
Tariq: <u>You're pulling my leg</u>, right? I thought you were totally in love with France.
Oki: That's true, but all of a sudden I've fallen out of love.
Tariq: What specifically is bothering you?
Oki: I'm not sure. <u>It's hard to put my finger on it</u> . . . Like <u>what's with</u> all those protests and student strikes? It seems like every other day they cancel classes for a demonstration. For goodness' sakes, aren't students here to study?
Tariq: <u>I'm with you there!</u> And the endless political discussions! Where I come from, it's not polite to ask people about their political opinions unless you're really close.
Oki: I know what you mean.

C **UNDERSTAND FROM CONTEXT** | With a partner, paraphrase the <u>featured</u> phrases and sentences your own way.

1. I'm feeling a little out of sorts.
2. Things have been kind of getting to me lately.
3. I feel like a fish out of water.
4. I'll get over it.
5. You're pulling my leg.
6. It's hard to put my finger on it.
7. What's with all those protests and student strikes?
8. I'm with you there!

D **THINK AND EXPLAIN** | With a partner, discuss the questions and explain your answers.

1. What's troubling Oki? What does he think is the problem?
2. What's one thing about French student culture that neither Oki nor Tariq can understand?

E **LOOK IT UP AND SHARE** | Find a word or phrase in Zoom-In that was new to you. Look it up and use it in a sentence. Share your sentence with a partner.

F **PAIR WORK** | Tell your partner about a time you felt "like a fish out of water."

UNIT 10

COMMUNICATION GOALS

Lesson 1 React to international news events
Lesson 2 Talk about the influence of foreign imports
Lesson 3 Discuss the ways your culture might cause culture shock
Lesson 4 Understand the impact of globalization

G TALKING POINTS | Take the quiz.

How much do you know about English in today's world?

1. English is not an official language in ___ .
   - ☐ the U.S. or the U.K.
   - ☐ South Africa
   - ☐ Canada
   - ☐ Nigeria

2. There are ___ speakers of English in the world.
   - ☐ 1.5 million
   - ☐ 10 million
   - ☐ 1 billion
   - ☐ 1.5 billion

3. Approximately ___ of the world's population are native speakers of English.
   - ☐ 5%
   - ☐ 10%
   - ☐ 20%
   - ☐ 30%

4. There are about ___ million people who speak English as a second or a foreign language.
   - ☐ 6
   - ☐ 10
   - ☐ 70
   - ☐ 700

5. ___ is the country with the most English speakers.
   - ☐ China
   - ☐ the U.K.
   - ☐ the U.S.
   - ☐ India

6. Approximately ___ million people are studying English in China.
   - ☐ 1
   - ☐ 10
   - ☐ 100
   - ☐ 400

7. In France, there are approximately ___ public and private university programs taught in English.
   - ☐ 20
   - ☐ 100
   - ☐ 500
   - ☐ 1500

8. Approximately ___ of online content is in English.
   - ☐ 10%
   - ☐ 30%
   - ☐ 50%
   - ☐ 80%

9. Which language has the largest vocabulary?
   - ☐ English
   - ☐ German
   - ☐ Chinese
   - ☐ French

Traffic signs in Québec, Canada

Many children in China study English in primary school.

English is the medium of instruction in many universities worldwide.

Answers 1. Neither the U.S. nor the U.K. has an official language. Both English and French are official languages in Canada. South Africa has 11 official languages, including English. Nigeria has only one—English. English is the main language in those countries by history and tradition. 2. Almost 1.5 billion people in the world speak English—that's one out of every six people, and the number is growing. 3. There are about 380 million native speakers of English, a little over 5% of the world's population. 4. There are about 700 million people who have learned English in addition to their own language. 5. The U.S. has the most English speakers, native and non-native, at 290 million. Ranking highest after that are India (125 million), Pakistan (108 million), Nigeria (79 million), the Philippines (64 million), and the U.K. (63 million). But there are more English speakers in Asia than in the U.S., U.K., and Canada combined. 6. 400 million people are learning English in China. 7. French universities offer approximately 1 500 programs in which English is the language of instruction. France attracts more foreign university students than any other non-English-speaking country. 8. 80% of the world's digitally stored information is in English, but the proportion of information stored in other languages is growing on the Internet. 9. English claims to have the largest vocabulary. Estimates range from 250,000 to 1 million words.

START TALKING

PERSONALIZE Complete the chart with details about the ways and places you expect to use English in your life. (Write N/A (not applicable) for situations you don't expect to occur.)

In my country	Outside of my country
With visitors from other countries:	For tourism:
In phone and video conferences:	For study:
In written communication for my job:	For my job:
Other:	Other:

PAIR WORK Compare charts and discuss the details you included in your chart.

1 COMMUNICATION GOAL: React to international news events

A VOCABULARY | Phrasal verbs for discussing events and issues | Read and listen. Then listen again and repeat.

Note: Phrasal verbs contain a verb and one or more particles that together have their own meaning. Particles are most commonly prepositions or adverbs.

bring about cause to occur or to exist
Rising temperatures have brought about many changes to the world's weather.

carry out achieve or accomplish a plan or a project
The Health Ministry has quickly carried out the ambitious vaccination plan it promised last month.

wipe out eliminate or destroy something completely
Agricultural science has wiped out many previously destructive plant pests.

come up with invent a novel plan or idea
Immunologists have come up with a cutting-edge approach to bee-sting allergy prevention.

go without live without something one needs or is accustomed to having
Our water filtration system has ensured that no town will go without clean, safe drinking water.

lay off end the employment of workers in response to poor economic conditions
During the period of widespread lockdowns in the pandemic, many businesses closed and laid off the majority of their employees.

put up with bear someone's behavior or a bad situation without complaining
Many people are willing to put up with terrible traffic jams during the national holidays.

run out of use one's entire supply of something and have no more
During the storm, stores ran out of essential supplies such as milk and bread.

come down with become sick with a particular illness
The increase in flooding has caused an increase in the mosquito population, and many people are coming down with dengue fever.

B ACTIVATE VOCABULARY | Circle the correct phrasal verb to complete each sentence.

1 The cruise industry shut down almost completely during the pandemic and had to (bring about / **lay off**) almost 100% of its non-technical staff.
2 Hopefully someone will (**come up with** / put up with) a way for employees working remotely to interact more frequently with their colleagues.
3 The catastrophic weather this last month forced us to (**put up with** / come down with) cancellations and delays to most flights.
4 The massive power outage that hit the East Coast caused millions of people to (put up with / **go without**) electricity for three days.
5 Smallpox vaccinations (**wiped out** / came down with) the disease all over the world in the mid-twentieth century.
6 Demand for fuel during the summer months last year caused many gas stations to (go without / **run out of**) gas.
7 When schoolchildren begin school after the summer vacation, lots of them (put up with / **come down with**) colds and other contagious diseases.
8 The soldiers came back exhausted after (wiping out / **carrying out**) the rescue mission in the mountains.
9 We're hoping the legislation just passed will (go without / **bring about**) a reduction in fossil fuel energy usage.

C LISTEN TO INFER MEANING | Listen to the conversations about news events. After each conversation, complete the statement.

Conversation 1 The refugees will ...... soon.
a go without food
b come down with something
c carry out a plan

Conversation 2 Lots of people have been ....
a putting up with vaccinations
b coming down with the disease
c coming up with a plan

Conversation 3 The government hasn't ....
a carried out the president's plan yet
b run out of supplies
c laid off anyone

D VOCABULARY PRACTICE | Complete the article, using the appropriate forms of the phrasal verbs from the Vocabulary.

PRONUNCIATION LESSON p. 143
Intonation of tag questions

Agencies merge to reduce hunger
Geneva, May 10

Last week the UN's World Food Program (WFP) and the International Global Food Fund (IGFF) met in Geneva and ....(1).................. a plan to temporarily combine their efforts for a more focused and efficient service delivery. These two hunger relief organizations' primary mission has been to implement programs that ....(2).............. malnutrition, especially among infants and children worldwide. Additionally, they will now collaborate to ....(3).............. increased food production and ....(4).............. plans to provide food assistance to people in each of their regions. In recent years, climate change has exacerbated food shortages, and the number of people who are currently forced to ....(5).............. food and potable water has skyrocketed. Increasingly, families are ....(6).............. being hungry for days on end. Making the issue even more urgent is the fact that malnourished people have weakened immune systems and readily ....(7).............. contagious diseases. In joining together, these two premier agencies have pledged to collaborate so no region ....(8).............. essential food supplies.

COMMUNICATION ACTIVATOR

Now let's react to international news events.

A CONVERSATION MODEL | Read and listen.
A: Can you believe all the humanitarian crises happening around the world?
B: Unbelievable. Starvation. Childhood mortality. You name it.
A: What's causing them?
B: Well, they say there are two major factors right now: conflict and the effects of climate change, like drought.
A: Right, and they both have a ripple effect. Look at the displacement of tons of people they cause.
B: To say nothing about millions of refugees migrating to other countries.
A: Makes you feel hopeless, doesn't it?
B: Actually, not really. There are places where you can make a donation.
A: You're right. At least we'd be doing something.

Social language
Say "You name it" to indicate the list could be a lot longer.
To add to an already long list, say "To say nothing about ___ ."

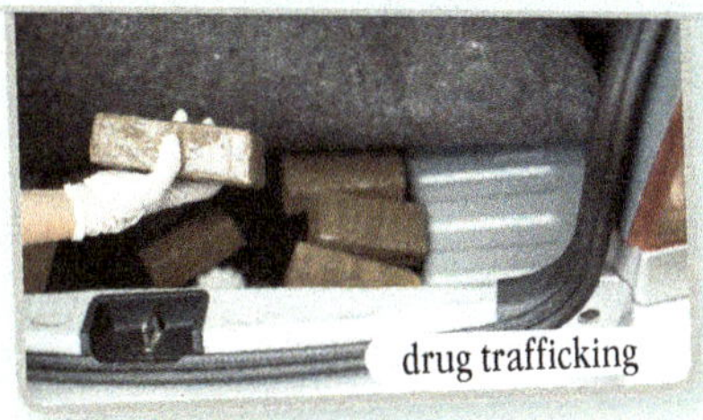

drug trafficking
conflict 

B PRONUNCIATION PRACTICE | Listen again
and repeat. Then practice the Conversation Model with a partner.

C IN YOUR OWN WORDS
Create a similar conversation about other crises happening in the world. Name the problem and any ripple effects. Start like this: *Can you believe . . . ?* Be sure to change roles and then partners. (Option: Use the Unit 10 Energizer Worksheet.)

KEEP TALKING!
- Describe the crisis in more detail.
- Say more about how you feel about the situation.
- Suggest ways to help.
- Say as much as you can.

▶ Watch the video for ideas!

Other crises
- childhood malnutrition
- epidemics
- victims of natural disasters
- childhood mortality
- homelessness
- scams
- drug use

migration
drought
street crime 
hunger 
terrorism

2 COMMUNICATION GOAL | Talk about the influence of foreign imports

A 🔊 **GRAMMAR CLOSE-UP** | Read the people's opinions. Notice the <u>featured</u> grammar.

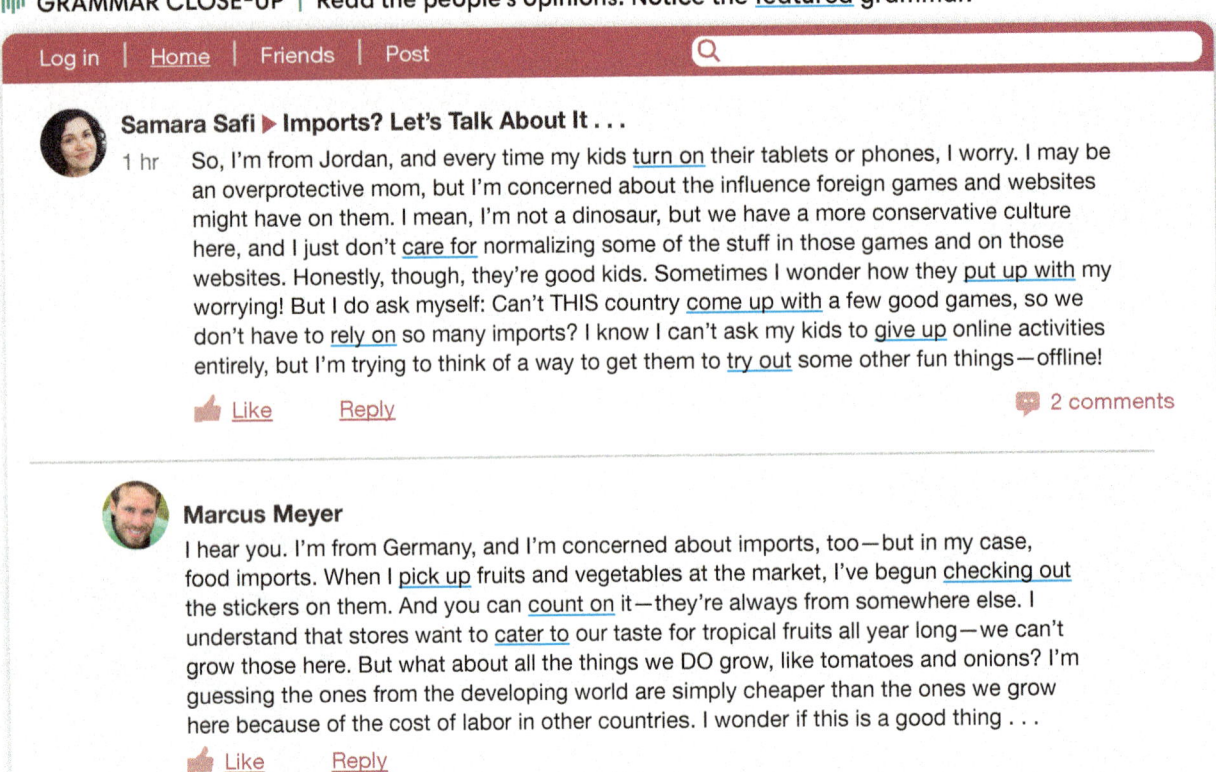

Log in | Home | Friends | Post

Samara Safi ▶ Imports? Let's Talk About It . . .
1 hr

So, I'm from Jordan, and every time my kids <u>turn on</u> their tablets or phones, I worry. I may be an overprotective mom, but I'm concerned about the influence foreign games and websites might have on them. I mean, I'm not a dinosaur, but we have a more conservative culture here, and I just don't <u>care for</u> normalizing some of the stuff in those games and on those websites. Honestly, though, they're good kids. Sometimes I wonder how they <u>put up with</u> my worrying! But I do ask myself: Can't THIS country <u>come up with</u> a few good games, so we don't have to <u>rely on</u> so many imports? I know I can't ask my kids to <u>give up</u> online activities entirely, but I'm trying to think of a way to get them to <u>try out</u> some other fun things—offline!

👍 Like   Reply   💬 2 comments

Marcus Meyer

I hear you. I'm from Germany, and I'm concerned about imports, too—but in my case, food imports. When I <u>pick up</u> fruits and vegetables at the market, I've begun <u>checking out</u> the stickers on them. And you can <u>count on</u> it—they're always from somewhere else. I understand that stores want to <u>cater to</u> our taste for tropical fruits all year long—we can't grow those here. But what about all the things we DO grow, like tomatoes and onions? I'm guessing the ones from the developing world are simply cheaper than the ones we grow here because of the cost of labor in other countries. I wonder if this is a good thing . . .

👍 Like   Reply

B **ACTIVATE PRIOR KNOWLEDGE** | Would people in your country express opinions similar to the ones in Grammar Close-Up? Explain.

C **GRAMMAR** | Separability of transitive phrasal verbs

Remember: Transitive verbs are verbs that can have direct objects. Transitive *phrasal verbs* can be separable or inseparable.

Separable
A direct object noun can generally come after or before the particle of a separable phrasal verb.
  I'd like to **try on** that blue blouse. OR I'd like to **try** that blue blouse **on**.
However, a direct object pronoun must come before the particle.
  I'd like to **try** it **on**. NOT I'd like to ~~try on it~~.

Inseparable
A direct object noun or pronoun always comes after the particle of an inseparable phrasal verb.
  They **cater to** younger customers. NOT They ~~cater younger customers to~~.
  I don't **care for** them. NOT I don't ~~care them for~~.

Be careful! Some phrasal verbs are always separated. The particle never comes directly after the verb.
  I **talked** them **into** contributing money. NOT I ~~talked into them~~ contributing money.

Separable		
blow away	find out	try out
bring about	give up	turn on / off
carry out	lay off	throw away
check out	pick up	try on
figure out	take up	wipe out

Inseparable		
care for	count on	put up with
cater to	do without	rely on
come across	go after	run into
come down with	go without	run out of
come up with		

Always separated
do (sth.) over   start (sth.) over   talk (s.o.) into (sth.)
For a more complete list with definitions, see pp. 114-116.

GRAMMAR EXPANDER p. 132
Phrasal verbs: expansion

D **UNDERSTAND THE GRAMMAR** | Which phrasal verbs in Grammar Close-Up are separable? On a separate sheet of paper, rewrite those sentences, with the direct object in a different position.

104   UNIT 10

E **GRAMMAR PRACTICE** | Complete the sentences, using a form of the phrasal verb with the pronoun it or them. Pay attention to whether or not the verb is separable.

1. Pilates is really popular. Even my great grandmother has (take up) ....
2. Although only a small number of people here can understand English, English words are everywhere. You often (come across) .... on signs, menus, ads, and clothing labels.
3. Many of the workers who were laid off during the pandemic had highly developed skills. It may not be so easy to (talk into) .... going back for more training.
4. Because young adults are tech-savvy and have tremendous economic power, Internet companies have developed marketing campaigns that (go after) .... aggressively.
5. At international food fairs, foreign companies offer samples of their products. Domestic suppliers can (try out) .... before deciding to import them.
6. Once a foreign brand has become popular, it's hard for people to (give up) ....

COMMUNICATION ACTIVATOR

Now let's talk about the influence of foreign imports.

A **TALKING POINTS** | On the notepad, list examples of imports from foreign countries or cultures that you come across regularly.

Foods:

Music:

Products for your house:

Clothing / personal care products:

Entertainment:

Vehicles:

Sports and games:

Other:

B **GROUP WORK** | Compare lists from Talking Points. Have the imports had a positive or negative influence in your country? Explain.

" There's been a trend here toward giving up local traditions and replacing them with imported things. Some of them are great, but I question the wisdom of throwing out our own traditions in their favor. Imported things aren't necessarily better than our own! "

KEEP TALKING!
- Agree or disagree, providing supporting details.
- Discuss recent trends in your country.
- Describe how imports can or do influence your home culture.
- Say as much as you can.

▶ Watch the video for ideas!

Spanish specialties are enjoyed in many places outside of Spain.

Asian martial arts are popular throughout the world.

Labels tell you where your garment was made.

3 COMMUNICATION GOAL: Discuss the ways your culture might cause culture shock

A **VOCABULARY** | Discussing culture shock | Read and listen. Then listen again and repeat.

culture shock *n.* the feelings of anxiety and confusion that people have when they spend time in a foreign country
Foreign students often experience culture shock.

homesick *adj.* feeling sad because of being away from home
The first time I went to summer camp, I was homesick.

overwhelming *adj.* more than one can bear; large enough in size, number, or amount to have a very strong effect
Homesickness can be overwhelming and hard to overcome.

disorienting *adj.* confusing, especially of new surroundings
If you come from a culture in which people often touch each other, it can be disorienting to be in a country where people generally do not.

belong *v.* feel happy or comfortable in a place or situation because one has the same interests and ideas as other people
It was so good to come home to a place where I belong!

miss *v.* feel sad because one doesn't have something or do something one had or did before
When Ella was in Europe, she found herself missing some of the foods from back home.

long for *v.* want something very much, especially when it seems unlikely to happen soon
Many people from the country long for a little quiet when they're in a busy city.

B **PERSONALIZE THE VOCABULARY** | Choose three of the words from the Vocabulary, and use them to write a true statement about yourself. Share statements with a partner.

C **LISTEN TO SUMMARIZE** | Listen to the radio program. In your own words, summarize the characteristics of each of the four stages of culture shock.

Stage one:

Stage two:

Stage three:

Stage four:

Susan Cahill

Berat Yildiz

D **LISTEN FOR DETAILS** | Listen again. Check the correct answers, according to the program.

1. Which of the following disorienting experiences did not cause negative feelings for Berat in London?
   ☐ the traffic ☐ the money ☐ the weather ☐ the food ☐ people's behavior

2. Which symptoms of culture shock did Berat experience?
   ☐ headaches ☐ disappointment ☐ sadness ☐ lack of sleep ☐ loneliness

3. Which of the following were mentioned as signs that Berat was in the final stage of culture shock?
   ☐ dressing right for cold weather ☐ making friends ☐ calling home
   ☐ appreciating cultural differences ☐ finding Turkish restaurants

UNIT 10

E **UNDERSTAND FROM CONTEXT** | Listen to the excerpts from the radio program. Use the context to help you complete each statement.

1 When Susan Cahill says that Berat Yildiz knows about culture shock "firsthand," she means he knows it from ....
   a experience   b his studies   c his culture

2 When Berat Yildiz says he felt like he was "in heaven," he means he felt ....
   a worried   b shocked   c great

3 When Susan says there is "a light at the end of the tunnel," she means that things will ....
   a get better   b get worse   c stay the same

4 When Berat says he got his "feet back on the ground," he means he stopped ....
   a feeling confused   b feeling happy   c thinking about Turkish food

COMMUNICATION ACTIVATOR

Now let's discuss the ways your culture might cause culture shock.

A **TALKING POINTS** | Check three aspects of your culture you think might cause a visitor to experience culture shock. Write those three on the notepad and write suggestions to help visitors overcome their discomfort with each one.

- [ ] local dishes
- [ ] eating and drinking customs
- [ ] etiquette at work
- [ ] local holidays
- [ ] sense of humor
- [ ] formality and informality
- [ ] punctuality
- [ ] traditional leisure activities
- [ ] socializing
- [ ] clothing do's and don'ts
- [ ] treatment of children
- [ ] customs of keeping pets
- [ ] public transportation
- [ ] driving behavior
- [ ] pedestrian behavior
- [ ] other: ....

1

2

3

B **PAIR WORK** | Use your notes from Talking Points to describe your ideas to help a visitor cope with culture shock in your country.

UNIT 10   107

4 COMMUNICATION GOAL: Understand the impact of globalization

A **READING** | Read the interview about the pros and cons of our increasingly interdependent world. What fact was most surprising to you?

WORLD GLOBALIZATION: A double-edged sword?
World interviewed sociologist Angela Kuhn about globalization.

WORLD: Professor Kuhn, you've been quoted as saying that globalization isn't a "Johnny-come-lately," having begun thousands of years ago. The popular perspective is that globalization, or the economic interdependence of nation states, is a phenomenon of the last hundred years that has accelerated rapidly in the Information Age past the point of no return.

KUHN: Most people do think of globalization as recent, but they're mistaken. The best known early example of economic interdependence is probably the Silk Road, the ancient network of trade routes across China, Central Asia, and the Mediterranean between 50 BCE and 250 CE. And just as today's globalization has been enabled by emerging technologies, so was the trade over the Silk Road.

WORLD: Which technologies could you be referring to, so long ago?

KUHN: Specifically, advances in metallurgy led to the creation of coins so that goods could be bought and sold and not simply exchanged, or "bartered," as they had been previously. And a developing infrastructure of roads and bridges played a key role just as they do today. Later, in the 15th century, advances in technology, such as improved ship design and the magnetic compass, made Columbus's four voyages to the New World possible. As it does today, trade impacted the lives and culture of ordinary people of the time—both for good and for bad. Heaven knows that much pain and suffering has always been a component of globalization.

WORLD: Can you elaborate on some ways the lives of ordinary people have been affected by globalization?

KUHN: Well, I'm simplifying, you understand, but in the Asian example, foods that had been eaten only locally began to be known elsewhere, and products such as Chinese silk and Arabian spices—along with the cultural exchange of religious beliefs—influenced the traditions and personal lives of people of the time. Similarly, Columbus's voyages opened the Age of Exploration, and repeated connections between Europe and the Americas introduced profound cultural change in the people of both places.

WORLD: So, fast forward to today—obviously, globalization still creates economic ties among the countries of the world, but the Internet has accelerated the process. And English has facilitated our ability to connect culturally with others. So, then, why are people so down on globalization?

KUHN: Well, I don't think we can state that categorically. Most people are ambivalent. They receive the benefits of globalization—economic growth, higher standards of living, enriched culture, more access to a wider range of products—but are also aware of some of its downsides.

WORLD: Such as?

In 2021, the cargo ship Ever Given *blocked the Suez Canal, disrupting the global trade the world's economies now depend on.*

KUHN: Well, companies in richer, developed countries often outsource manufacturing and customer service to poorer countries, where labor costs are lower. This has led to a widening gap between the rich and the poor in the more developed countries because jobs there are consequently lost. Since goods are imported and exported around the world, there has been a huge growth in shipping, and because of the lack of regulation in international waters, workers on merchant ships have been exploited and abused. Furthermore, ordinary people complain that their traditional culture and industries are being lost to an invasion of foreign brands and—lest we forget—our interconnectedness has created an increased risk of pandemic disease.

WORLD: Will a day come when we can offset the downsides and reap only the benefits of an interconnected world?

KUHN: As you said earlier, we may have reached the point of no return. World economies are interdependent, and there seems to be no Plan B when things go wrong; in other words, there's no alternative.

WORLD: As you said: it's a double-edged sword. Thank you, Dr. Kuhn.

B **UNDERSTAND FROM CONTEXT** | With a partner, answer the questions that contain key words and expressions from the interview.
1. What does Professor Kuhn mean that globalization isn't a "Johnny-come-lately"?
2. How does she define "globalization"?
3. What was the "infrastructure" of the Silk Road era?
4. Which "technologies" made Columbus's voyages possible?
5. How does "bartering" differ from buying and selling?
6. How would you describe the "outsourcing" of manufacturing and customer service?
7. What does it mean to be "ambivalent" about something?
8. What is meant by "the point of no return"?
9. How would you explain the meaning of a "Plan B"?

C **IDENTIFY SUPPORTING DETAILS** | Answer the questions, supporting your answers with information in the interview.
1. In what way has technology enabled growth in economic interdependence in the three time periods Professor Kuhn mentions?
2. How did the growth in metallurgy contribute to the shift from bartering to buying and selling traded goods?
3. What are the benefits of globalization that Kuhn points out?
4. Why is it easy for shippers to abuse and exploit workers on merchant ships?
5. Why has globalization multiplied the risk of pandemic disease?
6. Why was the incident of the Ever Given so significant?

COMMUNICATION ACTIVATOR

Now let's understand the impact of globalization.

A **TALKING POINTS** | On your notepad, write the names of international companies that have had an economic or cultural impact in your country.

have had an economic impact	have had a cultural impact

> I love things that come from other countries, like cool clothes, new music, and movies, but I feel sad that lots of our own traditions are changing. Whenever people visit from another country, I always take them out for some local culture. Unfortunately, though, it seems like it's harder and harder to find.

B **DISCUSSION** | What benefits or problems have the companies you identified in Talking Points brought to your country? Overall, do you think globalization is good or bad for your country? Do you think it's good or bad for the world as a whole? Explain. (Option: Use the Unit 10 Soft Skills Booster, p. 163.)

WRITING HANDBOOK p. 153
- **Skill:** Rebutting an opposing point of view
- **Task:** An essay about globalization

For more practice... Unit Review / Connect TV / Test-Taking Skills Booster

PROGRESS SELF-CHECK — NOW I CAN

- [ ] React to international news events.
- [ ] Talk about the influence of foreign imports.
- [ ] Discuss the ways my culture might cause culture shock.
- [ ] Understand the impact of globalization.

Soft Skills Workshop 5
A Panel Discussion

Outcome
You will prepare and present a panel discussion on a topic of your choice.

1 TEAMWORK — Choose a discussion topic and assign roles.

Form teams of four. With your teammates, discuss the topics and decide which would be most interesting to prepare. With your teacher, determine how much time you will have to conduct your team's panel discussion.

Assign roles. Choose one team member to be moderator. The other team members will be panelists. Choose a role for each panelist. Give each panelist a fictional name, an employer, and a job title, and invent other details as appropriate.

Research the topic for information, news, and any issues or controversies related to it. Share information to help frame your ideas and plan your points of view. Combine team members' notes.

Research notes
Important to include foods of many colors on the plate.

Tips for TEAMWORK

Support your colleagues' ideas.
 Makes total sense!   Good thinking!
 What a great idea!

Politely offer a different point of view.
 I see what you mean. But here's a question ___ .
 I get that. But I wonder what you think of this: ___ .
 Good point. But here's something to consider: ___ .
 True. But on the other hand, ___ .

DISCUSSION TOPICS

A Does healthy food have to be boring?
Moderator: a medical professional (doctor, nurse, physical therapist, etc.)
Panelist roles:
- a nutritionist
- a chef and restaurant owner
- a home cook with a large family

B How much discipline do children need?
Moderator: a parent of a teen in a multi-generational household
Panelist roles:
- a child psychologist
- a parent of a child with behavior problems
- a typical teenager

C What can we do about street crime?
Moderator: a small business owner in a large city
Panelist roles:
- a police officer
- a person recently released from prison
- a crime victim

D What is the future of English as an international language?
Moderator: a journalist from a business magazine
Panelist roles:
- a CEO of a company with offices around the world
- a student planning on a career in international business
- an English teacher in an adult language program

2 COLLABORATION — Work together to plan the panel discussion.

Using the team's notes from Activity 1, the moderator drafts five to ten questions to ask. At the same time, the panelists each think about and write notes about their general point of view of the topic. (For example: A chef might say that healthy food can be very exciting if it's spicy.)

Panelists and the moderator share their notes, giving each other feedback and suggestions.

As the moderator revises the questions, panelists brainstorm the answers they would give in the actual panel discussion, according to the point of view of the roles they will be playing.

Meet together again as a team to draft an introduction to the topic for the moderator to present at the beginning of the panel discussion, as well as brief (two or three sentences only) introductions to each panelist.

Tips for COLLABORATION

Offer suggestions.
 Have you thought about ___ ?
 What if we ___ ?
 Maybe we should give ___ a try.
 So what do you think of this? Let's ___ .

3 PRESENTATION Rehearse the panel discussion and then present a similar one to the class.

Rehearse: Using the notes and drafts from Activities 1 and 2, the moderator practices introducing the topic and then introduces the panelists in the order in which they are seated. Then he or she asks the questions that were planned, calling on one or more panelists to answer. Each panelist rehearses the answer he or she intends to give, based on the brainstorming in Activity 2. Discuss any last-minute changes you want to make.

Tips for PRESENTATION

Demonstrate respect for what others say.
[Ms. Bank] makes a good point.
That's definitely true.
I know what you meant when you said ___ .
I think [Mark]'s absolutely right.

Ask others to elaborate
Is there a particular reason you say ___ ?
Can you explain what you mean by ___ ?

Make name cards or tags that include each person's role.

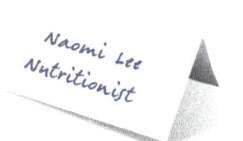

Naomi Lee — Nutritionist

Hello My name is Silvio Lagomarsino — Small business owner

Present: Conduct your panel discussion in front of the class. The moderator and all panelists should look at whoever is speaking, nodding and smiling to indicate they are paying attention.

The moderator can ask unrehearsed follow-up questions but should maintain control of the time any one person takes, in order to complete the discussion on time. Panelists who wish to respond spontaneously to something should raise their hand to be called on by the moderator and should not interrupt.

When time is up, the moderator thanks the panelists for their contributions and thanks the audience for its attention.

EVALUATE Improve your presentation skills.

Use the Key to answer the questions and evaluate each panel discussion. Discuss strengths and weakness and make suggestions about how each panel discussion might be improved.

KEY
Y = yes
U = usually
S = sometimes
N = no

1. The moderator introduced the topic in a way that made me want to hear something about it.
2. The panelists were clearly identified both by the moderator and with name cards or badges. They were seated in the order they were introduced.
3. The panelists acknowledged their introductions, waited to be called on, and didn't interrupt.
4. The panelists listened actively and attentively to the other panelists and the moderator.
5. The moderator retained control of the time limits and made sure all panelists had a chance to speak. When time was up, the moderator concluded the session appropriately.

REFERENCE CHARTS

IRREGULAR VERBS

base form	simple past	past participle	base form	simple past	past participle
be	was / were	been	mean	meant	meant
beat	beat	beaten	meet	met	met
become	became	become	mistake	mistook	mistaken
begin	began	begun	pay	paid	paid
bend	bent	bent	put	put	put
bet	bet	bet	quit	quit	quit
bite	bit	bitten	read /rid/	read /rɛd/	read /rɛd/
bleed	bled	bled	ride	rode	ridden
blow	blew	blown	ring	rang	rung
break	broke	broken	rise	rose	risen
breed	bred	bred	run	ran	run
bring	brought	brought	say	said	said
build	built	built	see	saw	seen
burn	burned / burnt	burned / burnt	sell	sold	sold
burst	burst	burst	send	sent	sent
buy	bought	bought	set	set	set
catch	caught	caught	shake	shook	shaken
choose	chose	chosen	shed	shed	shed
come	came	come	shine	shone	shone
cost	cost	cost	shoot	shot	shot
creep	crept	crept	show	showed	shown
cut	cut	cut	shrink	shrank	shrunk
deal	dealt	dealt	shut	shut	shut
dig	dug	dug	sing	sang	sung
do	did	done	sink	sank	sunk
draw	drew	drawn	sit	sat	sat
dream	dreamed / dreamt	dreamed / dreamt	sleep	slept	slept
drink	drank	drunk	slide	slid	slid
drive	drove	driven	smell	smelled / smelt	smelled / smelt
eat	ate	eaten	speak	spoke	spoken
fall	fell	fallen	speed	sped / speeded	sped / speeded
feed	fed	fed	spell	spelled / spelt	spelled / spelt
feel	felt	felt	spend	spent	spent
fight	fought	fought	spill	spilled / spilt	spilled / spilt
find	found	found	spin	spun	spun
fit	fit	fit	spit	spit / spat	spit / spat
fly	flew	flown	spoil	spoiled / spoilt	spoiled / spoilt
forbid	forbade	forbidden	spread	spread	spread
forget	forgot	forgotten	spring	sprang / sprung	sprang / sprung
forgive	forgave	forgiven	stand	stood	stood
freeze	froze	frozen	steal	stole	stolen
get	got	gotten	stick	stuck	stuck
give	gave	given	sting	stung	stung
go	went	gone	stink	stank / stunk	stunk
grow	grew	grown	strike	struck	struck / stricken
hang	hung	hung	string	strung	strung
have	had	had	swear	swore	sworn
hear	heard	heard	sweep	swept	swept
hide	hid	hidden	swim	swam	swum
hit	hit	hit	swing	swung	swung
hold	held	held	take	took	taken
hurt	hurt	hurt	teach	taught	taught
keep	kept	kept	tear	tore	torn
know	knew	known	tell	told	told
lay	laid	laid	think	thought	thought
lead	led	led	throw	threw	thrown
leap	leaped / leapt	leaped / leapt	understand	understood	understood
learn	learned / learnt	learned / learnt	upset	upset	upset
leave	left	left	wake	woke / waked	woken / waked
lend	lent	lent	wear	wore	worn
let	let	let	weave	wove	woven
lie	lay	lain	weep	wept	wept
light	lit	lit	win	won	won
lose	lost	lost	wind	wound	wound
make	made	made	write	wrote	written

VERBS FOLLOWED BY A GERUND

acknowledge	celebrate	discontinue	escape	imagine	postpone	recall	risk
admit	complete	discuss	explain	justify	practice	recommend	suggest
advise	consider	dislike	feel like	keep	prevent	report	support
appreciate	delay	don't mind	finish	mention	prohibit	resent	tolerate
avoid	deny	endure	forgive	mind	propose	resist	understand
can't help	detest	enjoy	give up	miss	quit		

EXPRESSIONS THAT CAN BE FOLLOWED BY A GERUND

be excited about	be committed to	make an excuse for	look forward to
be worried about	be opposed to	have a reason for	blame [someone or something] for
be responsible for	be used to	believe in	forgive [someone or something] for
be interested in	complain about	participate in	thank [someone or something] for
be accused of	dream about / of	succeed in	keep [someone or something] from
be capable of	talk about / of	take advantage of	prevent [someone or something] from
be tired of	think about / of	take care of	stop [someone or something] from
be accustomed to	apologize for	insist on	

VERBS FOLLOWED DIRECTLY BY AN INFINITIVE

afford	attempt	consent	fail	intend	neglect	pretend	struggle	want
agree	can't wait	decide	grow	learn	offer	promise	swear	wish
appear	care	demand	hesitate	manage	pay	refuse	threaten	would like
arrange	choose	deserve	hope	mean	plan	request	volunteer	yearn
ask	claim	expect	hurry	need	prepare	seem	wait	

VERBS FOLLOWED BY AN OBJECT BEFORE AN INFINITIVE*

advise	cause	enable	force	need*	persuade	require	want*
allow	challenge	encourage	hire	order	promise*	teach	wish*
ask*	choose*	expect*	instruct	pay*	remind	tell	would like*
beg	convince	forbid	invite	permit	request*	urge	

*In the active voice, these verbs can be followed by the infinitive without an object (example: *want to speak* or *want someone to speak*).

VERBS THAT CAN BE FOLLOWED BY A GERUND OR AN INFINITIVE

with a change in meaning

forget	remember
regret	stop

without a change in meaning

begin	continue	like	prefer	try
can't stand	hate	love	start	

ADJECTIVES FOLLOWED BY AN INFINITIVE*

afraid	ashamed	depressed	eager	fortunate	lucky	relieved	surprised
alarmed	certain	determined	easy	glad	pleased	reluctant	touched
amazed	content	disappointed	embarrassed	happy	prepared	sad	upset
angry	curious	distressed	encouraged	hesitant	proud	shocked	willing
anxious	delighted	disturbed	excited	likely	ready	sorry	

*Example: *I'm willing **to accept** that.*

PARTICIPIAL ADJECTIVES

alarming – alarmed	embarrassing – embarrassed	paralyzing – paralyzed
amazing – amazed	enlightening – enlightened	pleasing – pleased
amusing – amused	entertaining – entertained	relaxing – relaxed
annoying – annoyed	exciting – excited	satisfying – satisfied
astonishing – astonished	exhausting – exhausted	shocking – shocked
boring – bored	fascinating – fascinated	soothing – soothed
confusing – confused	frightening – frightened	startling – startled
depressing – depressed	horrifying – horrified	stimulating – stimulated
disappointing – disappointed	inspiring – inspired	surprising – surprised
disgusting – disgusted	interesting – interested	terrifying – terrified
distressing – distressed	irritating – irritated	tiring – tired
disturbing – disturbed	moving – moved	touching – touched

STATIVE VERBS

amaze	belong	dislike	feel*	include*	matter	please	resemble	surprise
appear*	care	doubt	forget	know	mean	possess	see*	taste*
appreciate	consist of	envy	hate	like	mind	prefer	seem	think*
astonish	contain	equal	have*	look like	need	realize	smell*	understand
be*	cost	exist	hear	look*	owe	recognize	sound	want*
believe	desire	fear	imagine	love	own	remember*	suppose	weigh*

*These verbs also have action meanings. Example: *I see a tree.* (non-action) *I'm seeing her tomorrow.* (action)

TRANSITIVE PHRASAL VERBS

Some transitive phrasal verbs have more than one meaning. Not all are included here.

Abbreviations
s.o. = someone
sth. = something
e.g. = for example
inf. = informal

SEPARABLE

blow sth. out	stop a flame by blowing on it
blow sth. up	1 make sth. explode 2 fill sth. with air, e.g., a balloon 3 make sth. larger, e.g., a photo
bring sth. about	make sth. happen
bring sth. back	1 return sth. to a store 2 revive or renew sth., e.g., a custom or tradition
bring sth. out	1 introduce a new product 2 make a quality more noticeable
bring s.o. up	raise a child
bring sth. up	start to talk about an issue
burn sth. down	burn a structure completely
call s.o. back	return a phone call
call sth. off	cancel sth.
call s.o. up	call s.o. on the phone
carry sth. out	conduct a plan
check s.o./sth. out	look at s.o. or sth. more closely
cheer s.o. up	make s.o. feel happier
clean s.o./sth. up	clean s.o. or sth. completely
clear sth. up	clarify sth.
close sth. down	force a business or institution to close
cover sth. up	1 cover sth. completely 2 change facts to avoid responsibility
cross sth. out	draw a line through sth.
cut sth. down	make sth. fall by cutting, e.g., a tree
cut sth. off	1 remove sth. by cutting 2 stop the supply of sth.
cut s.o. off	interrupt s.o who is speaking
dream sth. up	invent or think of a new idea
drink sth. up	drink a beverage completely
drop s.o./sth. off	leave s.o. or sth. somewhere
empty sth. out	empty sth. completely
figure s.o./sth. out	understand s.o. or sth. after some thought
fill s.o. in	tell s.o. about recent events
fill sth. out	complete a form
fill sth. up	fill a container completely
find sth. out	learn new information
follow sth. through	do everything to complete a task
get sth. across	help s.o. understand an idea
give sth. away	give sth. you do not need or want
give sth. back	return sth. to its owner
give sth. out	distribute sth.
give sth. up	quit doing sth.
hand sth. in	submit work, e.g., to a boss or a teacher
hand sth. out	distribute sth.
hang sth. up	put sth. on a hanger or hook, e.g., clothes
help s.o. out	assist s.o.
keep s.o./sth. away	cause s.o. or sth. to stay at a distance
lay s.o. off	fire s.o. because of economic conditions
leave sth. on	1 not turn sth. off, e.g., an appliance 2 not remove sth. such as clothing or jewelry
leave sth. out	omit sth.
let s.o. down	disappoint s.o.
let s.o./sth. in	allow s.o. or sth. to enter
let s.o. off	allow s.o. to leave a bus, car, taxi, etc.
let s.o./sth. out	allow s.o. or sth. to leave
light sth. up	illuminate sth.
look s.o./sth. over	examine s.o. or sth.
look s.o./sth. up	1 try to find s.o. 2 try to find sth. in a book, the Internet, etc.
make sth. up	create a fictional story
pass sth. out	distribute sth.
pass sth. up	decide not to take an opportunity
pay s.o. off	bribe s.o.
pay sth. off	pay back money one owes
pick s.o./sth. out	identify or choose s.o. or sth.
pick s.o. up	stop a vehicle so s.o. can get in
pick s.o./sth. up	lift s.o. or sth.
pick sth. up	1 get or buy sth. from somewhere 2 learn sth. new 3 get an infectious disease
point s.o./sth. out	show s.o or sth. to another person
put sth. away	put sth. in its appropriate place
put sth. back	return sth. to its original place
put s.o./sth. down	1 stop holding or lifting s.o. or sth. 2 insult s.o.
put sth. off	delay or postpone sth.
put sth. on	get dressed or place sth. on one's body
put sth. together	1 put sth. on a wall 2 build sth.
put sth. up	build or erect sth.
set sth. off	cause sth. to explode
set sth. up	1 establish a new business, organization, etc. 2 prepare equipment for use
show s.o./sth. off	display the best qualities of s.o. or sth.
shut sth. off	stop a machine or supply
straighten sth. up	make sth. neat
switch sth. on	start a machine, turn on a light, etc.
take sth. away	remove sth.
take sth. back	1 return sth. to a store 2 accept sth. returned by another person
take sth. down	remove sth. that is hanging
take sth. in	1 notice and remember sth. 2 make a clothing item smaller
take sth. off	remove clothing, jewelry, etc.
take s.o. on	hire s.o.
take sth. on	agree to do a task
take s.o. out	invite s.o. somewhere and pay for his/her meal, show, etc.
take sth. up	start doing an activity habitually
talk sth. over	discuss sth.
tear sth. down	destroy sth.
tear sth. up	tear sth. into small pieces
think sth. over	consider sth.

114 REFERENCE CHARTS

think sth. up	invent or think of a new idea	turn sth. off	stop a machine, light, etc.
throw sth. away	put sth. in the garbage	turn s.o. off	cause s.o. to lose interest (inf.)
throw sth. out	put sth. in the garbage	turn sth. on	start a machine, light, etc.
touch sth. up	improve sth. with very small changes	turn sth. out	make or manufacture sth.
try sth. on	try clothing to see if it fits	turn sth. over	turn sth. so the bottom is at the top
try sth. out	use sth. to see if one likes it or if it works	turn sth. up	raise the volume, heat, etc.
turn sth. around	1 turn so the front is at the back 2 cause things to get better	use sth. up	use sth. completely
		wake s.o. up	cause s.o. to stop sleeping
turn s.o./sth. down	reject s.o. or sth.	wipe sth. out	remove or destroy sth.
turn sth. down	lower the volume, heat, etc.	work sth. out	1 resolve a problem 2 calculate a math problem
turn sth. in	submit a paper, application, etc.	write sth. down	write sth. to have a record of it

ALWAYS SEPARATED

ask s.o. over	invite s.o. to one's home	see sth. through	complete a task
bring s.o./sth. down	remove a ruler or government from power	start sth. over	begin sth. again
do sth. over	do sth. again	talk s.o. into sth.	persuade s.o. to do sth.
keep sth. on	not remove sth. such as clothing or jewelry		

INSEPARABLE

cater to s.o.	provide what s.o. wants or needs	go over sth.	examine sth. carefully
carry on sth.	continue sth. another person has started	go without sth.	live without sth. one needs or wants
come across s.o./sth.	find s.o. or sth. unexpectedly	run into s.o.	meet s.o. unexpectedly
count on s.o./sth.	depend on s.o. or sth.	run into sth.	accidentally hit or crash into sth.
do without s.o./sth.	live without s.o. or sth. one needs or wants	stick with s.o.	stay close to s.o.
go after s.o./sth.	pursue s.o. or sth.	stick with sth.	continue doing sth. as before

INTRANSITIVE PHRASAL VERBS

Some intransitive phrasal verbs have more than one meaning. Not all are included here.

blow up	1 explode 2 suddenly become very angry	go off	explode; make a sudden noise
break down	stop functioning	go on	continue to talk about or describe sth.
break out	start suddenly, e.g., a war, disease, or fire	go out	1 leave a building 2 leave one's home to meet people, enjoy entertainment, etc.
burn down	burn completely		
call back	return a phone call	go up	be built
carry on	1 continue doing sth. 2 behave in a silly or emotional way	grow up	become an adult
		help out	do sth. helpful
catch on	become popular	hang up	end a phone call
check in	report one's arrival at an airport or hotel	hold on	wait during a phone call
check out	pay one's bill and leave a hotel	keep away	stay at a distance
cheer up	become happier	keep on	continue
clear up	become better, e.g., a rash or the weather	keep up	go or think as fast as another person
close down	stop operating, e.g., a factory or a school	lie down	rest on a bed
come along	accompany s.o.	light up	1 begin to shine brightly 2 look pleased or happy
come back	return	make up	end an argument and reestablish a friendly relationship
come in	enter	pass out	become unconscious
come off	become unattached	pay off	be worthwhile
come out	1 appear, e.g., the sun 2 be removed, e.g., a stain	pick up	improve, e.g., the economy
dress up	wear more formal clothes or a costume	play around	have fun or not be serious
drop in	visit unexpectedly	run out	no longer in supply
drop out	quit a class, school, or program	show up	appear
eat out	eat in a restaurant	sign up	register
empty out	empty completely	sit down	sit
fall off	become unattached	slip up	make a mistake
fill out	become bigger	stand up	rise to one's feet
fill up	become completely full	start over	begin again
find out	learn new information	stay up	not go to bed
follow through	continue working on sth. until it is completed	straighten up	make neat
fool around	have fun or not be serious	take off	depart by plane
get ahead	make progress or succeed	turn in	go to bed (inf.)
get along	to not argue	turn out	have a particular result
get back	return from a place	turn up	appear
get together	meet somewhere with a friend or acquaintance	wake up	stop sleeping
get up	get out of bed	watch out	be careful
give up	quit	work out	1 exercise 2 be resolved; end successfully
go along	1 accompany s.o. 2 agree		
go back	return		

THREE-WORD PHRASAL VERBS

Some three-word phrasal verbs have more than one meaning. Not all are included here.

catch up on sth.	1 do sth. one didn't have time to do earlier
	2 get the most recent information
catch up with s.o.	exchange information about recent activities
check up on s.o.	make sure s.o. is OK
come away with sth.	learn sth. useful from s.o. or sth.
come down to sth.	be the most important point or idea
come down with sth.	get an illness
come up against s.o./sth.	be faced with a difficult person or situation
come up with sth.	think of an idea, plan, or solution
face up to sth.	accept an unpleasant truth
fall back on sth.	use an old idea because new ideas have failed
follow through on sth.	continue doing sth. until it is completed
get around to sth.	finally do sth.
get away with sth.	avoid the consequences of a wrong act
get back at s.o.	harm s.o. because he / she harmed you
give up on s.o.	stop hoping that s.o. will change
give up on sth.	stop trying to make sth. happen
go along with sth.	agree to do sth.
go through with sth.	do sth. difficult or painful
grow out of sth.	stop doing sth. as one becomes an adult
keep up with s.o.	stay in regular contact
look down on s.o.	think one is better than another person
look out for s.o.	protect s.o.
look up to s.o.	admire or respect s.o.
make up for sth.	do sth. to apologize
put up with s.o./sth.	accept s.o. or sth. without complaining
run out of sth.	no longer have enough of sth.
stand up for sth.	support an idea or a principle
stand up to s.o.	refuse to let s.o. treat anyone badly
team up with s.o.	do a task together
think back on s.o./sth.	think about and remember s.o. or sth.
walk out on s.o.	end a relationship with a wife, boyfriend, etc.
watch out for s.o./sth.	protect s.o. or sth.

VERB FORMS: OVERVIEW

SUMMARY OF VERB FORMS

	Present time	Past time	Future time
Simple	Simple present walk / walks	Simple past walked	Simple future will walk
Continuous	Present continuous am walking / is walking / are walking	Past continuous was walking / were walking	Future continuous will be walking
Perfect	Present perfect have walked / has walked	Past perfect had walked	Future perfect will have walked
Perfect continuous	Present perfect continuous have been walking / has been walking	Past perfect continuous had been walking	Future perfect continuous will have been walking

SIMPLE VERB FORMS: USAGE

	Present time	Past time	Future time
Simple verb forms describe habitual actions or events that occur at a definite time.	Simple present[1] **Habitual action** The department **meets** once a month to review the status of projects. **Facts and generalizations** The Earth **rotates** around the sun every 365 days.	Simple past **Completed action that occurred at a definite time in the past** Last year researchers **discovered** a new cancer treatment. **Habitual action in the past**[2] When I was young we **visited** my grandparents every week.	Simple future[3] **Action that will occur at a definite time in the future** Next year they **will offer** a course on global trade. **Habitual action in the future** Next month I**'ll go** to the gym three times a week.

[1] The simple present tense can also express a future action: *Her flight arrives this evening at eight.*

[2] <u>Used to</u> and <u>would</u> also express habitual actions in the past: *When I was a child, we used to spend the summer in the mountains. In the mornings we would go hiking and in the afternoons we would swim in a nearby lake.*

[3] <u>Be going to</u> can also express a future action: *Next year they are going to offer a course on global trade.*

116 REFERENCE CHARTS

CONTINUOUS VERB FORMS: USAGE

	Present time	Past time	Future time
Continuous verb forms describe continuous actions or events that occur at a definite time.	**Present continuous*** **Action in progress now** The business managers **are discussing** next year's budget right now.	**Past continuous** **Action in progress at a definite time in the past** None of the computers **were working** when I came in this morning.	**Future continuous** **Action that will be in progress during a definite time in the future** We**'ll be listening** to the speech when you arrive.

*The present continuous can also express a future plan: They're getting married next month.

PERFECT VERB FORMS: USAGE

	Present time	Past time	Future time
Perfect verb forms describe actions or events in relation to other time frames.	**Present perfect*** **Completed action that occurred at an indefinite time before the present** She **has made** many contributions to the field. **Recently completed action** He **has** just **published** an article about his findings. **Uncompleted action (action that began in the past, continues into the present, and may continue into the future)** They **have studied** ancient cultures for many years.	**Past perfect** **Action that occurred at some point before a definite time in the past** By 2021, he **had started** a new business. **Action that occurred before another past action** They **had** already **finished** medical school when the war broke out.	**Future perfect** **Action that will be completed by some point at a definite time in the future** By this time next year, I **will have completed** my research.

*Many statements in the present perfect can also be stated correctly in the simple past tense, depending on the speaker's perspective: She made many contributions to the field.

PERFECT CONTINUOUS VERB FORMS: USAGE

	Present time	Past time	Future time
Perfect continuous verb forms describe continuous actions or events in relation to other time frames.	**Present perfect continuous** **Uncompleted continuous action (action that began in the past, continues into the present, and may continue into the future)** She **has been lecturing** about that topic since 2020. **Very recently completed action** The workers **have been protesting**. They're finished now.	**Past perfect continuous** **Continuous action that occurred before another past action or time** By 2020, researchers **had been seeking** a cure for this disease for more than 35 years.	**Future perfect continuous** **Continuous action that occurred before another action or time in the future** When the new director takes over, I **will have been working** at this company for ten years.

GRAMMAR EXPANDER (Optional)

The Grammar Expander is a source of additional instruction and practice. It offers learners a variety of information related to the unit's grammar, including more detailed explanations, descriptions of common errors; as well as new, related grammar topics. On occasion, students are given the chance to review previously taught grammar to support what they are learning in the unit. The Grammar Expander in *Connectivity* 4 and 5 also includes Grammar for Writing sections, which help students learn conventions of written English related to the unit's grammar. The optional *Connectivity* Workbook includes exercises aligned to the Grammar Expander. (Note: The Grammar Expander content is not tested on any *Connectivity* tests.)

UNIT 6

Real and unreal conditionals: summary and expansion

Type	Use	If clause (states the condition)	Result clause (states the result)	Examples
Factual conditional	To express a general or scientific fact	simple present Note: In this type of conditional, if can be replaced by when or whenever.	simple present	If it rains, the gardens close early. Water freezes if the temperature falls below zero degrees Celsius. Babies cry when they need to eat.
	To talk about what will happen in the future under certain conditions	simple present Note: Don't use a future form in the if clause.	will / be going to + base form of the verb Note: Use can, may, might, or should if the result is not certain.	If you plan your trip carefully, things will go smoothly. If we arrive late, they're going to start without us. If we hurry, we may be able to catch the train.
Present unreal conditional	To talk about present unreal or untrue conditions	simple past or were Note: Don't use would in the if clause.	would + base form of the verb Note: Use could or might if the result is not certain.	If I had the time, I would explain the problem to you. If he were here, he might make a lot of changes.
Past unreal conditional	To talk about past unreal or untrue conditions	past perfect Note: Don't use would have in the if clause.	would have + past participle Note: Use could have or might have if the result is not certain.	If they had known about the storm, they would have taken a different flight. If you had told us about the delay, we could have made other arrangements.
Mixed time frames	To talk about past unreal or untrue conditions in relation to the present	past perfect Note: Don't use would in the if clause.	would + base form of the verb Note: Use could or might if the result is not certain.	If I had prepared for the interview, I wouldn't be so nervous. If we had left earlier, we might be on time now.
	To talk about present unreal or untrue conditions in relation to the past	simple past or were Note: Don't use would have in the if clause.	would have + past participle Note: Use could have or might have if the result is not certain.	If she were honest, she would have told us the truth. If I spoke Russian, I might have understood the guide.

Extension: other uses

Use **should, happen to,** or **should happen to** in the *if* clause in factual conditionals when the condition is less likely.

If you { should / happen to / should happen to } see Peter, tell him to call me.

To express inferences in conditional sentences, different combinations of tenses can be used.
- If Julie **went** to the party last night, she definitely **saw** what happened.
- If you **don't know** the answer to this question, you **didn't do** your homework.
- If the results **didn't come out** yesterday, they**'ll** definitely **come out** today.
- If you still **haven't finished** packing by now, you**'re not going to catch** your flight.

A Circle the correct word or words to complete each sentence.
1. If Sam (does / will do) well this year, he'll apply to medical school.
2. Water (boils / is going to boil) when the temperature reaches 100 degrees Celsius.
3. If you (will / should) find my scarf, please hold it for me.
4. If you (happen / happen to) see a good camera at the market, please buy it for me.

(Continued on next page)

5 If it (wouldn't have been / hadn't been) for her savings, Anna wouldn't have been able to attend university.
6 If we (would have known / had known) that car insurance was so expensive, we wouldn't have bought a car.
7 If you didn't get a reply today, you (would definitely hear / will definitely hear) from us tomorrow.
8 If I (had / would have) a garden, I'd grow several types of flowers.
9 If I (would have practiced / had practiced) my speech a bit more, I might not be so worried now.
10 If I (should happen to / will) see John, I'll tell him you went home.

UNIT 7

Article usage: summary

Note where indefinite or definite articles are used or omitted.

	Indefinite article	Definite article	No article
General statement	Use with singular count nouns: *A cat* may symbolize good fortune.	Use with singular count nouns: *The cat* may symbolize good fortune. Use with non-count nouns: Freud called attention to *the importance* of dreams.	With plural count nouns: *Cats* may symbolize good fortune. With non-count nouns: *Misfortune* may strike at any time.
First mention	Use with singular count nouns: I found *a* lottery ticket.		With plural count nouns: I have (some) lottery *tickets*. With non-count nouns: I bought (some) *shampoo*.
Second mention		Use with singular count nouns: *The* lottery *ticket* was in my wallet. Use with plural count nouns: *The* lottery *tickets* were in my wallet. Use with non-count nouns: *The shampoo* is in the closet.	

A Rewrite the paragraph, correcting eleven errors and making any necessary changes.

The homes are expensive these days, but Peter got lucky and bought small house last week. A house has two bedrooms and one bathroom. It also has large kitchen and the living room. Peter will use a living room as his home office. Bedrooms are in bad condition, and Peter will need a help painting them. Then he wants to have the party so his friends can admire a house. Later Peter will buy a furniture—when he saves some money!

GRAMMAR EXPANDER 128

Definite article: additional uses

When a noun represents a unique thing	Use with singular count nouns: *The sun* rises in the east.		
With a comparative or superlative adjective to make a noun unique (or with right, wrong, first, only, or same)	Use with singular count nouns: Telling the truth is *the best course* of action. It's always *the right thing* to do. The robin is *the first sign* of spring.	Use with plural count nouns: People in different places often have *the same cultural traditions*.	Use with non-count nouns: That's *the only information* I was able to find on the Internet.
When context makes a noun specific	Use with singular count nouns: *The hospital* in this town has an excellent emergency room.	Use with plural count nouns: *The buildings* in this town are no higher than ten stories.	Use with non-count nouns: *The air* in this city is polluted.
When an adjective clause makes a noun specific	Use with singular count nouns: *The scam that he fell for* is very well known.	Use with plural count nouns: *The scams that people fall for* can end up costing a lot of money.	Use with non-count nouns: *The progress that she made* was due not to good luck but to hard work.
When an adjective represents a certain group of people	Use with a noun derived from an adjective, such as: the blind, the deaf, the dead, the living, the young, the old, the poor, the rich, the unemployed, the privileged, the underprivileged: *The unemployed* must often learn new job skills.		

B Complete the paragraphs with words from the box. Use a definite article when appropriate.

| tourists | gas | views | sport | world | wealthy | hot air | ballooning | first men |

On March 20, 1999, Bertrand Piccard of Switzerland and Brian Jones of Britain became ....1................ to travel around ....2................ in a balloon. The numerous balloonists who had been attempting this journey for decades beforehand ran into various problems with weather and equipment.

In the past several years though, ...3................ has become a popular adventure sport. Due to the high cost of ....4................, which is required to create ....5................ that lifts the balloon, ballooning tends to be a sport reserved for ....6................. However, ...7................ can get a taste of ....8................ by paying for a balloonist to take them on a breathtaking ride to enjoy ....9................ that they see from the sky during their travels.

Non-count nouns with both a countable and an uncountable sense

With some non-count nouns, the change in meaning is subtle: The countable meaning refers to something specific and the uncountable meaning refers to something general.

countable meaning	uncountable meaning
a fear = the anticipation of a specific danger; a phobia He had *two fears*: heights and open spaces.	**fear** = a general anticipation of danger Irrational *fear* can lead to anxiety.
a victory = a specific event in which mastery or success is achieved The battle of Waterloo was *a great victory* for the English.	**victory** = the phenomenon of winning She led her party to *victory*.
a time = a specific moment in the past or future; a specific occasion There was *a time* when food was much cheaper. How *many times* did you read it?	**time** = the general concept; clock time *Time* passes so quickly! What *time* did you arrange to meet?
a belief = something accepted on faith, not knowledge *A* common *belief* is that cold weather can cause a cold.	**belief** = general or religious faith Is *belief* more common in older or younger people?

129 GRAMMAR EXPANDER

C Write a before a noun where necessary. Write X if a noun should not have an article.
1. a Will people ever learn to control their spending? Only .... time can tell.
   b There has never been .... time when people didn't try to understand their dreams.
2. a If you have .... fear of flying, you shouldn't take a job that requires overseas travel.
   b Psychologists agree that .... fear is a universal emotion.
3. a Ignorance and fear may sometimes lead to .... conflict.
   b For the last few years, there has been .... serious conflict between local landowners and business owners.
4. a The coach's tactics helped the team win .... major victory in last night's game.
   b Everyone cannot always experience the joy of .... victory; someone has to lose.

GRAMMAR FOR WRITING: passive reporting verbs with an infinitive phrase

A passive reporting verb can be followed by an infinitive phrase.
Many insects **are believed to be** good for the garden.

The infinitive phrase can be simple, continuous, perfect, or perfect continuous.
This book is **said to be** excellent.
The robber **was reported to be running** away from the scene of the crime.
The car is believed **never to have been** in an accident before.
She was thought **to have been preparing** dinner when she got sick.

D Change each of the following sentences from the active voice to the passive voice.
1. Many people believe that flying isn't as safe as driving.
   ....
2. They reported that the driver was talking on his phone when he crashed into the back of that van.
   ....
3. Many people say the tour was overpriced, but others think the price was very fair.
   ....
4. People said the article was a lie, but it turned out to be perfectly true.
   ....

UNIT 8

GRAMMAR FOR WRITING: emphatic stress

In informal writing, you can underline the verb **be**, a modal, or other auxiliary verb to indicate emphatic stress. The addition of <u>do</u> for emphatic stress does not require underlining. In more formal writing, with the exception of adding the auxiliary <u>do</u>, underlining for emphatic stress is avoided.
She <u>is</u> good at math, isn't she?
Even though it was getting late, I <u>would</u> have liked to stay longer.
I suddenly realized that I <u>had</u> been there before.
BUT She didn't answer her phone, but she did text me.

> Be careful! In the modal-like expression <u>had better</u>, underline <u>better</u>, not <u>had</u>.
> He'd <u>better</u> pay attention in class!

If you want to indicate emphatic stress, don't contract the verb be, a modal, or an auxiliary verb.
I <u>will</u> tell her. NOT I'll tell her.

A Use the prompts to write B's response with emphatic stress. Add the auxiliary <u>do</u> if possible, and underline the stressed verb **be**, modal, or other auxiliary verb.
1. **A:** Do you worry much about global warming?
   B: .... (I think about it) from time to time.
2. **A:** Would you say you have a way with words?
   B: .... (I express myself) clearly.
3. **A:** I'm thinking of applying to medical school, but I haven't made up my mind yet.
   B: Well, ... (you should apply).
4. **A:** Do you have to pass any kind of tests to get a job at the Mason Corporation?
   B: .... (you have to take) an EQ test.

5 A: Shouldn't Jamie hurry if she wants to catch the 3:00 bus?
   B: .... (She'd better hurry). That's the last bus.

6 A: Would you like me to introduce you to my brother?
   B: .... (I'd like to meet) him.

7 A: Would you like to grab dinner somewhere together?
   B: .... (I've already had) dinner.

Infinitives and gerunds in place of the subjunctive

Certain statements in the subjunctive can be rephrased less formally by changing that to for and using an infinitive.
   It's essential **for** John **to find** the time each day to relax. (= It's essential that John **find** the time each day to relax.)

An infinitive can also be used without a for phrase. It usually refers to "people in general."
   It's essential **to find** the time each day to relax.

Certain statements in the subjunctive can be rephrased using a gerund if they refer to "people in general."
   Dr. Sharpe recommends **spending** a few moments relaxing. (= Dr. Sharpe recommends that people **spend** a few moments relaxing.)

B Rewrite each sentence less formally, using infinitives and gerunds. Make any necessary changes.
1. It's crucial that you practice feng shui.
2. The article suggests that you carry lucky charms.
3. The manager recommended that they finish the project fast.
4. It's important that we get enough sleep every night.
5. The directions advise that you add salt.
6. It's necessary that she arrive at the theater by 4:00 P.M.

UNIT 9

GRAMMAR FOR WRITING: when to use the passive voice

Passive sentences focus attention on the result of an action rather than on the performer (agent) of the action. Writers prefer the passive voice in the following situations:

1 To emphasize the result of an action, or if the agent is unimportant or unknown. This use is common in academic writing, scientific articles, and news reports.
   Some sophisticated treatments **have been developed**. (emphasizes the treatments, not the people who developed them)
   Hundreds of people **were made** homeless by yesterday's floods. (emphasizes the result, not the floods themselves)

2 To describe a process. This use is found in technical and scientific writing.
   There are four basic steps in the commercial production of orange juice. First the oranges **are unloaded** from trucks and **placed** on a conveyor belt. Then they **are washed** and **sorted**. Next they **are put** into machines that remove the juice and put it into cartons.

3 To use an impersonal or indirect tone, which suggests formality, impartiality, or objectivity. This use is favored in official documents, formal announcements, and signs, or to avoid placing blame.
   Walking on the grass **is prohibited**.
   An error **has been made** in your account. It **will be corrected** on next month's statement. (The writer avoids mentioning who made the mistake and emphasizes the fact that it will be corrected, rather than who will do the correcting.)

4 To keep the reader's attention focused on a previously mentioned noun, because it is the central topic of the paragraph.
   They caught the thief later that evening. He **was placed** in jail and **was allowed** to call a lawyer. (The topic is the thief. By using the passive voice in the second sentence, the writer shifts the reader's attention to what happened to the thief.)

5 To avoid using a "general subject." General subjects include the impersonal you, we, and they; people; one; someone / somebody; anyone / anybody. This use is common in formal documents, in official signs, and in newspaper editorials and other texts that express an opinion.
   People must show their IDs before boarding.   PREFERRED: IDs **must be shown** before boarding.
   Someone should inform consumers of their rights.   PREFERRED: Consumers **should be informed** of their rights.

6 To avoid awkward sentence constructions. This is a common solution when the agent has a long or complex modifier.
   The Tigers, whose new strategy of offense and defense seemed to be working, defeated the Lions.
   PREFERRED: The Lions **were defeated** by the Tigers, whose new strategy of offense and defense seemed to be working.

A Write each sentence in the passive voice. Don't include a <u>by</u> phrase unless you think it is required.

1 Construction workers built the museum in less than six months.
   ....
2 People must present their passports at the border.
   ....
3 First, engineers perfect the design for the new product. Then, workers build a prototype. Next, engineers test the prototype. After engineers approve the design, the factory begins production.
   ....
4 We have credited the sum of eighty-five dollars to your VISTA account.
   ....
5 The reporter, whose investigation uncovered many shocking details, exposed the mayor's pattern of corrupt behavior.
   ....

UNIT 10

Phrasal verbs: expansion

The passive form of phrasal verbs
Transitive phrasal verbs are always inseparable in the passive voice, even when they are separable or always separated in the active voice.
   I couldn't **turn on** the TV (OR **turn** the TV **on**). → The TV couldn't be **turned on**.
   They **turned** the empty lot **into** a beautiful garden. → The empty lot was **turned into** a beautiful garden.

> **Remember**
> Intransitive phrasal verbs are always inseparable. They can't be used in the passive voice since they don't have direct objects.

Transitive and intransitive meanings of phrasal verbs
Some phrasal verbs have both a transitive and an intransitive meaning.
   He went to bed without **taking off** his clothes. (transitive meaning: remove)
   What time does your plane **take off**? (intransitive meaning: leave)
   She **broke in** the new employees by showing them the procedures. (transitive meaning: train someone)
   Thieves **broke in** and stole her jewelry. (intransitive meaning: enter by force)
For a complete list of transitive and intransitive phrasal verbs, see the Reference Charts, pages 114–115.

Three-word phrasal verbs
A three-word phrasal verb consists of a verb, a particle, and a preposition that together have a specific meaning. The verb, the particle, and the preposition in three-word phrasal verbs are inseparable.
   As a result of his controversial ideas, the senator **came up against** members of his own party, who opposed him vigorously.
   Does society have an obligation to **look out for** people who are disadvantaged?
   Temper tantrums are not uncommon in young children. As children mature, they **grow out of** this behavior.
   I'm going to close my door and not take any calls today; I've just got to **catch up on** my work.
For a complete list of three-word phrasal verbs, see the Reference Charts, page 116.

A Rewrite each sentence in the passive voice. Do not include a <u>by</u> phrase.

1 We have to call the meeting off.
....

2 She talked the client into a better deal.
....

3 They covered the mistake up.
....

4 He dropped the children off in front of the school.
....

5 One of the applicants filled the form out incorrectly.
....

6 I paid the balance off last month.
....

7 Someone threw the document away.
....

8 The speaker handed pamphlets out at the end of the presentation.
....

B Underline the phrasal verb in each sentence. Then decide if it has a transitive or an intransitive meaning.

	transitive	intransitive	
1	☐	☐	The photographer blew up the photo 200 percent so we could use it for the poster.
2	☐	☐	The plane blew up shortly before it was supposed to land.
3	☐	☐	The workers won't give up until they're paid fair wages.
4	☐	☐	She has tried to give up smoking several times, without success.
5	☐	☐	Phil has to wake up at 5:00 A.M. every day to get to work on time.
6	☐	☐	The children played quietly in order not to wake up their parents.
7	☐	☐	He works out three or four times a week in order to stay healthy.
8	☐	☐	World leaders are meeting to work out a plan to eradicate poverty.

PRONUNCIATION TABLE

These are the pronunciation symbols used in *Connectivity 5*.

Vowels

Symbol	Key Word
i	beat, feed
ɪ	bit, did
eɪ	date, paid
ɛ	bet, bed
æ	bat, bad
ɑ	box, odd, father
ɔ	bought, dog
oʊ	boat, road
ʊ	book, good
u	boot, food, student
ʌ	but, mud, mother
ə	banana, among
ɚ	shirt, murder
aɪ	bite, cry, buy, eye
aʊ	about, how
ɔɪ	voice, boy
ɪr	beer
ɛr	bare
ɑr	bar
ɔr	door
ʊr	tour

Consonants

Symbol	Key Word
p	pack, happy
b	back, rubber
t	tie
d	die
k	came, key, quick
g	game, guest
tʃ	church, nature, watch
dʒ	judge, general, major
f	fan, photograph
v	van
θ	thing, breath
ð	then, breathe
s	sip, city, psychology
z	zip, please, goes
ʃ	ship, machine, station, special, discussion
ʒ	measure, vision
h	hot, who
m	men, some
n	sun, know, pneumonia
ŋ	sung, ringing
w	wet, white
l	light, long
r	right, wrong
y	yes, use, music
t̬	butter, bottle
tʼ	button

PRONUNCIATION LESSONS (Optional)

These Pronunciation Lessons are optional. The goal is to improve students' awareness of the pronunciation rules of Standard American English and to improve comprehensibility and fluency in speaking. Each lesson presents a new pronunciation feature, accompanied by audio for repetition and additional speaking or listening exercises for practice.

UNIT 6

Regular past participle endings

There are three pronunciations of the past participle ending -**ed**, depending on the final sound of the base form of the verb.

With voiced sounds (except /d/)
When the base form ends with a voiced sound, pronounce the -**ed** ending as /d/.
moved   canceled   described   stayed   agreed

With voiceless sounds (except /t/)
When the base form ends with a voiceless sound, pronounce the -**ed** ending as /t/.
helped   asked   crushed   watched

HOWEVER: When the base form ends with the sound /t/ or /d/, pronounce the -**ed** ending as a new syllable: /ɪd/ or /əd/. In American English, the final sound before the -**ed** ending is always /t̬/, no matter whether the base form ended in the sound /t/ or /d/. Link /t̬/ with the -**ed** ending.

| wai ted | → | /weɪt̬ɪd/ | nee ded | → | /nit̬ɪd/ |
| re por ted | → | /rɪpɔrt̬ɪd/ | in clud ed | → | /ɪnklut̬ɪd/ |

Voiced sounds		Voiceless sounds
/b/	/i/	/p/
/g/	/ɪ/	/k/
/ð/	/eɪ/	/θ/
/v/	/ɛ/	/f/
/z/	/æ/	/s/
/ʒ/	/ɑ/	/ʃ/
/dʒ/	/ɔ/	/tʃ/
/m/	/oʊ/	/t/
/n/	/ʊ/	
/ŋ/	/u/	
/r/	/ʌ/	
/l/	/d/	

Reduction in perfect modals

The auxiliary **have** in perfect modals is generally reduced. The /h/ is dropped and /æ/ is reduced to /ə/.

/wʊt̬əv/
If I'd looked at the expiration date, I **would have** renewed my passport.

/maɪt̬əv/
If I weren't Japanese, I **might have** needed a visa to enter the country.

/wʊt̬ənəv/
If we'd left on time, we **wouldn't have** missed our flight.

Perfect modals
would have
could have
should have   + [past participle]
might have
may have

(Continued on page 140)

A Listen and practice.

1 moved
2 canceled
3 described
4 stayed
5 agreed
6 helped
7 asked
8 crushed
9 watched
10 waited
11 reported
12 needed
13 included

B Listen and practice.

1 If I'd looked at the expiration date, I would have renewed my passport.
2 If I weren't Japanese, I might have needed a visa to enter the country.
3 If we'd left on time, we wouldn't have missed our flight.

C Circle the correct pronunciation of each -ed ending.

1 avoided	/ɪd/	/t/	/d/	9 promised	/ɪd/	/t/	/d/
2 looked	/ɪd/	/t/	/d/	10 covered	/ɪd/	/t/	/d/
3 summarized	/ɪd/	/t/	/d/	11 added	/ɪd/	/t/	/d/
4 arrived	/ɪd/	/t/	/d/	12 changed	/ɪd/	/t/	/d/
5 owed	/ɪd/	/t/	/d/	13 reported	/ɪd/	/t/	/d/
6 ruined	/ɪd/	/t/	/d/	14 discussed	/ɪd/	/t/	/d/
7 kicked	/ɪd/	/t/	/d/	15 investigated	/ɪd/	/t/	/d/
8 refunded	/ɪd/	/t/	/d/	16 enjoyed	/ɪd/	/t/	/d/

Now practice saying each word aloud and listen to compare.*

D Practice saying each sentence aloud, paying attention to reductions. Listen to compare.*

1 If I'd put my passport in my briefcase, it wouldn't have gotten lost.
2 If you'd checked the luggage limits, you might have avoided extra charges.
3 If my friend's luggage hadn't gotten stolen, he could have gone on the sightseeing tour.
4 I probably wouldn't have missed my flight if I had come on time.
5 If they'd taken a few simple precautions, their luggage might not have gotten stolen.

UNIT 7

Linking sounds

Link plural noun endings to the first sound in the word that follows.
Superstitions about animals are very common. /supərˈstɪʃənzəbaʊt/
Some say rats leaving a ship will cause it to sink. /ræt͡sˈslivɪŋ/

Link third-person singular endings to the first sound in the word that follows.
A belief in a superstition often results in fear. /rɪˈzʌltsɪn/

Remember: There are three different sounds for the endings of plural nouns and third-person singular verbs.

/z/	/s/	/ɪz/
diamonds	results	promises
superstitions	sharks	noises
bottles	types	matches
believes	beliefs	wishes
dreams	sleeps	judges

A Listen and practice.

1 Superstitions about animals are very common.
2 Some say rats leaving a ship will cause it to sink.
3 A belief in a superstition often results in fear.

B Practice reading each sentence aloud, paying attention to the linking sounds you have learned. Listen to compare.* (Note that your choices may differ from what you hear on the audio.)

1 A frog brings good luck to the house it enters.
2 Babies born with teeth become extremely selfish.
3 An itchy nose means you'll have a fight.
4 A lucky charm protects against the evil eye.
5 She keeps a large bowl of water near the front door.
6 Superstitions can be found in every culture.
7 A company claims to have invented a machine that allows people to talk with their pets.
8 Some fears are hard to overcome.
9 My sister believes in ghosts, avoids black cats, and carries a lucky charm in her pocket.

(End of lesson)

UNIT 8

Emphatic stress with auxiliary verbs

Use emphatic stress on an auxiliary verb to confirm or contradict.
- **A:** Do you think Jennifer Lawrence has a successful acting career?
- **B:** I think so. She **IS** getting a lot of lead roles these days.

- **A:** I wonder if I should take French lessons.
- **B:** Great idea! I think you **SHOULD** learn French.

- **A:** Have you eaten at the Blue Moon Café before?
- **B:** Actually, I think I **HAVE** eaten there before.

- **A:** Jan says you love coffee. Is that true?
- **B:** Not at all. I really **DON'T** like coffee.

Remember: The auxiliary <u>do</u> needs to be added for emphatic stress in affirmative statements in the simple present or past tense.
- **A:** Jan says you love coffee. Is that true?
- **B:** Yes, it is. I really **DO** like coffee.

A Listen and practice.
1. She **IS** getting a lot of lead roles these days.
2. I think you **SHOULD** learn French.
3. Actually, I think I **HAVE** eaten there before.
4. I really **DON'T** like coffee.
5. I really **DO** like coffee.

B Practice responding to each speaker, using emphatic stress on the auxiliary verb. Listen to compare.*

1. "I think Olivia's a great cook."
   RESPONSE: I agree. She does make great food.

2. "Your husband doesn't dance very well."
   RESPONSE: That's true. He really doesn't dance well.

3. "Can you eat seafood?"
   RESPONSE: Actually, I can't eat seafood. I'm allergic to it.

4. "Your cousins are hysterical!"
   RESPONSE: I agree. They really do tell a lot of funny jokes.

5. "Ana's report is late again."
   RESPONSE: Well, she does tend to procrastinate.

6. "Does Gary have a head for figures?"
   RESPONSE: No. But he is taking a math class on Tuesday evenings.

7. "I think it's time to tell everyone you're going to quit."
   RESPONSE: You're right. I should tell them sooner rather than later.

8. "Have you made up your mind yet?"
   RESPONSE: No. But I have been thinking about it.

(End of lesson)

UNIT 9

Reading aloud

Because it's more difficult to understand language when it's read rather than spoken in conversation, read with a regular rhythm and use fewer sound reductions. If there's a title, state it separately with falling intonation. Pause at all punctuation. Separate sentences into "thought groups," pausing after each one. Pause slightly longer between sentences.

Envisioning the Future
In the 1960s, / only large institutions, / such as banks, / corporations, / and the military, / had computers. // They were expensive, / slow, / and very large— / requiring a special air-conditioned room— / and access to them was limited / to only a few people. // In the 1970s, / computer prices came down / and then small businesses began to use them. // Nevertheless, / in 1977, / the CEO and founder of Digital Equipment, / Kenneth Olsen, / predicted that computers would never be used in the home.

A Listen to the selection. Then practice reading it aloud.

Envisioning the Future
In the 1960s, only large institutions, such as banks, corporations, and the military, had computers. They were expensive, slow, and very large—requiring a special air-conditioned room—and access to them was limited to only a few people. In the 1970s, computer prices came down and then small businesses began to use them. Nevertheless, in 1977, the CEO and founder of Digital Equipment, Kenneth Olsen, predicted that computers would never be used in the home.

B Practice reading each selection aloud. Then listen to compare.* (Note that thought groups can vary, so your choices may differ from what you hear on the audio.)

1 **Birth of the Personal Computer**
In the early 80s, Steve Jobs and Bill Gates introduced the personal computer—the Macintosh and the IBM PC, respectively—which made computing at home possible. In 1983, Jobs gave a speech about the future, in which he predicted that, for most people, a great deal of time would be spent interacting with personal computers. He also predicted that, within ten years, computers in the office and at home would be connected so people would be able to use them to communicate.

2 **Predicting Social Media**
In 1999, Gates predicted that small devices would be carried around by everyone so that they could get instant information and stay in touch with others. He also claimed that, by the early twenty-first century, Internet communities would have been formed, based on one's interests or to connect with friends and family.

(End of lesson)

UNIT 10

Intonation of tag questions

When a tag question follows a statement to which a speaker anticipates agreement, both the statement and the tag question are said with falling intonation. The main stress in the tag question falls on the auxiliary verb and not on the pronoun. Note that there is generally no pause at the comma.

It's really shocking, isn't it?

They'll come up with a solution, won't they?

It's not really surprising, is it?

She didn't speak out against that project, did she?

It really makes you feel angry, doesn't it?

When the tag question represents a genuine question to which the speaker expects an answer, the statement is said with falling intonation, but the tag question is said with rising intonation.

It's really shocking, isn't it?

They'll come up with a solution, won't they?

It's not really surprising, is it?

She didn't speak out against that project, did she?

It really makes you feel angry, doesn't it?

A Listen and practice. (Each sentence is said two ways.)
1. It's really shocking, isn't it?
2. It's not really surprising, is it?
3. It really makes you feel angry, doesn't it?
4. They'll come up with a solution, won't they?
5. She didn't speak out against that project, did she?

B Listen to the following tag questions. Check to indicate if each one anticipates agreement or expects an answer.

		Anticipates agreement	Expects an answer
1	That's really appalling, isn't it?	☐	☐
2	He's worried about his children, isn't he?	☐	☐
3	It really makes you feel good, doesn't it?	☐	☐
4	It wasn't really true, was it?	☐	☐
5	They're going to do something about that problem, aren't they?	☐	☐
6	It's not really important, is it?	☐	☐
7	You heard that on TV, didn't you?	☐	☐
8	You'll support us, won't you?	☐	☐

Now practice saying each tag question aloud and listen to compare.*

C Practice saying each tag question two ways, first to express anticipated agreement and then to express a genuine question. Listen to compare.*
1. It really makes you stop and think, doesn't it?
2. They're concerned about global warming, aren't they?
3. The president's economic policy is effective, isn't it?
4. The benefits of globalization are very clear, aren't they?
5. The benefits of globalization aren't very clear, are they?
6. There's no turning back, is there?

(End of Pronunciation Lessons)

WRITING HANDBOOK (Optional)

For each unit in the *Connectivity* Student's Book, this Writing Handbook provides a succinct lesson focused on one key principle of good writing in English. In addition to the presentation of each principle, the Handbook includes clear examples and models. To ensure students put each principle into practice, the Handbook provides a Unit Writing Task and a Self-Check for students to evaluate their progress.

UNIT 6 — A comparison and contrast essay

A   WRITING SKILL | Study the rules.

Choose one of these formats for organizing your supporting paragraphs when you want to compare and contrast places, objects, people, ideas, etc., in an essay. (Be sure to include expressions of comparison and contrast.)

I. Introductory paragraph
Begin with an explanation of what you are going to compare and contrast.

WRITING MODEL

Public and private transportation both have upsides and downsides, so it is fortunate that we have options. To help us choose, we can take into account convenience, cost, destination, and the needs and preferences of the people with whom we are traveling. Other factors we might consider are the length of the trip and the environmental impact of the means of transportation we choose.

II. Supporting paragraphs
Choose Format A or B to present and support your ideas.

Format A: Discuss the similarities in one paragraph and the differences in another.

Format B: In each paragraph, focus on one specific aspect of the topic and discuss the similarities and differences within the paragraph

(Format A)

Both public and private means of transportation provide clear advantages. *They are similar in certain ways.* Both are convenient and cut travel time, allowing people to travel farther than traveling on foot. In addition, they are capable of providing comforts such as air-conditioning and heating.

Nevertheless, public and private means of transportation are different in more ways than they are similar. Private cars offer a level of security, comfort, and convenience not necessarily available in public transportation. You can make your own schedule, take a different route, and avoid paying fares. Plus, you don't have to travel with strangers. However, only on public transportation can you sit back and relax, or even move around, and not have to pay attention to your driving or to traffic and weather conditions.

-- OR --

(Format B)

Regarding scheduling, private and public means of transportation are very different. When you travel by car, you can make your own schedule and stop anywhere and anytime you want. On the other hand, when you travel by public bus or train, you know exactly when you are going to arrive, making planning easy.

In terms of comfort, private transportation has the clear advantage. Public transportation is often crowded and . . .

III. Concluding paragraph
Summarize your main ideas.

Most people choose to use a mix of private and public transportation, depending on their circumstances. However, if I could choose only one means of transportation, I'd go with the car. It has its downsides, but I enjoy the privacy of traveling alone, or only with my family, and the convenience of being able to make my own schedule. All in all, driving in my own car is the way to go.

B   UNIT 6 WRITING TASK | Write an essay comparing and contrasting two means of transportation. Use Format A or Format B, depending on what you want to communicate. Use expressions of comparison and contrast.

Comparison	Contrast
Similarly,	While / Whereas . . .
Likewise,	Unlike [buses],
In similar fashion,	Nonetheless, / Nevertheless,
In the same way,	In contrast,
. . . as well.	On the other hand,
. . . don't either.	However,

SELF-CHECK

☐ Does my essay have an introductory and a concluding paragraph?
☐ Did I use one of the two formats for organizing the supporting paragraphs?
☐ Did I use expressions of comparison and contrast?

UNIT 7 — Subject-verb agreement: expansion

A WRITING SKILL | Study the rules.

When the subject and verb are separated by other words, the subject and verb must still agree.
   Beliefs in bad omens and curses **are** common in many cultures.
   The smart thing to do when someone tells you something is unlucky **is** to just listen.

When two subjects are connected with <u>and</u> in a sentence, the verb must be plural.
   A black cat and **a broken mirror are** symbols of bad luck in several cultures.

When verbs occur in a sequence, all the verbs must agree with the subject.
   My sister **has** a lucky horseshoe, **avoids** the number 13, and **wears** a good luck charm on a chain around her neck.

When the subject is an indefinite pronoun like <u>each</u>, <u>everyone</u>, <u>anyone</u>, <u>somebody</u>, or <u>no one</u>, use a singular verb.
   Nobody I know **worries** about sweeping a house in which a funeral has taken place.

When the subject is <u>all</u>, <u>some</u>, or <u>none</u> and refers to a singular count noun or a non-count noun, use a singular verb. Otherwise use a plural verb.
   If salt is spilled by accident, **some is** immediately thrown over the shoulder.
   Some superstitions are old-fashioned, but **some are** not.

> **Remember:** Subjects and verbs must always agree in number.
> - **A superstition is** a belief many people think is irrational.
> - **Many people believe** certain objects can bring good luck.

B PRACTICE | Read the paragraph and rewrite it on a separate sheet of paper, correcting the errors in subject-verb agreement.

ERROR CORRECTION

One common superstition in Western countries concern the number 13. Because they are considered unlucky, many situations involving the number 13 is frequently avoided. For example, in the past, the thirteenth floor of tall apartment buildings were often labeled "fourteen." While that is rare today, there are still many people who are uncomfortable renting an apartment on the thirteenth floor. In addition, there is a general belief that Friday the thirteenth brings bad luck, increases the chance of mishaps, and make it more difficult to get things done effectively.

C UNIT 7 WRITING TASK | On a separate sheet of paper, write a four-paragraph essay. In your first paragraph, introduce the topic of superstitions in general, explaining what they are and why people might believe them. Then write two supporting paragraphs, each with a topic sentence about a different superstition. End with a concluding paragraph that summarizes your main points. Be sure all your verbs and subjects agree in number.

SELF-CHECK
- ☐ Did I introduce the topic of superstitions in general in my first paragraph?
- ☐ Did my second and third paragraphs each include a clear topic sentence?
- ☐ Did I summarize my main points in a concluding paragraph?
- ☐ Did all my subjects and verbs agree?

UNIT 8 Explaining cause and result

A WRITING SKILL | Study the rules.

In formal writing, connecting words and phrases are commonly used to clarify relationships between ideas. Use the following to focus on causes or results.

Causes
Use one of these phrases to focus on a cause.

> Due to ___ ,   Because of ___ ,
> As a result of ___ ,   As a consequence of ___ ,

┌─── cause ───┐
As a result of my lack of organization, I can never find things on my desk when I need them.

                                          ┌─── cause ───┐
It may be diffcult to stay on task **due to constant interruptions by colleagues**.

Results
Begin a sentence with one of these words or phrases to focus on a result.

> As a result,   Consequently,
> As a consequence,   Therefore,

                                              ┌─── result ───┐
Colleagues may constantly interrupt your work. **Consequently**, it may be difficult to stay focused.

B PRACTICE | In the Writing Model, underline four sentences with connecting words or phrases that clarify causes and results. Then, on a separate sheet of paper, rewrite each sentence twice, using a different connecting word or phrase.

C UNIT 8 WRITING TASK | Write a three-paragraph essay about the challenges of staying focused while trying to study or complete a task at work or at home. Use the "outline" below as a guide. Be sure to include connecting words and phrases to signal causes and results.

Paragraph 1
Describe the things that make staying focused difficult.

Paragraph 2
Describe the results of not being able to stay focused.

Paragraph 3
Suggest some ways one might overcome the challenges and become more focused on completing a task.

SELF-CHECK
- [ ] Did my paragraphs follow the content and sequence suggested in Exercise C?
- [ ] Did I use connecting phrases to focus on causes?
- [ ] Did I introduce sentences with connecting words or phrases to focus on results?

WRITING MODEL

When trying to focus on a task at work, you may discover numerous distractions that can keep you from completing what you planned to do. You may find it difficult to stay focused due to your staying up late the night before. Or, as a consequence of frequent interruptions by colleagues, you may feel like you are always starting the task all over again. Many other things can distract you from a task, and the results can be significant.

Not being able to stay focused can have serious consequences. You may not be able to produce a report for your manager by the time it's due. As a result, your manager may wonder whether he or she can count on you to achieve your commitments. Your colleagues may depend on you to finish your part of a collaborative task, but you are unable to. Consequently, when these things happen, your reputation at work can suffer.

If you are having difficulty completing a task, it is important that you take action to help you stay on task. If you are frequently interrupted, you may have to close your office door or ask your colleagues not to disturb you. If you are suffering from a lack of sleep, you may have to take a break or grab a cup of coffee for a burst of energy. It's useful to have a strategy to cope with distraction and fatigue because those will probably always occur.

UNIT 9 | The thesis statement in a formal essay

A | WRITING SKILL | Study the rules.

A **thesis statement** presents the main idea of an essay, for example, by making an argument or stating a point of view. A formal essay should include a thesis statement somewhere in the **introductory paragraph**. The **supporting paragraphs** that follow should be organized to provide reasons, facts, or examples to support your thesis. A **concluding paragraph** should restate your thesis and summarize the main points of the supporting paragraphs. The outline below shows an effective way to organize a formal essay to support a thesis.

To write a thesis statement . . .
- Narrow the topic to one or two main ideas.
- Make sure it expresses a point of view.

I. Introductory paragraph
- Include a thesis statement.
- Provide a hint of the topics the essay will include.

II. Supporting paragraphs
- In each paragraph, include a topic sentence that supports your thesis statement.
- Provide examples that support your topic sentence.

III. Concluding paragraph
- Summarize the main points of your essay.
- Restate your thesis.

WRITING MODEL

There are good reasons to be optimistic about the future of the automobile. Manufacturers are already increasing their focus on providing alternative energy sources and technologies for self-driving vehicles. Gas-powered engines and human drivers will almost certainly be replaced over the next few decades.

Most experts today are confident that, in the future, the majority of cars will be powered by electricity. Unlike today's electric cars, which are not as popular as gas-powered vehicles, the cars of the future will be affordable and easier to maintain. For example, . . .

Recent advances in artificial intelligence will soon make human drivers obsolete. Tomorrow's electric cars will have advanced technological features that will dramatically increase safety on the road. First of all, cars will all be able to drive themselves. In addition, . . .

Based on the direction the auto industry is heading in today, we can predict these advances will come sooner rather than later. Manufacturers already offer both electric and hybrid choices that include a number of driverless features, so it's only a matter of time before gas-powered vehicles, and knowing how to drive them, become a memory.

B | PRACTICE | Essay tests often suggest topics in the form of a question. On a separate sheet of paper, write a thesis statement for each topic. Be sure to apply the guidelines above.

1. How can we end poverty? *Poverty will be ended only if world leaders make finding a solution a top priority.*
2. What are the best ways to learn about other cultures?
3. How can urban crime rates be improved?
4. What can be done to prepare for the next pandemic?
5. How can jobs be automated without causing massive unemployment?
6. Is the population shift from rural to urban areas a problem?

C | UNIT 9 WRITING TASK | Write a four- or five-paragraph essay on one of the suggested topics. State your argument in the introductory paragraph with a thesis statement. Support your argument with two or three supporting paragraphs, each with a topic sentence. In a concluding paragraph, restate your argument and summarize the main points.

Suggested topics
- How will transportation in the next century differ from today's?
- What technological developments do you predict will change the way people communicate with each other?
- What do you think will be the greatest improvements in medical care over the next fifty years?
- What are the most important issues educators need to pay attention to in order to ensure quality education for all in the future?
- In what ways do the world's leaders need to cooperate in order to ensure a future for our planet and the people living on it?
- Your own idea: ....

SELF-CHECK
- ☐ Did I include a thesis statement that clearly states my argument?
- ☐ Does each of my supporting paragraphs have a topic sentence that supports my point of view?
- ☐ Does my conclusion summarize my main points and restate my thesis?

UNIT 10 Rebutting an opposing point of view

A WRITING SKILL | Study the rules

When writing a rebuttal to an opposing argument or point of view, support your ideas by presenting them one by one. Following is an outline to organize your essay effectively.

I. Introductory paragraph
First, explain the issue and summarize the opposing point of view. Then include a thesis statement that states your own point of view.

II. Supporting paragraphs
In each paragraph, state one argument supporting the point of view you are rebutting. Use details and examples to support your own point of view.

III. Concluding paragraph
Summarize your point of view.

Expressions for introducing others' arguments:
According to [Dr. Kuhn], . . .
Some people [say / think / feel] that . . .
Many experts [argue / believe] that . . .
It may be true that . . .
It has been [argued / said / pointed out] that . . .

Transitions and subordinating conjunctions for your rebuttal:
However, . . .   All the same, . . .
Nevertheless, . . .   In spite of this, . . .
Even so, . . .

WRITING MODEL

There are many people who feel that globalization is causing more problems than it is solving. **Nevertheless, it is my opinion that, overall, globalization has contributed to a better world.** We need to accept it as the reality of today's world and do what we can to make it work for everyone.

Critics argue that many countries have not benefitted as much as others. **All the same**, we shouldn't assume that all countries will benefit at the same speed or time. It is a fact that free trade has greatly benefitted nations in East and Southeast Asia. Their economies have grown substantially in this century and their standard of living has greatly improved. There's no reason to believe this won't happen elsewhere, for example in West Africa.

It has been argued that globalization has caused an increase in the spread of disease, worsened pollution, and made it easier for criminals to cross borders. **In spite of this**, I believe that free trade and increased international cooperation have also made it easier for nations to fight these problems more effectively. With attention, these are problems that can be solved.

Clearly, globalization has created problems that need to be overcome. **Even so, I believe the advantages of globalization far outweigh the problems.**

B PRACTICE |
Look at the interview with Angela Kuhn on page 108. Find five arguments that support or argue against the idea that globalization has been a positive force for change. On a separate sheet of paper, paraphrase each argument in your own words and introduce each with the expressions from Exercise A.

> *It has been argued that globalization has improved the quality of life in many places.*

C PRACTICE |
Now write statements to rebut each of the arguments that you introduced in Exercise B. Use the suggested transitions and subordinating conjunctions.

> *Even so, the outsourcing of manufacturing has reduced job opportunities in some countries.*

D UNIT 10 WRITING TASK |
Write an essay of at least four paragraphs in which you present your point of view about globalization and rebut the opposing point of view. Or summarize and rebut Kuhn's arguments for or against globalization in the interview on page 108.

SELF-CHECK
☐ Did I summarize the point of view I want to rebut in my introduction?
☐ Did I rebut each argument by providing details and examples to support my own?
☐ Did I use the suggested expressions and transitions or subordinating conjunctions to link my ideas clearly?
☐ Did I summarize my point of view in my conclusion?

SOFT SKILLS BOOSTER (Optional)

The Soft Skills Booster helps develop the soft skills increasingly valued and required by employers to ensure employees' effective interaction with colleagues, management, partners, and clients in work settings. The target skills in the *Connectivity 5* Soft Skills Booster also contribute to students' success in academic settings and in everyday life. Each Soft Skills Booster unit focuses on one soft skill, which is then practiced with a partner. Finally, students are directed to apply the soft skill in a Communication Activator exercise from the unit in the Student's Book. As students become proficient with each soft skill, they should be encouraged to use it in all speaking activities in order to maximize the quality of their relationships with others.

UNIT 6 | Soft skill: PROBLEM SOLVING — Give constructive feedback non-judgmentally

(For Exercise B, page 63)

A Use the expressions on the left to give constructive feedback and advice non-judgmentally. Use the expressions on the right to respond. Listen and repeat each one.

TIP: Not judging someone else's previous error or misfortune makes it easier for him or her to accept constructive feedback.

Giving advice	Responding to advice
Next time, you might want to think about (not) . . .	You're absolutely right.
Did you consider (not) . . . ?	Yeah, you're right.
Well, if I were you, next time I would (not) . . .	Yeah, you may be right.
If you ask me, it probably would have been better (not) to have . . .	Maybe, but . . .
The way I see it, you probably should (not) have . . .	

B PAIR WORK | Take turns reading each problem aloud. Your partner gives you constructive feedback and you respond. Use expressions from Exercise A.

Student A (Student B gives feedback)

I got to the airport at 6:45 for a 7:30 flight, but I got bumped. They said the flight was full, and I'd have to wait ten hours for the next one!

Someone stole my camera and wallet out of my backpack. I'd left my backpack on the beach while I was swimming.

The taxi driver was going so fast! I was terrified, and I was holding onto my seat. Suddenly the car swerved. I hit the door and got a bad bruise on my arm.

The food at the street market had a funny taste—I thought it was a spice I hadn't tried before. But then after I got back to the hotel, I started throwing up and was terribly ill for three days.

When I got to the hotel, they couldn't find my reservation. I got angry at the clerk and started yelling. He called security and they grabbed me and led me outside.

Student B (Student A gives feedback)

I made a reservation by phone, but when I got to the hotel they didn't have any record of it. It took me hours to find a hotel that had a room.

We had some drinks and snacks from the little fridge in our hotel room. When we checked out, we were shocked at how much we were charged for them!

When I returned the rental car, they noticed a broken taillight. I knew it hadn't been my fault—it must have already been there when I rented the car. But they charged me for it anyway.

I had my wallet in my back pocket. When I got off the subway, a couple of guys bumped into me. Next time I checked, my wallet was gone! They got away with all my cash!

I took a six-day tour of Europe. We saw London, Paris, Madrid, Rome, Vienna, and Berlin. But by the fourth day of the trip I was totally exhausted and got totally confused about which city I was in!

C Now practice giving feedback about the past as you do Exercise B on page 63.

UNIT 7 — Soft skill: LEADERSHIP — Encourage others to support their ideas

(For Exercise B, page 75)

TIP: Asking others to elaborate on their ideas helps build mutual respect and a habit of critical thinking among people who work together.

A Use these expressions to encourage others to provide examples that explain or support their ideas. Listen and repeat each one.

Asking for examples

- What led you to that conclusion?
- Can you explain what led you to that?
- What are some examples of that?
- For example? / For instance? / Such as?

> Really? What led you to that conclusion?

> Have you been following the news? Some fans really crossed the line this week by yelling ethnic jokes at some of the players on the opposing team.

B PAIR WORK | Take turns reading a statement as a conversation starter. Using expressions from Exercise A, ask your partner to explain or support his or her statement.

Student A	Student B
Advertisements use various strategies to persuade people to buy a product.	Unfortunately, racism still influences people's behavior.
Movies can affect people in profound ways.	The news doesn't always report a story in an objective way.
What celebrities do has a huge effect on popular culture.	A person's family and friends probably have the most influence on his/her belief system.
Many people depend on expert opinions to help them make decisions on difficult or complicated issues.	Schools, companies, or other institutions also shape people's values.
Although not as widespread as in the past, sexism still exists in the workplace.	Hypnosis can be used to affect people's behavior.
Your own idea:	Your own idea:

C Now practice asking for and giving examples as you do Exercise B on page 75.

UNIT 8   Soft skill: RESPECTFULNESS   Interrupt and delay an interruption

(For Exercise B, page 83)

A   Use these expressions to politely interrupt, or to delay an interruption, during a discussion. Listen and repeat each one.

TIP: In a lively group discussion, knowing how to interrupt and how to delay someone's interruption enables others to fully complete their thoughts and cuts down on frustration.

Interrupting	Delaying an interruption
Sorry / Excuse me, but . . .	Let me just finish this thought.
I hate to interrupt, but . . .	First let me say . . .
Yes, but let me just say that . . .	Just one second.
I don't mean to butt in, but . . .	I'm almost finished.

B   PAIR WORK | Read your script aloud. Your partner tries to interrupt you as you read, and you try to delay each interruption. Use expressions from Exercise A.

Script 1

Student A

A: I work in an office where I have to do a lot of paperwork, but I also get a lot of phone calls—I can't stand getting all those calls—I lose my concentration and I can't focus on the paperwork . . . But I've got to answer the phone because no one else will—my co-workers are all really lazy—so I get very frustrated and hardly get any work done . . . Though I've tried to talk to my boss about it, she says I should be able to get the paperwork done AND answer the phone—but she's quite wrong—and I just don't think there's anything I can do about it! I think I'm just going to have to quit!

Student B tries to interrupt

B: ___ I work in an office where I have to do a lot of paperwork and answer the phone, too. And there's a pretty simple solution.

B: ___ I really think there's probably a simple solution. I would suggest not answering the calls but instead listening to them later on voicemail.

B: ___ If you can just answer the voicemail once every hour or so, you could get an hour's worth of paperwork done uninterrupted.

Script 2

Student B

B: I sit at a desk all day, and I've got this terrible chair—it's very cheap and old, and it's hard on my back—lower back pain—you can imagine how terrible that must feel . . . And I also get pain in my shoulders—so I have this awful pain all day long, even after work . . . And I've gone to see a doctor about it and he gave me some medication, but it makes me sleepy—so I can't take it at work—but my back hurts so much that the pain interferes with the quality of my work—and my boss is too cheap to get me a good chair! He gets angry when I complain, which I do a lot, but I don't know what else to do!

Student A tries to interrupt

A: ___ I used to have a bad chair in my office, too, and I had some back pain. So let me tell you what I did about it.

A: ___ There are some good chairs that are designed to support your lower back.

A: ___ A better chair might be a bit expensive, but if you're in so much pain, I'd recommend going ahead and buying one with your own money.

A: ___ You really should get a better chair.

C   Now practice interrupting and delaying interruptions as you do Exercise B on page 83.

SOFT SKILLS BOOSTER   161

UNIT 9 Soft skill: CONFLICT RESOLUTION — Respectfully acknowledge that others may disagree with you

(For Exercise B, page 99)

TIP: Acknowledging that your colleagues may have different points of view from your own enables them to hear yours with an open mind.

A Use these expressions to respond to complex or controversial questions. Listen and repeat each one.

> **Responding to complex or controversial questions**
>
> You may disagree, but I believe . . .
> It's a complicated issue, but I guess . . .
> It's a controversial subject, but I think . . .
> There's not a simple answer, but I suppose . . .

B PAIR WORK | Take turns asking the questions below. Use expressions from Exercise A when responding.

Student A

- What do you think is the most serious problem the world is facing?
- What do you think the biggest problem with the news media is?
- What do you think the most serious problem with our government is?
- Your own idea:

Student B

- What do you think is the biggest problem in our country?
- What do you think the most serious problem with our education system is?
- What do you think is the biggest threat families are facing today?
- Your own idea:

C Now practice using these phrases for responding to complex or controversial questions as you do Exercise B on page 99.

SOFT SKILLS BOOSTER

UNIT 10 — Soft skill: NEGOTIATION

Attempt to come to agreement by respectfully acknowledging an opposing point of view

(For Exercise B, page 109)

A Use these expressions to politely disagree with others but to indicate that you are open to their ideas as well.

TIP: It's easier to negotiate differences of opinion when you show acceptance of an opposing view and provide reasons for your own point of view.

Disagreeing politely

Maybe, but don't you think . . . ?
I hear what you're saying, but the way I see it . . .
That's one way to look at it, but from my point of view . . .
I understand what you're saying, but if you ask me, I think . . .
I understand where you're coming from, but I tend to think that . . .

B PAIR WORK | Take turns reading the prompts and politely disagreeing with your partner. Use expressions from Exercise A to acknowledge your partner's opinion and introduce your own.

Student A

I believe globalization is helping raise wages and living standards for everybody all over the world.

(globalization has generated most of the jobs we have in this country)

(the large multinationals are investing a lot in our country and helping our economy)

(globalization is spreading money around the globe and helping poor people become rich)

(globalization is letting us export more and more — and bringing in new imports that we can't make in our own country)

Student B

(globalization has hurt all the people who live in developing countries)

(the large multinational corporations only bring in low-wage jobs)

(the large multinationals are taking all the money they make here out of the country)

(globalization is bankrupting all the small shops and family-owned businesses in this country)

(globalization is totally destroying our culture and way of life)

C Now practice disagreeing politely as you do Exercise B on page 109.

SOFT SKILLS BOOSTER

# Connectivity
LEVEL 5B

WORKBOOK

Joan Saslow
Allen Ascher

UNIT 6 On the Move

Preview

1 Complete each conversation with an expression from the box. There are two extra choices.

| are playing with fire | can't be too careful | can't beat | leave me be |
| over the top | Take my word for it | the umpteenth time | What are the odds |

1. **A:** Mary?
   B: Sheila! This is incredible! I didn't know you were traveling to Paris!
   A: I can't believe we bumped into each other on the street! ....?

2. **A:** Are you kidding? Can't they ....?
   B: What's the matter?
   A: I'm tired of ads popping up in this travel app. It's so annoying.

3. **A:** Did you see Sharon's new hairstyle?
   B: I did, and I really don't like it. It seems to be a bit .... for a pilot.

4. **A:** I heard that you just returned from a trip to Panama. What did you think?
   B: ...., you don't want to travel there during this busy time of year. Flights were being delayed and canceled daily.

5. **A:** Have you booked your cabin on the group cruise yet?
   B: No, not yet. I'm waiting to see if there are any last-minute specials.
   A: You .... If you don't book soon, you might not get a room.

6. **A:** What did you think of Bali?
   B: Oh, you .... Bali for a beautiful, relaxing vacation!

2 Think about the worst travel hassles you or someone you know have experienced. Write a paragraph. How did they affect the trip? How have you changed your travel habits to avoid similar troubles in the future?

_____
_____
_____
_____
_____

LESSON 1

1 Complete each statement. Circle the correct verb phrases.

1. If we (**had taken** / would be taking) the train, we (wouldn't sit / **wouldn't be sitting**) in traffic right now.
2. If she (hadn't talked / **hadn't been talking**) on her phone, she (would have been hearing / **would have heard**) the boarding announcement.
3. If the children (had slept / **had been sleeping**) better, they (**wouldn't be arguing** / would argue) so much today.
4. If she (isn't traveling / **weren't traveling**) outside the country, she (**wouldn't need** / didn't need) her passport.
5. I (**wouldn't be using** / wouldn't have been using) my smart phone if the plane (would be taking off / **were taking off**).

2 Read each sentence. Complete the unreal conditional sentences with the correct form of the verb phrases. Use at least one continuous verb form in each sentence. Some may have more than one correct answer.

1. **Alan:** It's too bad they overbooked the flight. I was supposed to fly to Spain tonight.
   If they _hadn't overbooked_ (not overbook) the flight, I _would be flying_ (fly) to Spain tonight.
2. **Jules:** I'm so glad I sat in this seat. I got to meet Sam.
   If Jules _____ (not sit) in this seat, she _____ (not met) Sam.
3. **Cara:** I wish I'd used the bathroom before we left! Now I can't find one.
   If Cara _____ (use) the bathroom before she left, she _____ (not look) for one now.
4. **Rob:** I'm glad I'm not hanging out at home tonight. There's nothing to do but watch TV.
   If Rob _____ (hang out) at home tonight, he _____ (watch) TV.
5. **Tim and Marcy:** We're glad we're traveling during the week. This train is very crowded on the weekend.
   If we _____ (travel) on the weekend, the train _____ (be) much more crowded.
6. **Sara and Jeff:** We should have packed some snacks to take on the plane. We really don't like the airline food.
   Sara and Jeff _____ (not eat) the airline food now if they _____ (pack) some snacks.

3 Complete the unreal conditional sentences. Use continuous verb forms and your own ideas.

1. If I were with my family right now, I _____.
2. If it were the weekend, I _____.
3. If I hadn't decided to study English, I _____.
4. If I could be doing anything I wanted right now, I _____.

W48 UNIT 6

LESSON 2

1 Complete each polite request with a phrase from the box. There is one extra choice.

> Could I ask   Could you possibly   Do you think
> you be nice enough to   you please let   Would you mind

1 .... giving me a hand with this?
2 .... you could point me in the right direction?
3 .... you to keep an eye on my things?
4 .... grab that for me?
5 Would .... save my place in line?

2 Complete the conversations. Use the correct words to politely ask for a favor.

1 **A:** Excuse me, ... you could open the door for me? My hands are full.
   B: Of course!
2 **A:** Excuse me, ... possibly tell me what time it is?
   B: It's 10:00 A.M.
3 **A:** Do you need any help?
   B: Yes, please—would .... telling me where the check-in counters are?
4 **A:** Could .... you to move your bag off this chair? I'd like to sit here.
   B: No problem.
5 **A:** Would you .... to swap seats with me? I'd like to sit next to my friend.
   B: Sure, I don't mind.

3 Look at the pictures. Write a request for a favor for each situation. Use phrases from the box in Exercise 1.

1 ....

2 ....

3 ....

4 ....

UNIT 6   W49

4 Complete each statement of relief or regret. Use **if it weren't for** or **if it hadn't been for**.

1 .... the express bus, we would have missed our flight.
2 I would go for a walk with you .... my sore ankle.
3 .... Angela, our travel agent, we might have been waiting overnight for a flight.
4 .... the icy roads, we wouldn't have had an accident.
5 We would be in the museum by now .... these long lines.

5 Rewrite each statement of relief or regret. Use **if it weren't for** or **if it hadn't been for**.

1 Without your help, I never would have passed this class.
   ....
2 This would be a perfect flight, except for the uncomfortable seats.
   ....
3 Without the confusion at the airport, our bags wouldn't have gotten lost.
   ....
4 If we didn't have a scheduling conflict, we would go to your party.
   ....
5 We would have gotten lost without that stranger's help.
   ....
6 If you hadn't hired that speaker, this would have been a boring meeting.
   ....

6 Put the sentences in order. Write the number on the line.

.... **Brian:** Thanks so much. I really appreciate it.
.... **Amy:** What's that?
...1... **Brian:** Amy, could you do me a favor?
.... **Amy:** I'd be happy to.
.... **Brian:** I've got a horrendous headache. Would you mind getting me some aspirin?

7 Choose one of the situations in Exercise 3. Write a conversation in which someone asks for a favor and expresses gratitude. Refer to the Conversation Model on Student's Book page 61 as an example.

LESSON 3

1 Read the advice column. What type of advice are the people asking for? Circle the letter.

a how to avoid losing a phone or passport while traveling

b what essentials to pack for a long backpacking trip

c which smart phone apps to use while traveling

Lost, Stolen, or Damaged
featuring Tom Kramer

Dear Tom,
Next month, I'm going on a big backpacking adventure. I'm not packing a lot—but I am taking my smart phone! I'll be using it as a camera, boarding pass, watch, alarm clock, map, you name it. I'm worried that losing it will ruin my entire trip. What can I do to avoid this?—*Isla, Melbourne, Australia*

There are a few things to do before you leave. First, buy travel insurance that covers your phone against theft and loss. Second, make sure your phone's security is up to date. Back up your personal information and photos. Third, turn on remote tracking so that you can locate it in the event it gets lost. And finally, consider making room in your bag for a few old-fashioned backups, like a watch with an alarm clock and paper maps. These could really save the day if your phone loses service or runs out of battery!

If you do lose your phone, don't panic. These things happen, no matter how carefully you look after your phone. Just access your phone from another device to try and locate it, and also to delete everything on it so that strangers can't access your sensitive information even if they manage to crack your security. Then contact your insurance company to get a replacement. Above all, have an amazing adventure!

Dear Tom,
The last time I traveled abroad, my passport got stolen. It was a total disaster! Now I'm about to go to Paris on business, and I'm very nervous. What if it happens again?—*Ricardo, Guadalajara, Mexico*

You're not alone: at least a million passports are reported as stolen or missing across the world each year. And as you obviously know, replacing a passport while traveling can be difficult and stressful. You can avoid some of the hassle, however, by taking some precautions. Each country has its own passport rules and regulations. Before you leave, check your government's website to find out what to do and where to go when you lose your passport. Second, have digital copies of your passport and passport photos. These will come in very useful when you need to replace your travel documents.

To avoid this bad situation in the first place, keep your passport as safe as you possibly can. The best thing is to leave it in your hotel safe. If that's not possible, keep it on your person. Make sure it's not visible to anyone else, and never, ever hand it to strangers. Good luck—and enjoy Paris!

2 Read the advice column in Exercise 1 again. Then read the statements. Check True, False, or No information (NI).

	True	False	NI
1 Isla is planning on traveling for business.	☐	☐	☐
2 Tom suggests traveling with low-tech devices like watches and alarm clocks.	☐	☐	☐
3 Your insurance company won't replace your stolen phone unless it was insured against theft.	☐	☐	☐
4 Tom warns that a thief can use remote access to steal private information on a stolen phone.	☐	☐	☐
5 Ricardo's passport was stolen last year while he was on a business trip to Paris.	☐	☐	☐
6 Every year, more than a million smart phones are stolen or lost globally.	☐	☐	☐
7 Every country has a different process for replacing a lost or stolen passport.	☐	☐	☐
8 According to Tom, it's best to carry your passport with you at all times.	☐	☐	☐

3 Read the advice column in Exercise 1 again. Complete the summary of Tom's advice to each traveler.

Advice for Isla

Before your trip:

....

....

In case of loss or theft:

....

....

Advice for Ricardo

Before your trip:

....

....

To prevent loss or theft:

....

....

DID YOU KNOW...?
Of the 4 billion bags that passengers check in each year, 28 million are mishandled by the airlines. 18%, or 5,040,000 bags, are damaged and 77%, or 21,560,000 bags, are delayed. Sadly, 5%, or 1.4 million bags, are lost and never returned to their owners.

LESSON 4

1 Read the interview with an Internet hacker. Answer the questions.

The Public Wi-Fi Blues

DD: This is Donald Dean, your roving reporter, going all over the city to give you information on the things that matter in your life. Thanks for listening. I know one of the things that matters to you is security—for your information, for your money, and for your identity. You may feel pretty safe, but in the first six months of this year, there were 1,860 incidents of hacking reported, exposing 228 million records. And we don't know how many went unreported. Of course, most hacking targets business and industry. But you could be a target, too, if you're not careful.

So, today I'm talking to a hacker! Well, she's not really a hacker. Veronica Tyler is a computer security specialist, a real expert. But if she hadn't learned how hackers get into your personal computer, she couldn't help you keep them out. So, Veronica, thank you for agreeing to talk to me and my listeners.

VT: It's my pleasure, Donald.

DD: We're here at Ground Up coffee shop so that you can show me up close what hackers can do in a place like this. Where do we start?

VT: Well, we already took the first step. When we ordered our coffee, we got the Wi-Fi password. Now, I'm turning on my laptop and this clever, but nasty little device.

DD: What's it doing? What's that on your monitor?

VT: Information. I'm intercepting signals from laptops, tablets, and smart phones all over the café. This is really basic hacking, and I can already tell you a lot. For example, I can see what Wi-Fi networks each of these people has joined before. And that means I know a lot about them.

DD: Like what?

VT: The guy in the red baseball cap has recently been to Boston. He was logged in to the Logan International Airport network. He stayed at the Morris Hotel, which is very expensive. If I were a real hacker, I would pay close attention to him. He also likes to play golf and eat at fast food places, which are often Wi-Fi hotspots. But let's get serious now. One of the most effective hacking techniques involves setting up an evil twin.

DD: What in the world is an evil twin?

VT: On a soap opera, it's a character who is supposed to be the twin brother or sister of one of the regular characters. But while the regular character is good and moral, the twin is evil and dangerous.

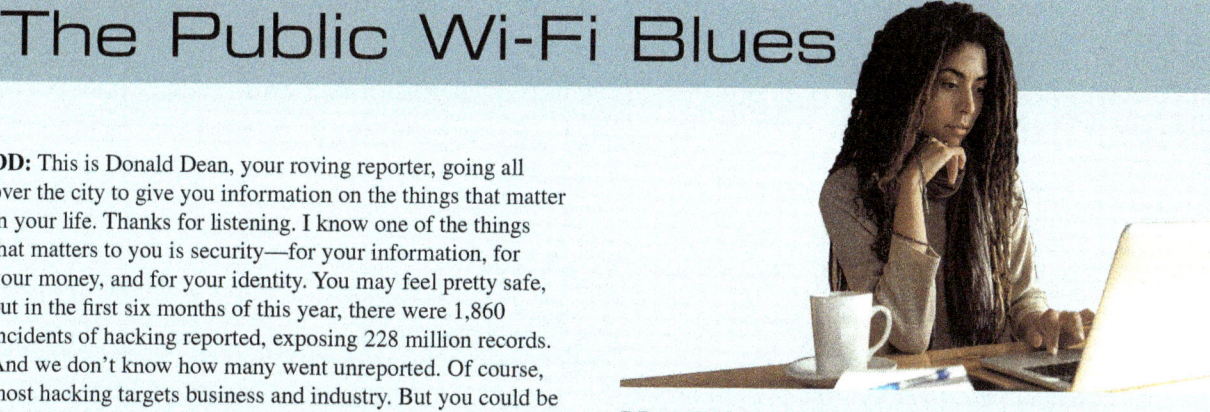

DD: OK. If we were talking about soap operas, I would know exactly what you mean. But we're talking about hacking.

VT: And in hacking, an evil twin is a hidden WiFi access point that impersonates a legitimate access point. Hackers use it to get sensitive information, like usernames and passwords to various accounts.

DD: How does that work?

VT: Well, when someone tries to log in, they see a list of possible networks, right? The name of this coffee shop's Wi-Fi network is on that list, but it's not the same as the name of the shop. It's just a selection of letters and numbers. Now, people are more comfortable with names than with random letter and number combinations. So, on my access point, I've set up another network called GroundUp. It's now on the list, too. Now I'm going to disrupt service for a moment. OK. Everybody's Wi-Fi connection is now off. Let's see what happens when people try to reconnect.

DD: They're connecting to GroundUp! The evil twin! So they don't remember or care that what they originally logged in to, the actual coffee shop network, was not named for the shop at all?

VT: No. They happily log in to the evil twin because it's named GroundUp.

DD: I'm afraid I would, too. That's scary.

VT: So, at this point, I can get into their computers and get anything I want. Their online banking credentials, credit card numbers, even Social Security numbers. If it weren't for my honesty and integrity, I could cause a lot of trouble, even commit identity theft. But I couldn't touch the young woman in the green shirt. Her information is encrypted, and I wouldn't be able to break the code.

DD: Fascinating. Well, that's all the time we have, Veronica. Thank you for some great information. And now, this is Donald Dean saying, "See you next time."

1. What is Veronica Tyler's job? How does she use her hacking skills? ....
....
2. What does Tyler's little device allow her to do? ....
....
3. Why does knowing what Wi-Fi networks people have joined before tell Tyler a lot about them? ....
....
4. Why would a hacker pay close attention to the man in the red baseball cap? ....
....
5. What is an evil twin? What does it allow hackers to do? ....
....
6. What information can't be accessed using the evil twin? ....
....
7. Before reading this interview, if you were using the Internet, and the Wi-Fi connection were interrupted, do you think you would pay much attention to the name of the network when you logged back in? ....
....
8. Did anything in the interview surprise you? What was it? ....
....

2 After reading the interview in Exercise 1, what will you (or should you) do differently the next time you use a public Wi-Fi network?

_____
_____
_____
_____

3 Complete the sentences. Use the verb in the first sentence as a past participial adjective to modify the noun in the second sentence.

1. On my last vacation, my luggage was lost. When the airline was unable to locate my ......*lost*...... luggage, they reimbursed me promptly.
2. A waiter spilled a glass of red wine, staining the front of my dress. I took the .... dress to the dry cleaners, but they couldn't get the stain out.
3. My son accidentally broke a vase in a souvenir shop. Of course, we had to pay for the .... vase.
4. A thief stole my laptop while I was eating in an outdoor café. Surprisingly, the police caught the thief and recovered the .... laptop within 24 hours.
5. I dropped my new camera and damaged the lens. Luckily, it's still under warranty, so when I called customer service they offered to repair or replace the .... lens.
6. Someone burglarized a suite in the hotel. The police are now searching for evidence in the .... suite.

W54 UNIT 6

GRAMMAR EXPANDER

1 Read each conditional sentence. Then read the two statements. Check <u>True</u> or <u>False</u>.

	True	False
1 If Dave were here, he'd tell us what to do.		
Dave is here.	☐	☐
Dave is going to tell us what to do.	☐	☐
2 If she hadn't read the letter, she would have been shocked by the news.		
She didn't read the letter.	☐	☐
She wasn't shocked by the news.	☐	☐
3 We might be on the train now if we hadn't gotten stuck in traffic.		
We're not on the train.	☐	☐
We got stuck in traffic.	☐	☐
4 If I have time, I may be able to help you out.		
I am certain that I'll have time.	☐	☐
I will definitely help you out.	☐	☐

2 Complete the sentences. Circle the letter.

1 If the park gets too full, you .... wait for some people to leave before they let anyone else in.
   a had to   b wouldn't have had to   c have to   d didn't have to

2 The air-conditioning automatically turns on if the temperature .... above 27 degrees Celsius.
   a goes   b will go   c would go   d would have gone

3 If we had gotten the call earlier, we .... help.
   a would   b will   c were going to   d might have been able to

4 Kyle studied very hard for his test. But if he ...., he would be really nervous.
   a had studied   b would have studied   c hadn't studied   d doesn't study

5 I .... so excited to go to Paris tomorrow if I had been there before.
   a wouldn't have been   b wouldn't be   c won't be   d hadn't been

6 If we had time, we .... the Grand Canyon.
   a would visit   b had visited   c visited   d visit

3 Complete the conditional sentences with your own ideas.

1 If I had more free time, ...

2 If we arrive at English class late, ...

3 If I hadn't decided to ....

4 If I spoke English fluently, ...

WRITING HANDBOOK

1 Complete the chart. Compare two vacation destinations that you'd like to visit. Write each destination name at the top. Then describe how they are similar and how they are different.

COMPARING VACATION DESTINATIONS

DESTINATION 1: _____   **DESTINATION 2:** _____

Similarities

_____
_____
_____

Differences

_____	_____
_____	_____
_____	_____

2 On a separate sheet of paper, compare and contrast the two destinations. Use the information in your chart. Explain which place you would prefer to visit for a vacation. Use expressions of comparison and contrast.

3 Read the following self-check questions. Check those that apply to your work in Exercise 2.

☐ Did I use expressions of comparison and contrast?

☐ Does my essay have an introductory and a concluding paragraph?

☐ Do the supporting paragraphs follow one of the formats illustrated on Student's Book page 149?

WRITING MODEL

Two places that I'd love to visit for a vacation are Nice in France and Cinque Terre in Italy. Both places are very beautiful and great vacation destinations. However, there are some differences.

Nice is a busy, beach city. There are people from all over the world shopping, eating in world-class restaurants, and going to dance clubs that stay open very late. Similarly, Cinque Terre is also by the water, but the environment is very different. It is still undiscovered by many tourists. In contrast to the fast pace of Nice, most visitors to Cinque Terre spend their days hiking, swimming, and visiting olive groves and vineyards.

Both Nice and Cinque Terre are great for vacation. But if I had to choose just one of those places, I think I would choose Cinque Terre. For me, it would probably be more relaxing.

UNIT 7 Belief and Reality

Preview

1 Complete the conversations with expressions from the box. There is one extra choice.

| a grain of salt | a safe bet | wishful thinking | raise a red flag | run something by | one catch |

1. **A:** Is Dana still in her office? I'd like to .... her.
   B: I think so. Actually, I'll come with you. I need to ask her opinion about something, too.
2. **A:** Did you hear about the amazing offer Milton got for a free stay at a beautiful resort? There was only ....
   B: Let me guess. He had to sit in on a timeshare presentation.
   A: Yes! How did you know?
3. **A:** Oh, look! This email says I won a free big-screen TV. All I have to do is pay for delivery.
   B: Don't fall for it! Offers like that always .... for me.
   A: You're right. It's probably a scam to get my credit card information.
4. **A:** What do you think about purchasing company stocks with our discount?
   B: Well, the company is doing well. So, it sounds like .... to me.
5. **A:** I heard that Eli got a new boat and it's very luxurious. Maybe he'll invite us to go out on it.
   B: I think that might be .... on your part. He doesn't even know us.

2 Think about a time when something you thought sounded good at first ended up not being trustworthy. What raised a red flag for you? Describe your experience.

_____
_____
_____
_____
_____

LESSON 1

1 Write **a**, **an**, or **the** before the noun where necessary. Write X if the noun should not have an article. Then write **definite**, **indefinite**, **unique**, or **generic**.

1. *The* ingredients in this soup are all organic. — *definite*
2. .... CEO of our company announced budget cuts. — ....
3. .... Apples are a very popular fruit. — ....
4. You should eat .... apple a day. — ....
5. .... rain is coming down really hard now. — ....
6. It's so dry out. Our garden needs .... rain. — ....
7. .... scam that fooled you also fooled me. — ....

2 Read the paragraphs. Complete the sentences. Write a, an, or the before the noun or noun phrase where necessary. Write X if the noun should not have an article.

1. Phishing is .... a .... scam designed to steal a person's identity. Victims of .... the .... scam receive .... an .... email that appears to come from .... a .... trusted website such as their bank or favorite shopping site. .... The .... email attempts to trick people into disclosing valuable personal information like credit card numbers, passwords, or account data.

2. Until the 1800s, British doctors believed that .... X .... tomatoes were poisonous and caused conditions like "brain fever" and cancer. In fact, ... the .... tomato is highly nutritious and a good source of vitamin A, which is important for healthy hair and skin.

3. There's .... a .... new product being marketed on .... the .... Internet called "Exercise in a Bottle." In pop-up ads, the company claims that .... the .... product will burn fat while the user is just sitting around doing nothing or even sleeping. .... The .... ads also state that consumers can enjoy fried chicken, pizza, and other high-calorie, high-fat products and still lose weight.

4. .... A .... U.S.-based company is in the business of selling stars. For US $48, you can purchase .... a .... star and name it. .... The .... company has faced a great deal of criticism from .... X .... astrologers and consumer groups, who point out that the certificates of purchase issued by the company aren't recognized by any other organization. "They can't sell .... the .... sun because it's not theirs to sell," states one critic of the company.

3 Complete the conversation with phrases from the box. There are two extra choices.

a drug trafficking scam	Don't ask	Don't tell me	exactly what happened
hear what happened	That seems a little fishy	the foreign lottery scam
there's one catch	Why am I not surprised	why she was so gullible

A: Did you **(1)** .... to Tracey?

B: No, what?

A: She got an email saying she'd won the lottery in a different country.

B: Oh, no. **(2)** .... she fell for **(3)** ....—the one where someone tells you you've won a lot of money, but **(4)** ....

A: You have to pay a fee first before you can collect your money? Yeah, that's **(5)** .... She paid the "tax" ... and that was the last she heard from them.

B: **(6)** .... ? How much did she lose?

A: **(7)** .... Let's just say she won't trust emails from foreign lotteries again!

B: Right. I wonder **(8)** .... in the first place.

4 Have you ever received an email or phone call that was a scam? Describe the message that you received. What did you do?

LESSON 2

1 Complete the sentences. Replace the subject and active verb with <u>it</u> + a passive reporting verb.

1. Many people believe that hanging a horseshoe with the ends pointing up brings good luck.
   It is believed that hanging a horseshoe with the ends pointing up brings good luck.

2. They say that picking up a penny on the sidewalk will bring good luck.
   .... that picking up a penny on the sidewalk will bring good luck.

3. Estimates are that 25% of Americans are superstitious.
   .... that 25% of Americans are superstitious.

4. People once thought that lightning during a summer storm caused crops to ripen.
   .... that lightning during a summer storm caused crops to ripen.

5. People used to say that taking someone's picture was like taking that person's soul.
   .... that taking someone's picture was like taking that person's soul.

6. People used to believe that a clap of thunder after a funeral meant that the person's soul had reached its final resting place.
   .... that a clap of thunder after a funeral meant that the person's soul had reached its final resting place.

7. People used to feel like they had no choice but to live with a phobia or fear, no matter how irrational.
   .... that one had no choice but to live with a phobia or fear, no matter how irrational.

8. Some suggest that therapy offers a potential "cure" or relief for people with phobias.
   .... that therapy offers a potential "cure" or relief for people with phobias.

2 Complete the chart about phobias. Write the correct noun or adjective form in each category.

Name of phobia	What you call a person who suffers from it	How you describe the person
acrophobia [heights]	an acrophobe	(1) *acrophobic*
agoraphobia [being outside of the home]	(2)	agoraphobic
(3) .... [spiders]	an arachnophobe	arachnophobic
aerophobia [flying]	an aerophobe	(4) ....
(5) .... [enclosed spaces]	a claustrophobe	claustrophobic
ophidiophobia [snakes]	an ophidiophobe	(6) ....
xenophobia [foreigners]	(7)	xenophobic

3 Complete the sentences. Choose the correct word from Exercise 2.

1 Kate is an ………………………………… . She wouldn't even go near the window of our high-rise apartment.
2 I have ………………………………… . I get scared in elevators even if they're very large.
3 The candidate's speech showed his distrust of foreign culture. He was widely criticized for being ………………………………… .
4 Ariana is an ………………………………… . She refuses to fly and always travels by car.
5 Bill must be ………………………………… . He screamed when a little spider landed on him.
6 If you're an ………………………………… , don't go in the reptile house at the zoo!
7 Ken always prefers to stay at home. I think he's a little ………………………………… .

4 Complete the chart. Answer the questions.

1 List a few things that many people are afraid of. Why do you think people fear these things?

Common fear or phobia	Reason
bees	bee stings are painful and some people are allergic

2 Do you know anyone who has an irrational fear or phobia? What is it? Do you feel sympathy for the person? Why or why not?

……
……

3 What advice would you give to someone who wants to get over a phobia?

……
……
……

DID YOU KNOW…?
Glossophobia, or the fear of public speaking, is believed to be the most common phobia in the world, affecting as many as 75% of all people.

LESSON 3

1 Read the article. Answer the questions.

VISUALIZING THE WAY TO VICTORY

It's often said that sports are 90% mental and 10% physical. It may be a cliché, but many athletes and trainers now place a strong emphasis on the mental aspect of training. As many elite athletes will tell you, mental toughness and focus is often the difference that separates the very best (think Olympic gold medal) athletes from the second-best. For almost all elite athletes, *visualization*, or as some prefer to call it, *using imagery*, is now a crucial part of their training.

What is visualization? In a nutshell, it involves mentally simulating every aspect of an event, competition, or race. It can be thought of as "athletic training for the brain." Athletes use visualization to build focus, reduce stress, and tune out distractions. While visualization cannot replace physical practice, it can greatly enhance it. Studies have shown that the brain patterns activated when someone visualizes performing a sport are the same brain patterns as those activated by actually doing the sport.

"Visualization might be a misleading term, since using *mental imagery* involves all five senses," says sports psychologist Dr. Dana Carter. Athletes focus on how things feel, smell, and sound as they go through every moment of their event in their mind. For example, a bobsledder will visualize his or her way down the bobsled track, slowing down the process and "seeing" every inch of the track. "Athletes are actually feeling the ice or the track beneath them, feeling the wind hit their skin, seeing the turns in the track or the moguls on the mountain, hearing their skates on the ice or their body in the water," says Carter. Many athletes even move their bodies as they practice mental imagery because their muscles are responding to the brain signals created as they visualize themselves performing. "It can be a little weird to watch," says Chelsea Yost, an elite skier who has worked with Dr. Carter. "People might be moving their arms, bouncing back and forth, all with their eyes closed and this look of intense concentration on their faces."

Another aspect of mental imagery is known as *instructional self-talk*. As athletes imagine themselves going through the motions of their event, they tell themselves what to do, step by step—for example, "Point your toes," "Glide, then pull," or "Push off quickly, arms up." Some athletes record this step-by-step instruction aloud, along with what they're seeing and feeling at every moment. They then play it back over and over, feeling muscles in their bodies responding as they would during the actual event. It's believed that mental exercises like this actually train the muscles to respond more quickly.

Yet another aspect of mental imaging is called *pattern-breaking*. Pattern-breaking uses imagery to get rid of fear or nervousness. For example, if an athlete has had an accident or been injured while competing, images of the trauma may pop into his or her head before a similar competition. With practice, visualization can help the athlete push out the negative images. Some athletes use an image of a physical action, such as a balloon popping or an elastic band snapping, that they can summon up as a *trigger* to dispel the negative thoughts. Once athletes become adept at pattern-breaking, they are able to banish negative thoughts and maintain positive focus much more easily, which is crucial in competition.

Visualization is not just for elite athletes. Studies have shown that it significantly improves performance in beginner athletes as well. But you need to do more than just think about performing your sport. You need to focus on every little detail: how every moment of the event feels, sounds, looks, smells. Slow down and imagine each step in the event, or in a portion of the event, such as the beginning of a race, or the last hundred yards. You never know—it may just give you the edge over the local competition that you need in your next 5K race!

1 What is *visualization* or *mental imagery*? ....
....

2 How is it used by athletes? ....
....

3 What is *instructional self-talk*? ....
....
4 What effect might instructional self-talk have on the body? ....
....
5 What is *pattern-breaking*? ....
....
6 When using pattern-breaking, what images might be used as a *trigger*? ....
....
7 How can pattern-breaking be valuable in competition? ....
....
8 How is visualization different from just thinking about performing a sport? ....
....
9 Is visualization only beneficial for elite athletes? ....
....

2 Answer the questions with your own ideas.

1 Name a sport or an activity that you do. If you were to try visualization, what details would you need to imagine? What senses might be involved?
....
....
....

2 If you were to try instructional self-talk, what words or phrases might you use?
....
....

3 In what situations could pattern-breaking help you overcome fear or nervousness?
....
....

4 What image might you visualize as your trigger to help you banish negative thoughts?
....
....

LESSON 4

1 Match the words with their definitions. Write the letter on the line.

.... 1 a superstition
.... 2 bad luck
.... 3 a good luck charm
.... 4 a curse

a an object that some people believe can bring them good luck
b a belief that some objects or actions are lucky or unlucky
c the expression of a wish that someone will face misfortune
d a misfortune that happens by chance

2 Complete the conversation. Circle the correct word or phrase.

A: Don't walk under that ladder! It will bring you **(1)** (a good luck charm / bad luck / a superstition).

B: That's just **(2)** (a good luck charm / a curse / a superstition). It's a silly belief that's not real.

A: How do you know? I know someone who walked under a ladder, and a day later they crashed their brand new car!

B: Hmm, that was very unlucky. But I'm still not sure I believe all that stuff.

A: Well, I do. That's why I always wear this necklace. It's my **(3)** (good luck charm / curse / bad luck). If I wear this, I know nothing bad will happen to me.

B: I see. And does it protect you from **(4)** (curses / superstitions / bad luck), too? You know, when someone says something or looks at you in a funny way to make something bad happen to you?

A: Don't be silly—of course not! Everybody knows that's not real.

3 What are some superstitions that you know? Complete the sentences with your own ideas.

1 In some cultures, it is considered good luck ....
....

2 In some cultures, ... is considered to be bad luck.

3 The numbers .... are thought to be .... luck in some countries.

4 An animal that is believed to be good luck in .... is the ....

5 If you want your child to be .... , you should ....

4 Answer the questions in your own way.

1 What numbers are considered lucky or unlucky in your country? Why?
....
....

2 Are there any numbers that you personally consider lucky or unlucky? Why or why not?
....
....

DID YOU KNOW...?
In much of the Western world, it's long been thought that the number 13 is bad luck. Next time you're traveling by air, try looking for row number 13 on your airplane. Chances are, there isn't one. Few airlines have a row 13, and most airlines don't offer flight numbers that contain that number. A spokesperson for one airline admitted that the airline omits row 13 because too many passengers refuse to sit in those seats. Travel industry studies even show that travel declines on "unlucky" days, such as the thirteenth day of the month.

GRAMMAR EXPANDER

1 Complete the sentences. Write <u>a</u> or <u>the</u>. Write X if the noun should not have an article.

1 People in different parts of .... world have varied superstitions. For example, in some cultures .... number 13 is considered unlucky, while in others 4 is an unlucky number, and in still others 17 is thought to be .... bad luck.

2 Bill gave me .... glass of water to drink. He said that .... water at his house goes through .... special filtering system.

3 Lucy bought .... car last month. .... car isn't brand new; she bought it from .... neighbor who had driven it for less than .... year. But it's in .... good condition, and Lucy thinks she paid .... fair price for it.

4 If you're in the mood for Japanese food, I know .... good restaurant that's not too far from here. .... restaurant just opened recently, but it's already become one of .... most popular places in town.

5 .... success that Jackie has had is because she's .... hard worker. It has nothing to do with .... luck.

2 Complete the sentences with a word from the box. Add <u>a</u> if necessary. Each word may be used more than once.

| fear | superstition | time | victory |

1 I remember .... when life was simpler. Things were very different then.
2 Deborah Richard's election to the presidency represents .... for women.
3 My mother had a .... that it was bad luck to put a hat on a bed.
4 Hearing the strange noise, we all felt alarmed and looked at one another with ....
5 Athletes experience the joys of .... as well as the pains of defeat.
6 According to .... that I heard, it's bad luck to walk under a ladder.
7 Neil is afraid of flying. It's .... he's had since he was a child.
8 Do you have .... to go get something to eat?

3 Rewrite each sentence in the passive voice.

1 The newspaper reported that the politicians were getting close to a deal.
The politicians ....

2 They say that tennis player has never lost a match when wearing his lucky tennis shoes.
That tennis player ....

3 Most people think my doctor is one of the best in the country.
My doctor ....

4 They say that scams affect elderly people far more than the rest of the population.
Scams ....

5 In the past, people didn't think the brain had much effect on physical performance.
In the past, the brain ....

WRITING HANDBOOK

1 Think about your own fears. Read and follow the steps. Write notes.

- Choose a fear that you have. Write for five to ten minutes any words, phrases, statements, or questions about the topic that come to mind.
- Consider exactly what you are afraid of, where the fear came from, how it makes you feel, how it affects your life, and how you might overcome it.
- Write quickly. Do not take time to correct spelling, punctuation, organization, etc.
- Read what you wrote. Circle ideas that go together and add more details.

WRITING MODEL

I'm afraid of upsetting other people. It's not a fear that actually causes me fright—for me it's more like I feel very nervous about doing something that someone else won't like. This fear probably stems from my childhood when my mother insisted that I always consider how my words and actions would affect other people. Now I rarely do anything without thinking about what other people will think.

This fear is actually a bit annoying because it means that I feel inhibited to do a lot of things that other people do easily. For example, if I receive poor service at a restaurant, I likely won't complain because I think the waiter will get angry with me. I know in my head this doesn't make much sense, but it still feels real for me.

I want to overcome my fear, and I think the way to do that is by doing things that I'm afraid of or anxious about. I think that little by little I might be able to overcome my fear.

2 Describe your fear in your own words. Use your notes above for ideas.

3 Read the following self-check questions. Check those that apply to your work in Exercise 2.
- ☐ Did I introduce the topic of my fear in general in my first paragraph?
- ☐ Did all my paragraphs include topic sentences?
- ☐ Did all my subjects and verbs agree?

UNIT 8 Achievement and Intelligence

Preview

1 Match the phrases with their definitions. Write the letter on the line.

..... 1 narrowed down
..... 2 making up my mind
..... 3 being on the cutting edge
..... 4 having second thoughts
..... 5 a gut feeling
..... 6 the polar opposite
..... 7 the best of both worlds
..... 8 start from scratch
..... 9 you can't go wrong

a being at the forefront; being where new developments are taking place
b an instinctive feeling not based on facts
c begin with nothing
d deciding between multiple choices
e your actions will always be suitable or successful
f completely different
g rethinking your position
h reduced options; closer to making a decision
i all the advantages of two different situations

2 Write complete sentences. Use your own ideas and the phrases in parentheses.

1 (narrow down)   *We've narrowed down the candidates for Assistant Manager to three people and hope to to make a decision soon.*

2 (make up my mind) ....

3 (on the cutting edge) ....

4 (have second thoughts) ....

5 (a gut feeling) ....

6 (the polar opposite) ....

7 (best of both worlds) ....

8 (can't go wrong) ....

3 Think about when you need to focus on a single task for a long period of time. What makes it easy or hard for you to focus? What helps you focus?

LESSON 1

1 Read the descriptions of the zodiac signs. Then find your sign. Do you think your strengths and weaknesses match the description? Explain your answer.

....
....
....
....

Characteristics of the Zodiac Signs

AQUARIUS (January 20–February 18) You are intelligent and inventive. With an independent (and rebellious) mind, you have your own unique way of thinking and refuse to follow the crowd. You have a talent for discovering new ways of doing things. You love electronic gadgets and figuring out how they work. Your unusual lifestyle and unpredictable nature may seem odd to some people.

PISCES (February 19–March 20) You have a vivid imagination and have a talent for writing poetry, creating art, and performing on stage. You care deeply for other people and devote time to helping those who are sick. A daydreamer, you have a habit of seeing life as you want it to be, rather than how it really is. You sometimes allow your emotions to control your behavior.

ARIES (March 21–April 19) You are adventurous and not afraid to try new things. You are always busy and never lazy. You prefer to work independently and don't have patience with people who are slower or less talented. You're not afraid to fight with others to achieve your goals. In your enthusiasm to get things done, you sometimes work too quickly and don't notice smaller points.

TAURUS (April 20–May 20) You have a fondness for luxury and relaxation. You have excellent taste in food, art, and music. After hearing a song just once, you can sing the lyrics or play the melody. Slow to act and speak, you view all sides of a situation before making decisions, and you choose your words carefully. Although some may find you too quiet, you are a loyal friend.

GEMINI (May 21–June 20) A smooth talker, you have the ability to communicate ideas clearly and persuade others to agree with your point of view. Always the life of the party, you have many friends. You are skilled at using tools and fixing machines. Your love of talk sometimes gives you the reputation of being a gossip.

CANCER (June 21–July 22) You are sensitive and emotional. Your love of family is strong, as is your need to protect and care for the people close to you. When making decisions, you have a talent for sensing the correct choice. However, you have a tendency to allow your emotions to get in the way of rational judgments. Shy and easily hurt, you are slow to make friends.

LEO (July 23–August 22) You are a born leader and others naturally look to you for advice and inspiration. An independent spirit, you don't like being told what to do. You love being the center of attention and dislike being ignored. You enjoy playing sports of all kinds, especially in front of an audience. Your desire to be a star sometimes causes you to forget to be a team player.

VIRGO (August 23–September 22) A perfectionist, you are highly critical of anything that is not done properly. You notice small things that less perceptive people miss. You pick up foreign languages easily. You are highly organized and dislike messiness. With your irresistible urge to improve everything and everyone, you are sometimes seen by others as being fussy and narrow-minded.

LIBRA (September 23–October 22) Easygoing and charming, you get along with almost everyone. A skilled diplomat, you are good at solving problems and convincing people to compromise. You have a need for peace and avoid conflict and arguments. Because you always see both sides of any issue, you have difficulty making decisions.

SCORPIO (October 23–November 21) Watchful and perceptive, you quickly sense other people's true thoughts or feelings. You are a good judge of people and a patient listener. However, you are intensely private, and hold back expressing your own emotions. This lack of openness prevents others from getting to know you well.

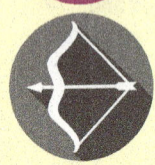

SAGITTARIUS (November 22–December 21) Fun-loving and free-spirited, you are happiest when on the move or trying new things. You learn foreign languages easily, and your open-mindedness about other cultures makes travel a rewarding experience. A natural storyteller, you love recounting your adventures, although you often exaggerate the facts. You are easily bored.

CAPRICORN (December 22–January 19) Disciplined and hardworking, you know how to get things done. Determined to succeed, you set goals for yourself and patiently take steps until you achieve them. Shy and cautious with new people, you are often uncomfortable in social situations. You prefer to work independently and have trouble asking others for help.

2 Read the statements. Check <u>True</u> or <u>False</u>. Read the descriptions of the zodiac signs in Exercise 1 again, if necessary.

	True	False
1 Aries signs have an eye for detail.	☐	☐
2 Taurus signs have an ear for music.	☐	☐
3 Gemini and Aquarius signs tend to be mechanically inclined.	☐	☐
4 Pisces signs have a way with words.	☐	☐
5 Leo, Libra, and Gemini signs have a way with people.	☐	☐
6 Virgo signs have a head for figures.	☐	☐
7 Sagittarius signs have a knack for learning languages.	☐	☐
8 Capricorn signs have a way with people.	☐	☐
9 Aquarius and Scorpio signs have a good intuitive sense.	☐	☐
10 Gemini signs are not good with their hands.	☐	☐

3 Complete the sentences in your own words. Use <u>do</u> or <u>did</u> for emphasis.

1 I don't have an ear for music. I _do like to listen to it, though_.
2 Sam doesn't have a way with words. He ....
3 Even though we didn't make it to your art show, we ....
4 I don't usually have a way with people. I ....
5 Luke doesn't have a knack for learning languages. He ....
6 .... I didn't like her mother, though.

LESSON 2

1 Complete the sentences. Circle the correct words.

1. It's essential that you (were / **be**) on time for your interview.
2. Do you recommend that he (**call** / calls) about the job rather than email?
3. I hoped that I (be / **would be**) invited back for a second interview.
4. They suggested that every employee (**take** / took) the training.
5. Is it really necessary that every employee (will be given / **be given**) the IQ test?
6. I agree that he (**talk** / should talk) with a career counselor.
7. They requested that I (**come** / came) back for another meeting.

2 Complete the sentences. Use the correct active or passive form of the verb in parentheses. Use the subjunctive when necessary.

1. It is crucial that he .... his taxes on time. (pay)
2. I believe that he .... able to do the job very well if we hire him. (be)
3. We insist that women .... the same as men when they do the same work. (pay)
4. The judge demanded that the man who was shouting .... from the courtroom. (remove)
5. We hoped that we .... to the dinner, but we weren't. (invite)
6. It is essential that she .... afraid to speak up during the meeting. (not be)

3 Mark the grammatically correct sentences with a checkmark. Mark incorrect sentences with an X. Then correct any errors in the incorrect sentences.

- [X] 1. A psychologist suggested that Kim ~~reduces~~ *reduce* her stress levels.
- [ ] 2. It is agreed that measuring intelligence is very complicated.
- [ ] 3. The company will insist that people will not smoke on company property.
- [ ] 4. I've suggested that she talk to her doctor about ways to stimulate her brain's activity.
- [ ] 5. It's important that you be willing to try new things.
- [ ] 6. It's desirable that no one knows the details of the project before it is announced.
- [ ] 7. It's essential that each person remembers his or her role in the process.

4 Think about strategies you use when you need to study for an exam or complete a project. What are they? What are some strategies that aren't successful for you? Explain your answers.

Strategies
- avoid junk food
- get plenty of sleep
- study my class notes
- listen to music
- make quizzes for myself
- read what I've written aloud
- make to-do lists
- work with a partner

LESSON 3

1 Read the live report of a panel discussion. What point are the experts debating? Circle the letter.

a the reasons why brain training has become so popular

b the role of genetics, education, and health in determining IQ

c whether daily mental exercise can improve intelligence

City University Quarterly Debate: Live Analysis

Topic: "Increasing IQ: Can we train our brains to become more intelligent?"
Panelists:
- Brian Hanson, developer of brain training app "IQ gym"
- Dr. Sandra Kimura, educational psychologist
- Amy Aldington, author of *Brain Lifting: Can Cognitive Training Make You Smarter?*
- Prof. Michael Clayton, psychometrician

4:02 P.M.
The moderator welcomes everyone to the City University Debating Society's event and introduces the panelists.

4:11 P.M.
Mr. Hanson starts the discussion by explaining what brain training is. "By challenging your brain with daily memory games and word or math puzzles, you can improve your cognitive abilities. It's similar to the way regular physical exercise makes your heart stronger," he says. "And it works! Just ask the people who buy our apps." According to his data, consumers worldwide spend close to $2 billion a year on apps like "IQ gym" with the hope of increasing their IQs.

4:28 P.M.
Dr. Kimura now talks about her experience as a psychologist, describing how young children with developmental delays have shown an increase in their IQ scores after three years of cognitive therapy. "I guess you could call it a form of brain training," she concludes. "But this was really *intense* training from a *very young* age."

4:45 P.M.
Ms. Aldington: "I have to disagree. There's no scientific evidence that so-called brain training can improve your IQ score or overall intelligence," she says. She explains that, according to research, the only benefits are a temporary increase in the ability to perform specific tasks, like puzzles or games. She points out that it's essential to consider genetics. "Someone without a natural aptitude for numbers might pass their school exams by studying hard. But can they become brilliant mathematicians just by doing simple puzzles?"

4:56 P.M.
Prof. Clayton interjects, "I'm afraid the question itself is flawed. It equates IQ scores with intelligence. But IQ tests aren't a reliable measure of intelligence at all." He cites a recent study in which 100,000 participants completed 12 IQ tests that examined memory, reasoning, attention, and planning abilities. None of these tests were able to accurately evaluate how well a person could perform cognitive tasks. He further explains that while genetics play a role in determining our intelligence at birth, our environment—including the quality of our education and our physical health—affects how well our brains develop. This, in turn, can impact our intelligence.

5:03 P.M.
Dr. Kimura questions the use of the word *intelligence*. "Usually, when we talk about intelligence, we think of academic ability, especially in math and language. But what about musical, creative, physical, interpersonal, and intrapersonal intelligence?"

2 Read the live report in Exercise 1 again. Then answer the questions. Circle the letter.

1 Why do people buy brain training apps?
   a They believe it will improve their cognitive abilities.
   b They think it's better than doing physical exercise.
   c They want to find out what their IQ scores are.
2 What has helped Dr. Kimura's patients to increase their IQ scores?
   a They used brain training apps such as "IQ gym."
   b They did intense cognitive therapy from a young age for three years.
   c They've done brain training since at least the age of three.
3 Why does Ms. Aldington believe that brain training doesn't work?
   a There isn't any scientific evidence that proves its effectiveness.
   b Brain training apps are difficult to use and unpopular.
   c Brain training is only effective for very young children.
4 Why does Prof. Clayton say that "the question itself is flawed"?
   a It assumes that improving your IQ means you've become more intelligent.
   b It doesn't take the role of genetics into account.
   c It doesn't mention the role of education or physical health.
5 What does Dr. Kimura believe about academic ability?
   a It cannot be improved through brain training.
   b It's an example of interpersonal intelligence.
   c It's not the only type of intelligence.
6 Which kind of intelligence do puzzles in brain training apps tend to focus on?
   a academic ability
   b physical intelligence
   c creative intelligence

DID YOU KNOW...?
The Stanford-Binet Intelligence Scale is the usual standard by which IQs are measured. An average adult IQ score on this scale ranges from 85 to 115. Approximately 1% of people in the world have an IQ of 135 or higher (a score indicating genius or near genius). According to estimates, which of course are an inexact science, Leonardo da Vinci had a staggering IQ of 220!

3 Match each speaker's idea to the information from the report that supports it. Write the letter on the line.

.... 1 Mr. Hanson: Many people believe that memory games can improve cognitive ability.
.... 2 Dr. Kimura: There is evidence that some forms of brain training can affect IQ.
.... 3 Ms. Aldington: There's no evidence that brain training can improve IQ.
.... 4 Ms. Aldington: Genetic ability is the most important factor in determining IQ.
.... 5 Prof. Clayton: IQ tests aren't a reliable measure of intelligence.
.... 6 Dr. Kimura: Intelligence isn't limited to academic abilities like math and language.

a Research shows that brain training only offers a temporary increase in the ability to perform specific tasks.
b Customers across the world spend $2 billion a year on brain training apps.
c Other types of intelligence include musical, creative, physical, interpersonal, and intrapersonal intelligence.
d A study showed that IQ tests can't judge how well a person could perform cognitive tasks.
e Intense cognitive therapy can increase the IQ of very young children with disabilities.
f Without natural aptitude, a person cannot become brilliant just by studying hard.

LESSON 4

1 Read the definitions. Choose the correct words. Circle the letter.

1 the ability to understand one's own feelings, fears, and motivations
   a interpersonal intelligence   b intrapersonal intelligence   c social skills

2 the ability to understand the intentions, motivations, and desires of others
   a interpersonal intelligence   b intrapersonal intelligence   c self-regulation

3 knowing one's own emotions, strengths, and weaknesses, and recognizing their impact on others
   a self-awareness   b interpersonal intelligence   c empathy

4 managing relationships to get along well with others
   a empathy   b intrapersonal intelligence   c social skills

5 controlling one's negative impulses in order to adapt to a particular environment
   a self-awareness   b self-regulation   c social skills

6 being aware of or sensitive to other people's feelings
   a self-awareness   b self-regulation   c empathy

2 Complete the interview with words from the box.

| empathy | interpersonal | intrapersonal | self-awareness | self-regulation | social skills |

Career counselor: Let's talk about your soft skills. First of all, would you say you have high (1) .... intelligence? For example, do you get along well with other people?

Job candidate: Yes, I do. In fact, I'm still friends with a lot of my old classmates.

Career counselor: That's great! Sounds like you have strong (2) .... And do you see yourself as a compassionate and considerate person?

Job candidate: Um, yeah, I guess so. I try to show (3) ....

Career counselor: That's great. And what would you say are your weaknesses?

Job candidate: Weaknesses? I'm not sure. Well, my teacher used to say that I'm not great at adapting to new situations, and that I should learn to control my temper a bit more.

Career counselor: So, in other words, you need to work on your (4) ....

Job candidate: Well, that's what she said, but I'm not sure I agree.

Career counselor: I see. Any other weaknesses?

Job candidate: I don't think so.

Career counselor: Right. I'd say you need to work on your (5) .... I mean, you already know what your strengths are, which is great. But you also need to understand which areas you need to improve. After all, everyone has weaknesses!

Job candidate: Is that really important?

Career counselor: Absolutely! Employers want to hire people with good (6) .... intelligence.

Job candidate: Oh, I see. Thank you.

3 Think about the interpersonal and/or intrapersonal intelligence of someone you know or a character in a book, movie, or on television. What are that person's strengths and weaknesses? Write a description. Give examples.

GRAMMAR EXPANDER

1 Write two sentences about each person. In the second sentence, use emphatic stress by adding the auxiliary verb <u>do</u> or by underlining the stressed verb <u>be</u>, the modal, or other auxiliary verb.

1 (Derek) not really very observant / has a way with people
   Derek isn't really very observant. He does have a way with people, though.

2 (Amy) isn't good with her hands / has an ear for music

3 (Gail) doesn't have a knack for learning languages / is talented in other ways

4 (Kyle) doesn't have much confidence / has all the skills he needs to succeed

5 (Victor) doesn't have a lot of experience / has a good intuitive sense

6 (Suri) hasn't found a job yet / is persistent

7 (Tara) hasn't been to Africa / has traveled to many other countries

8 (Travis) doesn't have a teaching certificate / would make a great teacher

2 Complete each sentence. Circle the correct words.

1 If you have time, I suggest (**stopping** / to stop) for lunch at one of those restaurants.
2 The coach recommends (to get / **getting**) a good night's sleep before each game.
3 For the team to be successful, it's essential (**to work** / working) together.
4 Mr. Hammond said it's critical (getting / **to get**) the package to Shanghai by tomorrow morning.
5 It's urgent for you (**to start** / starting) the process today.
6 The airline suggests (to arrive / **arriving**) at the airport two hours before an international flight.

3 Complete the sentences. Use the infinitive or gerund forms of the verbs in parentheses.

1. Doctors recommend .... (exercise) at least three times a week.
2. It's critical that people work .... (protect) the environment.
3. I heard that it's best .... (arrive) at the theater two hours before the show starts if you want to get tickets.
4. She advised .... (seek) help from a local historical society.
5. The teacher suggested .... (write) an outline to help us organize our ideas.

4 Complete the sentences with your own ideas. Use infinitive and gerund phrases.

1. When I was younger, people advised me ....
2. If a person wants to be healthy, I recommend ....
3. If a person wants to be successful in life, it's important ....

WRITING HANDBOOK

1 Think about your strengths. Choose one of them. On a separate sheet of paper, brainstorm ideas and write notes. Include ideas about how you learned or inherited the strength, its effects on your life, and ways in which you might use it to your advantage in the future.

2 On another sheet of paper, write about your strength. Develop the ideas you brainstormed about in Exercise 1. Use your notes and the outline below as a guide. Make sure to include connecting words and phrases.

Paragraph 1: State the strength and describe how you think you got that ability.

Paragraph 2: Explain what you have gained as a result of having that strength. Support your ideas with examples.

Paragraph 3: Describe how your strength might help you in the future.

3 Read the following self-check questions. Check those that apply to your work in Exercise 2.

- [ ] Did my paragraphs follow the outline in Exercise 2?
- [ ] Did I use connecting phrases to focus on causes?
- [ ] Did I introduce sentences with connecting words or phrases to focus on results?

WRITING MODEL

One of my strengths is my ability to communicate with others. I think I really have a way with people. Because my mom is the same way, and I never really had to work at it, I probably inherited the trait.

I think that I have a way with people because they really listen to me. For example, I was class president when I was in high school, and I was able to convince the other student leaders to change their points of view on a few issues. As a result, we made some changes to the school's policies. When I was in college, I had a part-time job at a store in a shopping mall. I learned quickly and was able to teach other co-workers how to do things. Consequently, I was promoted to manager in less than a year.

My dream job definitely includes working with people. I can't imagine a job where I worked by myself all day. I'm studying right now to become a teacher. I think I'll be a good teacher because I'll be able to use my people skills to connect with students.

UNIT 9 Looking Ahead

Preview

1 Match the words with their definitions. Write the letter on the line.

.... 1 not being facetious
.... 2 jumping the gun
.... 3 enhance
.... 4 slippery slope
.... 5 massive unemployment
.... 6 to master
.... 7 go poof
.... 8 hoopla

a excitement and discussion
b when large numbers of people don't have jobs
c to learn and be able to do something perfectly
d not joking
e disappear
f when something leads to unanticipated negative changes
g improve or increase
h reaching a conclusion before knowing all the facts

2 What aspects of the future do you feel optimistic about? What things make you feel pessimistic? Explain.

_____
_____
_____
_____

DID YOU KNOW...?
Some of the worst predictions of all time include:

1. *"The horse is here to stay but the automobile is only a novelty, a fad."*
   —1903, Anonymous banker advising Henry Ford's lawyer against buying stock in Ford Motor Company

2. *"Nobody wants to hear actors talk."*
   —1927, H.M. Warner, co-founder of Warner Bros. Studios

3. *"There is no reason for any individual to have a computer in their home."*
   —1977, Ken Olson, Founder of Digital Equipment Corporation

4. *"Everyone's always asking me when Apple will come out with a cell phone. My answer is 'Probably never.'"*
   —2006, David Pogue, *New York Times* tech writer

UNIT 9   W75

LESSON 1

1 Complete the chart. Write sentences from the box in the correct category.

> You might be going overboard.   I don't see it that way at all.   I guess I just see things differently.
> I think that's a little exaggerated.   ~~It's a slippery slope.~~   It's like opening a can of worms.
> It's like opening Pandora's Box.   It's playing with fire.

To express concern	To dismiss concern
It's a slippery slope.	

2 Complete the conversations. Circle the correct phrases.

1 Mark: How do you feel about artificial intelligence?

Chris: Personally, I think **(1)** (you might be going overboard / it's playing with fire / that's a little exaggerated). One of these days we'll lose complete control over the machines and have disastrous results.

Mark: **(2)** (That's a little exaggerated / It's a slippery slope / It's like opening Pandora's Box), don't you think? Surely that won't happen!

2 Sam: I'm very concerned about genetic engineering. **(3)** (I don't see it that way at all / I guess I just see things differently / It's like opening Pandora's Box).

Filipe: **(4)** (I don't see it that way at all / It's playing with fire / It's like opening a can of worms). Personally, I think it's fantastic that we can modify genes to suit our needs!

3 Eric: Did you see this article on nuclear power?

Tony: The one saying how terrible it is? I did, but **(5)** (it's a slippery slope / it's like opening a can of worms / I guess I just see things differently). I think it's a necessary, sustainable way to generate electricity.

Eric: You don't think **(6)** (it's a slippery slope / you might be going overboard / I just see things differently)?

Tony: Not at all!

3 Complete the passive unreal conditional sentences. Write the correct forms of the words in parentheses.

1 Can you imagine having a computer chip put inside your body? According to one company that makes computer chip implants, that reality might not be too far away. The company claims that cases of identity fraud _might / would be reduced_ (reduced) if implants _were used_ (use) for identification.

2 At the present time, human cloning is illegal in this country. But some people argue that it should be allowed. They say that if human cloning .... (permit), information about how certain illnesses develop .... (learn) from cloning diseased cells.

W76   UNIT 9

3 If the severe side effects of the drug .... (make) public, patients .... (warned) about them by their doctors. But the company hid the information, causing many people unnecessary pain and suffering.

4 It seems like the possible future applications of innovative technologies are endless. For example, if the technology .... (develop) further, computer chip implants .... (use) instead of keys. Imagine waving your computer-chipped hand at your front door to open it instead of inserting a key to unlock it.

5 Several non-governmental organizations are working to achieve equal rights for all people. The organizations' supporters say that if equal rights .... (grant) to all people, opportunities for a new way of life .... (create) for them.

6 In the past, consumers didn't know a lot about the dangers of certain genetically modified foods, so they were popular. If consumers .... (inform) about the dangers, then the foods .... (not buy).

4 Complete the passive unreal conditional sentences. Write the correct forms of the words in parentheses and use your own ideas.

1 If computer chip implants .... (use) instead of credit cards, ...

2 If companies .... (allow) to clone human beings, ...

3 If the Internet .... (not / developed), ...

4 If the electric car .... (introduce) sooner, ...

5 Complete the conversation with phrases from the box. There are three extra choices.

be perfectly honest   genetic engineering   hit the nail on the head   little exaggerated
makes two of us   playing with fire   remote surgery   see things differently
still think twice   suddenly goes poof   what do you think

A: So **(1)** .... about doctors performing surgery over videoconferencing?

B: They can do that? But why?

A: Well, they say that **(2)** .... is great when doctors can't physically be present where they're needed for very specialized and complicated operations—for example if they live on the other side of the world.

B: Seriously? It's **(3)** .... , if you ask me. I mean, it can be hard enough to have a simple business meeting through videoconferencing. What about the time lags? Or what if you're in the middle of a critical operation when the Wi-Fi network **(4)** .... ?

A: You've **(5)** .... The stability of Internet connections is one of the main reasons why remote surgery hasn't become more common yet—although, apparently, 5G technology has solved that.

B: Well, I'd **(6)** .... before trusting a Wi-Fi network with my life, to **(7)** ....

A: Right—that **(8)** .... !

UNIT 9   W77

LESSON 2

1 Complete the sentences. Use the words in parentheses and the passive voice to express the future, the future as seen from the past, or the future perfect. Some may have more than one correct answer.

1. Because of an increase in automated jobs, fewer people _will be needed_ (need) by manufacturers in the future.
2. In 1970, a telephone that offered both sound and video was developed. Company executives confidently predicted that 3 million of these Picturephone sets ………………………… (sell) by 1980. However, the Picturephone was a flop.
3. Before the next big outbreak of disease, we hope that emergency plans ………………………… (make) and precautions ………………………… (take) by governments.
4. Experts now say that hydrogen fuel cells ………………………… (accept) as an alternative source of energy within ten to twenty years.
5. By the time the average person can travel to outer space for recreation, many trips ………………………… (make) to all the planets in our solar system.

2 Rewrite the sentences. Change the underlined part of each sentence from the active to passive voice. Include a <u>by</u> phrase if necessary.

1. Within the next fifty years, <u>scientists will introduce technologies that we can't even imagine now</u>.
   Within the next fifty years, technologies that we can't even imagine now will be introduced.
2. By the year 2050, <u>people will have accepted inventions that seem incredible now</u> as a common part of life.
   …………………………
3. I thought <u>an assistant would answer the phone</u>, not the boss.
   …………………………
4. At this time tomorrow, <u>the courier will have delivered the package</u>.
   …………………………
5. Because of its global themes, <u>audiences all over the world are going to appreciate the film</u>.
   …………………………

3 Make predictions about what will or won't be done in the future. Write your opinions in the passive voice. Use ideas from the box or your own ideas.

> achieve world peace   control the weather   discover new energy sources
> establish one international language   increase food production   protect the environment
> provide education for all children   reduce costs of medication

1. _In my opinion, the costs of medication won't be reduced for a long time. Drug companies are making too much money, and they have a lot of power._
2. …………………………
3. …………………………
4. …………………………

LESSON 3

1 Read the article. What is the main idea? Circle the letter.

a The world has entered an era characterized by frequent and deadly epidemics.
b Governments worldwide are unprepared to deal with future outbreaks of disease.
c The world's medical industries are not equipped to deal with outbreaks of disease.

Opinion: Are we prepared for the next pandemic?

Many governments have plans in place to deal with pandemics. Yet, when the COVID-19 pandemic started in 2020, such plans did very little to avoid chaotic government responses. So has this recent experience taught us enough to prevent similar crises in the future? Sadly, the experts say, the answer is no.

According to the world's leading disease experts, we have entered an "era of epidemics." The frequency of disease outbreaks is increasing, with more and more new viruses spreading from wild animals to humans. And with an increasingly larger, more connected world population, diseases are able to spread faster and further than ever before. More epidemics and pandemics like Covid are inevitable—yet studies show that governments remain unprepared.

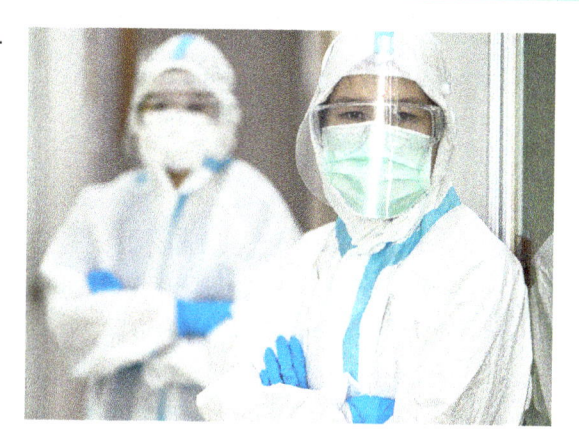

Why are they not better equipped? First, existing pandemic plans often focus on known diseases such as influenza. But as the Covid pandemic showed, the next outbreak might be caused by a whole new pathogen for which we have few or no defenses.

Second, even a perfect plan means nothing if it's not supported by the necessary infrastructure. For example, you need a strong, well-staffed medical industry before a pandemic starts. Yet, according to a recent report on global health security, 70% of the world's countries are not investing enough in medical staff or facilities—including some of the wealthiest countries such as the U.K., where the national healthcare system was under severe strain even before the pandemic hit.

Furthermore, the public must be able to comply with government regulations. In some countries, people found it impossible to follow mandates to self-isolate during the Covid pandemic without paid sick leave and income, food, and housing assistance.

Understandably, such measures require massive amounts of funding. And many governments are less inclined to fund potential risks when they are already facing political, security, and economic threats. The U.S., for example, spends at least twice as much money on its military each year than on public health programs or infectious disease research—which, according to experts, impaired the government's ability to deal with the pandemic in 2020. And although the government has now earmarked tens of billions of dollars toward pandemic preparedness, similar promises after previous pandemics failed to materialize.

Simply having a plan is not enough. Governments need to be able and willing to put those plans into action—and they need to start right now instead of waiting for the next, perhaps even more deadly, pandemic.

2 Read the article in Exercise 1 again. Complete the sentences with words from the box. There are three extra choices.

> a strong healthcare system | Covid virus | era of epidemics | financial support | governments
> influenza virus | medical infrastructure | military infrastructure | political threats

1 According to the writer, ... are to blame for ineffective reactions to the 2020 pandemic.
2 In an ...., disease outbreaks happen frequently and spread fast.
3 Existing pandemic plans often assume that the next outbreak will be caused by another ....
4 Most of the world's countries are not spending enough on their ....
5 Without ...., even the world's wealthiest countries are unable to deal effectively with pandemics.
6 In some countries, people were given .... to enable them to stay at home instead of going to work during the Covid pandemic.

3 Complete the definitions. Circle the letter.

1 When something is "inevitable," it is ....
   a certain to happen and impossible to avoid
   b likely to happen unless you do something to avoid it
   c something you can't prepare for

2 A "pathogen" is ....
   a a new type of influenza
   b a medication used to treat influenza
   c something that causes disease in your body

3 When you "comply" with regulations, you ....
   a agree to do it
   b refuse to do it
   c get paid to do it

4 If you are not "inclined" to do something, you ....
   a are likely to do it
   b are unlikely to do it
   c absolutely refuse to do it

5 To "impair" something means to ....
   a strengthen or fix something that is broken
   b use it effectively and innovatively
   c make it not as good as it should be

6 When you've "earmarked" something, you've ....
   a borrowed it from someone and failed to return it
   b used it in a way that is not effective or sensible
   c decided to use it for a particular purpose in the future

LESSON 4

1 Match the words with their definitions. Draw a line.

1 statistic   a how often or how fast something happens in a certain period of time
2 rate   b a part of the population that is identified as a specific group
3 trend   c a number that represents a fact or measurement
4 demographic   d a general way something is changing

2 Complete the sentences with words from the box. There are three extra choices.

birth   crime   demographic   divorce   fertility   literacy   mortality   statistic   trend

1 Mongolia has one of the highest .... rates in the world, which means that nearly all its adults are able to read and write.
2 The Solomon Islands has one of the highest .... rates in the East Asia and Pacific region, with 4.4 births per adult woman in 2019.
3 The .... rate in Latin America has decreased significantly over the past 30 years, from an average of 54.8 deaths per 1,000 people in 1990, to 16 in 2020.
4 Different sources often use different methods and numbers to represent facts and measurements, which can make it hard to know whether or not to trust a ....
5 With 6.8 births per 1,000 people, Niger has one of the highest .... rates in sub-Saharan Africa.
6 Because of its high number of births every year, Niger is the country with the youngest .... With half of its population under the age of 14, the country is often nicknamed "the youngest country in the world."

3 Look at the graphs showing world population trends. Then read the statements. Check True or False.

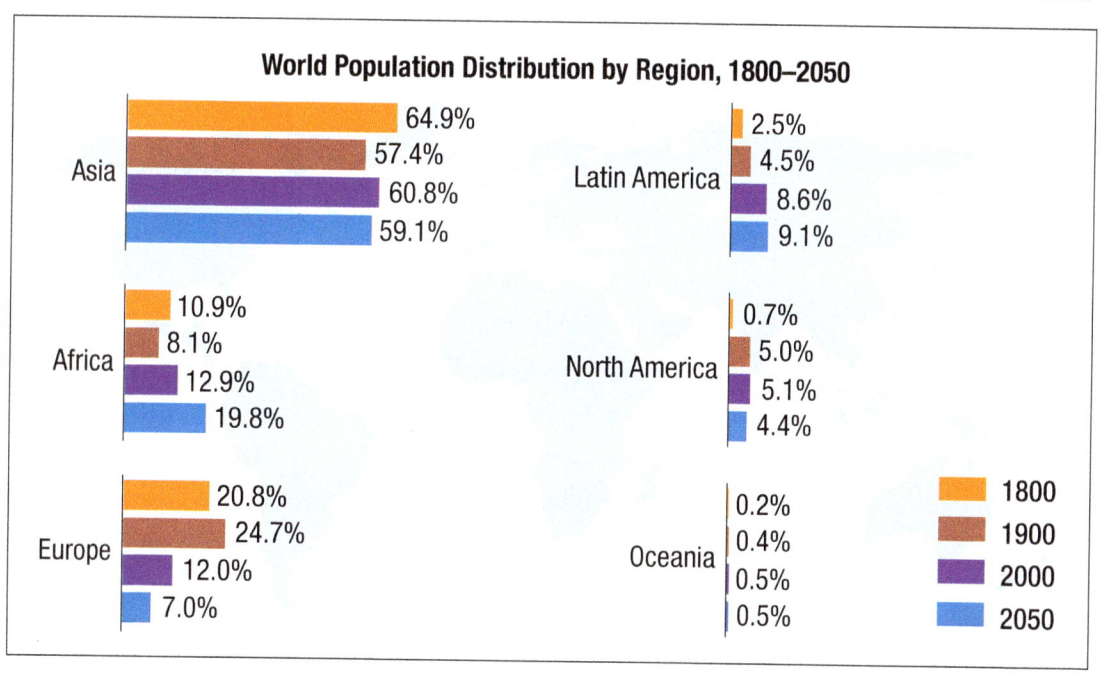

World Population Distribution by Region, 1800–2050

Region	1800	1900	2000	2050
Asia	64.9%	57.4%	60.8%	59.1%
Africa	10.9%	8.1%	12.9%	19.8%
Europe	20.8%	24.7%	12.0%	7.0%
Latin America	2.5%	4.5%	8.6%	9.1%
North America	0.7%	5.0%	5.1%	4.4%
Oceania	0.2%	0.4%	0.5%	0.5%

	True	False
1 The percentage of population increase from 2000 to 2050 is expected to be greater in Africa than the percentage of population increase in Latin America.	☐	☐
2 The largest percentage of the world's population is expected to live in Asia in 2050.	☐	☐
3 Latin America is the only region to show a consistent increase in its percentage of the world's population.	☐	☐
4 North America made the greatest increase in its percentage of the world's population in the last century.	☐	☐

4 What social or demographic changes do you think your country will experience in 2050? What are some possible benefits or consequences?

GRAMMAR EXPANDER

1 Read the sentences. Write <u>A</u> if the sentence is active or <u>P</u> if it is passive. Circle the passive verbs.

.... 1 Laws to protect the environment must be passed by the legislature.
.... 2 If the company's policy isn't working, then the managers should change it.
.... 3 The president was interviewed by a famous reporter whose articles have been published in magazines around the world.
.... 4 Citizens must show identification in order to vote.
.... 5 The party will be attended by government officials and other dignitaries.

2 Complete the sentences. Circle the correct words.

1 My hair (had been cut / had cut) right before that picture (took / was taken).
2 After the apples (pick / are picked), workers (wash / are washed) them in cold water.
3 Managers (have reduced / have been reduced) prices on everything in the store.
4 A number of possible solutions (will be discussed / will discuss) at the conference.
5 Caution (should be taken / should take) when storing household cleaners. Parents (must be kept / must keep) all hazardous materials out of children's reach.

3 Rewrite each sentence in the passive voice. Include a <u>by</u> phrase if necessary.

1 Researchers have conducted numerous studies on the topic.
　...
2 First the chef chops onion, basil, and tomatoes. Then he combines all the ingredients.
　...
3 Patients should take this medication with food to avoid stomach discomfort.
　...
4 Passengers must provide tickets and identification before boarding.
　...
5 Members of the health board, who make sure that restaurants meet state health standards, visited The Good Table Café.
　...

WRITING HANDBOOK

1 Prepare to write an essay about life in the future. Choose a topic from the box or your own idea. Write a thesis statement.

Thesis statement:

Possible topics about life in the future:
- New technologies
- New uses for existing technologies
- Future population trends
- The environment
- Your own topic: ....

2 Write an outline to organize the supporting paragraphs of your essay. Write a topic sentence for each paragraph you plan to write. Follow each topic sentence with a list of supporting examples.

3 On a separate sheet of paper, write an essay about the topic you chose in Exercise 1. Follow your outline. Use your thesis statement and topic sentences. Develop your supporting examples. Don't forget to include an introduction and a conclusion. Refer to the Writing Model on Student's Book page 152 as an example.

4 Read the following self-check questions. Check those that apply to your work in Exercise 2.
- [ ] Does my thesis statement clearly state my argument?
- [ ] Does each of my supporting paragraphs have a topic sentence that supports my point of view?
- [ ] Does my conclusion summarize my main points and restate my thesis?

UNIT 10 Global Ties

Preview

1 Complete the conversations with expressions from the box. There are two extra choices.

a little out of sorts	a fish out of water	getting to me	get over it
I'm with you	put my finger on it	What's with	pulling my leg

1. **A:** What do you find difficult about learning English, Mei?
   B: I'm not sure. It's hard to .... Maybe it's because English grammar is so different from Chinese.

2. **A:** We missed you in English class yesterday, Toby. I hope you weren't ill.
   B: No, I'm fine. I was just feeling .... , so I was avoiding people.

3. **A:** Did you see that Professor Krum's class was filled up already? He's not accepting any more students.
   B: You're .... How did that happen? No one even likes him or his course.

4. **A:** All this political talk on campus has really been .... lately. It's creating such a negative vibe.
   B: I know what you mean. In my country, it's not polite to talk about political matters with strangers.

5. **A:** .... all the traffic today? Is someone important coming to the university?
   B: Um, not that I know of. But you're right, there sure were a lot of cars out. There must be something going on.

6. **A:** I thought you were going to join the debate club. What happened?
   B: Well, I showed up at their last meeting, but honestly, I felt like .... Everyone seemed so much smarter and more talented than me.

2 Describe how you expect to use English in your life. Where will you speak it? With whom? For what purpose?

DID YOU KNOW...?
There are 2,700 languages with over 7,000 individual dialects spoken around the world today. It's estimated that nearly half will disappear in the next century as communities abandon native tongues in favor of more widely spoken languages such as Mandarin, English, or Spanish.

LESSON 1

1 Match the phrasal verbs with their definitions. Write the letter on the line.

..... 1 put up with   a completely destroy
..... 2 carry out   b accept without complaining
..... 3 come up with   c cause to happen
..... 4 wipe out   d use up; not have any more of
..... 5 lay off   e to not have; be deprived of
..... 6 bring about   f think of; produce
..... 7 come down with   g become sick with
..... 8 go without   h achieve; accomplish
..... 9 run out of   i end the employment of workers

2 Complete the conversations. Circle the correct phrasal verbs.

1 **Debra:** Why do you look so worried?
  Don: I'm afraid I might be out of work soon. My company is in financial trouble, and I've heard they're going to (put up with / lay off / bring about) some employees next week.

2 **Nico:** Are you going to eat that hamburger?
  Ella: No, I'm a vegetarian.
  Nico: I don't understand how you can (go without / carry out / come up with) meat, but I guess that means I can have the last hamburger. Thanks!

3 **Yolanda:** Did you finish the exam?
  Min-jun: Yes. Did you?
  Yolanda: No, I (ran out of / came down with / wipe out) time before I got to the last section. I need to work faster next time.

3 Complete the conversation with phrases from the box. There are three extra choices.

childhood malnutrition	don't tell me	makes you feel hopeless	no end in sight
that makes two of us	the ripple effect	To say nothing about	victims of natural disasters
we'd be doing something	What's causing it	You name it	

A: Can you believe what's been happening in Asia?
B: A real environmental and humanitarian crisis. Floods, landslides, hurricanes . . . (1) ....
A: (2) .... ? I mean, these are natural disasters, but why are there so many?
B: Environmentalists say that, because of climate change, we're experiencing more and more extreme weather events. They say there's (3) ....
A: And there's (4) .... Food shortages, hunger, starvation . . .
B: (5) .... the displacement of thousands of people!
A: It (6) .... , doesn't it?
B: Actually, not really. There are things we can do to help—like make donations to charities that support (7) ....
A: I guess you're right. At least (8) .... !

UNIT 10 W85

4 Think about a crisis that is currently in the news. Explain the problem and the effects it is having on the world. Describe how the situation makes you feel and what you could do to help.

LESSON 2

1 Complete the conversations. Circle the correct phrases. Some may have more than one correct answer.

1

Jack: This project isn't coming out the way that I imagined it at all. I think we should **(1)** (start it over / start over it).

Ben: I disagree. People are **(2)** (counting us on / counting on us) to finish it before the deadline. We have a good plan. We just need to **(3)** (carry it out / carry out it).

2

Amy: Have you been to the new Asian fusion restaurant? I'd love to **(4)** (try it out / try out it).

Jason: No, actually I haven't. We could go tonight, but we might have to **(5)** (put up with a crowd / put up a crowd with).

Amy: Hmm. Maybe we should **(6)** (put off our visit / put our visit off). A weeknight might be better.

Jason: Good idea.

3

Iris: You know, I'm really interested in **(7)** (taking up knitting / taking knitting up).

Mary: Really? You should do it. I'm sure you could **(8)** (pick it up / pick up it) easily.

Iris: You're right. I'd better start looking for a place that offers classes. Is there any chance I can **(9)** (talk into you / talk you into) taking them with me?

Mary: Actually, that sounds like fun. Let's do it.

2 Complete the sentences. Circle the correct letter.

1 I hope the company doesn't ....
   a lay me off   **b** lay off me

2 Please help me figure ....
   a it out   **b** out it

3 You can always count ....
   a Helen on   **b** on Helen

4 I tried ...., and they didn't fit.
   a on them   **b** them on

5 I ran .... downtown today.
   a into your brother   **b** your brother into

6 I made so many mistakes. I want to do ....
   a over my homework   **b** my homework over

7 It may be the most popular sport in the world, but I just don't care ....
   a for it   **b** it for

8 That would be an improvement, so I hope you can bring ....
   a about it   **b** it about

3 Complete the sentences. Use the correct form of the phrasal verb in parentheses + <u>it</u> or <u>them</u>.

1 It's a complicated plan. Will they be able to ....? (carry out)
2 I'm afraid I can't come to dinner tonight because I've got a cold. I just
.... yesterday. (come down with)
3 Those people are so annoying! I don't know how you can ....
(put up with)
4 There was a false start to the race, with two runners starting too soon, so the officials had to
.... (start over)
5 The library is holding two books I requested. Can you .... for me when
you go there? (pick up)
6 His favorite T-shirts were full of holes, so he finally .... (throw away)
7 Jack and Rose didn't want to go at first, but we .... coming with us.
(talk into)
8 What a clever idea! How did you ....? (come up with)

4 Describe some examples of imports that you regularly enjoy from foreign countries or cultures. Do you believe these imports have had a positive or negative influence on your own culture? Explain.

_____
_____
_____
_____
_____
_____

LESSON 3

1 Match the words with their definitions. Write the letter on the line.

.... 1 culture shock
.... 2 homesick
.... 3 overwhelming
.... 4 disorienting
.... 5 to belong
.... 6 to miss
.... 7 to long for

a the feelings of anxiety and confusion that people may have when they spend time in a place with different behaviors, languages, traditions, and customs
b confusing, especially of new surroundings
c to feel sad because one doesn't have something or do something one had or did before
d feeling sad because of being away from home
e to feel happy or comfortable in a place or situation because one has the same interests and ideas as other people
f to want something very much, especially when it seems unlikely to happen soon
g more than one can bear; large enough in size, number, or amount to have a very strong effect

2 Complete the conversation with words from the box.

| belonged | culture shock | disorienting | homesick | longing for | miss | overwhelming |

Jerry: Hey, Clive! Welcome home. How was your trip to South Korea?

Clive: Hi Jerry! Thanks. It was amazing—I loved every moment.

Jerry: Really? You were away for three months! Didn't you (1) .... home?

Clive: I did get a bit (2) .... whenever I thought of my family back home, but most of the time I was just having too much fun to feel sad.

Jerry: But wasn't it a big (3) .... ? South Korea must be very different from the U.S.!

Clive: Not really. Everyone I met there was extremely friendly and welcoming. It wasn't long before I felt like I (4) .... there!

Jerry: That's good to hear.

Clive: The only thing I found a little bit (5) .... was the fact that Koreans have a different alphabet. I found it confusing at first, but then I discovered that it's actually easy to learn to read Korean.

Jerry: I don't know. I think I would find it very (6) .... to be in a new country for that long. It would all be too much for me.

Clive: You'd be surprised! I used to feel the same way, until I went to South Korea. Now I'm already (7) .... my next adventure!

3 Read about one person's experience with culture shock.

I have been a student here in the United States for three years. It's almost time for me to return to my home country, Slovakia. I'm excited but also a little sad. It took me a while, but I've grown to love living here in New York City. It wasn't always that way, however.

When I first arrived, I was a bit overwhelmed. Some things were the same as at home, but so much was different! All the new stuff was fun for me for a while. I loved trying new food, like New York pizza and sushi. Then there were the stores—such huge stores, with so many items. It was overwhelming trying to figure out what to buy, but all the choices were also fascinating. There were also so many people from different cultures and countries. That was very different from my hometown, where it was unusual to see someone from another country. I loved just people-watching.

Jozef Soroková

But after a few weeks, I began feeling more overwhelmed and less enchanted. Having so many people around me all the time started to get on my nerves. It didn't help that my English needed some work; I couldn't always understand what people were saying. And of course, my lack of fluency in English made my classes a little difficult. I was also having a hard time figuring out what kinds of things were OK to talk about and what were not. For example, I learned the hard way that it's not OK to ask someone how much money he or she makes. At home, that wasn't considered rude. And believe it or not, having all those choices when I went shopping started to get annoying, too. I mean, who wants to choose between fifteen different kinds of toothpaste?

I guess I had come down with a case of homesickness. I missed my family, and I missed hanging out with my friends and being able to communicate easily. Speaking of friends, I was having a hard time making any close friends in New York. My difficulty making friends was in part because I hadn't met the right people, and, in addition, I think I was a little withdrawn and depressed.

Finally, though, things started to get better. That was in the spring. I had been here for several months, and my English had improved enough that communicating had become much easier. I made a couple of friends in my classes, and that really helped. One friend was from Japan, and one was actually from New York. She took us to all her favorite places in the city, and I discovered some places of my own, including the Conservatory Gardens in Central Park, which were a perfect place to escape the crowds. But you know what? After a while the crowds didn't bother me like they used to. I guess I had just become part of the crowd myself.

Write the positive and negative things that Jozef experienced in each stage of culture shock.

Stage 1 — honeymoon stage:

Stage 2 — frustration stage:

Stage 3 — depression stage:

Stage 4 — acceptance stage:

4 What aspects of your culture might cause a visitor to experience culture shock? What advice could you give to help visitors navigate these cultural differences?

LESSON 4

1 Read the article. What problem is described? ....

SWEATSHOPS: The Price of Development?

One of the most publicized results of globalization in recent years has been the transfer of well-paid manufacturing jobs from developed countries to less-developed ones, where workers can be paid much less, and goods are significantly cheaper to produce.

Critics of this trend have been vocal. In the developed countries where manufacturing jobs are disappearing, labor protesters claim that the resulting rise in the unemployment rate is hurting the national economy. Critics also point out that when the jobs move to developing countries, the working conditions at many facilities in developing countries are far below the accepted standards in developed countries. At these facilities, commonly known as "sweatshops," employees work long hours, often in dangerous conditions, for low pay. Without government laws against child labor, some workers are as young as five years old.

A typical Western response to sweatshops has been to boycott, or refuse to buy, any imports made under these conditions. Surprisingly, however, opinion polls show that most people in developing countries view these sweatshop jobs positively. Although sweatshop workers in developing nations hope for better wages and working conditions, they don't want consumers in developed nations to protest the situation by refusing to buy the products they make. These boycotts could lead to the closing of factories and employees losing their jobs. Many workers feel that working under these conditions is better than having no job at all.

Moreover, some experts point to statistics showing that sweatshop labor has had a positive economic impact on some developing countries. Average incomes for sweatshop workers are now 5 times what they were less than 20 years ago. The working conditions at some factories have improved, as each company tries to attract the best workers. Decreasing infant mortality rates and rising levels of education are indications of an increased standard of living.

While the pros and cons of sweatshop labor continue to be debated, one fact remains clear—the world economy is rapidly changing into one free-flowing global market. The challenge will be to come up with a way to make globalization work for the benefit of everyone.

2 Read the article in Exercise 1 again. Then read each statement. Check <u>True</u> or <u>False</u>.

		True	False
1	The article describes workers moving from developing countries to developed countries in search of jobs.	☐	☐
2	The number of manufacturing jobs in developed countries is rising.	☐	☐
3	Factories with poor working conditions are known as "sweatshops."	☐	☐
4	The article presents arguments both for and against sweatshop labor.	☐	☐
5	Products that are made by low-paid workers are commonly known as "imports."	☐	☐
6	Some workers in developed countries have decided to stop buying products made in sweatshops.	☐	☐
7	Statistics show that wages for sweatshop workers in some countries are rising.	☐	☐
8	Statistics suggest that sweatshop jobs have increased the level of wealth and comfort in some developing countries.	☐	☐
9	The article recommends that the globalization of the world economy be stopped.	☐	☐

3 Complete the chart. Look at the labels of some things you own. List each item and its country of origin. Then answer the questions.

Item	Country of origin

1 Do you think it's important to buy products that are made in your own country, rather than goods imported from other countries? Explain.

....
....
....

2 Have you ever participated in a product boycott? Do you think that boycotts can be effective in changing bad company practices? Why or why not?

....
....
....

GRAMMAR EXPANDER

1 Underline the phrasal verbs in each sentence. Write T if the sentence has a transitive meaning or I if it has an intransitive meaning.

.... 1 It's a formal event, so everyone should dress up.
.... 2 After hearing the news, the committee called off the celebration.
.... 3 When I think back on those times, they seem like so long ago.
.... 4 The girl grew up in a small fishing village in the north.
.... 5 It's incredibly rude to cut someone off when they're speaking.
.... 6 Please look your essay over before you send it to your teacher.
.... 7 He agreed to go along with the story, but he wasn't happy about it.

2 Read each sentence. Write T if the sentence has a transitive meaning or I if it has an intransitive meaning. Match each definition with the way the phrasal verb is used in each sentence. Draw a line.

...I... 1 You're being ridiculous. Stop carrying on like that! — continued
...T... 2 We've carried on many of the traditions from when we were children. — behaving in a silly way

.... 3 We blew up balloons to decorate the room for the party.
.... 4 A devoted Tigers fan, John blew up when he heard they had lost the game.

suddenly became very angry
filled with air

.... 5 I don't want to fight anymore. Let's make up.
.... 6 My grandfather used to make up stories that even the adults loved to hear.

end the argument
created

UNIT 10   W91

3 Underline the phrasal verbs in each sentence. Write <u>A</u> if the sentence is active or <u>P</u> if it is passive.

.... 1 The memo was thrown out because we thought it was trash.
.... 2 Someone used up all the hot water before I could take a shower.
.... 3 The poster had to be done over again because the first one was a disaster.
.... 4 They passed out coupons and prizes at the door.
.... 5 That group of kids always leaves Ginny out when they play games.
.... 6 The passengers on the bus were let off at the corner.
.... 7 The application had been filled out with a blue pen.

WRITING HANDBOOK

1 Prepare to write a rebuttal to an opinion or point of view that you disagree with.

Choose a controversial issue in your city or country that you're concerned about. For ideas, consider current news topics; governmental laws and policies; or social, cultural, and economic issues.

First, list the opposing point of view. Then list two or three key aspects of that point of view, with your opposing arguments. Use a separate sheet of paper if you need more space for your notes.

Example:
Opposing point of view: *We should not raise taxes on the wealthy*
Key argument: *If the wealthy pay higher taxes, they will spend less, hurting the economy.*
My rebuttal: *The increase in taxes will not be enough to change spending habits.*

Opposing point of view:
Key argument:

My rebuttal:

2 Many publications include a special section for letters they receive from their readers. Writing a letter to the editor is one way to express your opinions on issues that concern you. Choose a newspaper or magazine to write to. On a separate sheet of paper, write a letter stating a point of view that you oppose and your rebuttal arguments.

3 Read the following self-check questions. Check those that apply to your work in Exercise 2.

☐ Did I summarize the point of view I want to rebut in my introduction?
☐ Did I rebut each argument by providing details and examples to support my own?
☐ Did I use the expressions and transitions or subordinating conjunctions from Student's Book page 153 to link my ideas clearly?
☐ Did I summarize my point of view in my conclusion?